# POLICY STABILITY AND DEMOCRATIC CHANGE

Energy in Spain's Transition

# POLICY STABILITY AND DEMOCRATIC CHANGE

## Energy in Spain's Transition

Thomas D. Lancaster

The Pennsylvania State University Press
University Park and London

Library of Congress Cataloging-in-Publication Data

Lancaster, Thomas D.
  Policy stability and democratic change.

  Bibliography: p.
  Includes index.
  1. Representative government and representation—
Spain.  2. Spain—Politics and government—1975–  .
I. Title.
JN8341.L36  1989          946.083          87–43185
ISBN 0-271-00634-X

*In loving memory of the life and work of*
*my maternal grandfather, Hiel D. Bollinger*

# Contents

# Preface

The United States makes much ado about democracy. We verbally and physically defend our democratic system of government, seldom seriously questioning what we mean by "democracy." We exhort its virtues, taking pride in its existence. We are harsh on those who do not hold the system in equal esteem. Our contention is that democracy allows the best in human nature to reach its potential, while permitting a maximum of individualistic freedom. We seldom question the validity of this governmental form for ourselves.

Convinced of democracy's fundamental goodness, Americans generally contend that other political systems should also be democratic. The rhetoric of American foreign policy is frequently cloaked in a veil of democratic goals, even if perceived by some to be hypocritical. U.S. leaders speak often and loudly in international circles, arguing on behalf of democratic principles. They harshly criticize nations that relinquish the pursuit of democratic principles, e.g., Greece under the Colonels, Franco's Spain in its early years, contemporary Turkey, and various Latin American countries. With actions not always consistent with these words, American troops, advisers, and military materiel have been sent to Korea, Vietnam, El Salvador, Honduras, Nicaragua, and other nations in the name of democracy and against nondemocratic expansionism. The United States's propensity to support democracy in other political systems has spent many lives and much in resources.

This clamor about the virtues of democracy implicitly assumes that democracy and authoritarian political systems are intrinsically different. Spain, with its many changes during the decade after 1975, certainly appears to have reinforced this assumption. Spain's peaceful political transition from authoritarianism to a European-style parliamentary democracy following Franco's death in November 1975 unquestionably brought many changes: the right to vote, to organize collectively in both political and economic affairs, and to dissent; greater freedoms in speech and the press; more regional autonomy; and a new role in international relations, particularly vis-à-vis the nations of the European Community and NATO. Such changes clearly reflect significant differences between the most recent examples of authoritarian and democratic politics in Spain. On the other hand, while broad in its scope of political reform, Spain's transition to democracy was not revolutionary in the sense of total destruction of the old order. This political transformation followed a model of *reforma* rather than *ruptura*. Highlights were the Francoist Cortes's passage of the Reform Law, the referendum, the Union of the Democratic Center's incorporation of political leaders from the past regime along with past oppositional members, the 1977 elections, the ratification in 1978 of a new Constitution, and ultimately the peaceful transition of power to the Socialist party in 1982. Such political changes, however, left intact much of the country's *economic* policy-making structure.

I argue in this book that little significant change occurred in Spanish energy policy-making and planning during the early years of the Spanish transition from an authoritarian political system to a parliamentary democracy. I offer an explanation as to why few significant changes were found. I attempt to provide insight into the many different relationships found among the events and actors involved in the political transition and energy policy in Spain. This book does not, it should be noted, attempt to explain why the transition actually occurred. That is altogether another task, one which requires focusing on many additional political participants and groups including the unique role played in Spain by King Juan Carlos I. The current work is concerned with gaining a more general understanding of the policy-making consequences of such a regime change. The analysis focuses on the key political and economic participants that made Spanish energy policy decisions, considering their relationships to each other before and after Spain's transition to democracy. The logic of this argument is that regime form or the type of political system is, up to a point, unrelated to economic policy. The influence key economic institutions and interests exert in either an authoritarian or a democratic type of government better explain many policy orientations than does the regime type itself. Stated differently, with regard to fundamental macro-economic outcomes, when political or governmental structures change but economic structures remain essentially unaltered, policy orientations generally remain unaltered. Change in economic structure is a necessary condition to produce fundamental change in macro-economic policy. In some situations, change in political or governmental structure may be a necessary condition to produce significant change in macro-economic policy, but it is generally not a sufficient condition. A transition to democracy that leaves political accountability for macro-economic policy unaltered does not provide the necessary conditions for significant economic policy changes. A political transition to democracy must change ultimate accountability for macroeconomic policy if it is to produce fundamental and long-term change in policy.

A central point to our discussion is that political institutions offer the opportunity for strategic participants in the economic structure to continue dominant roles in spite of a transition to democracy. While the questions of how a transition to democracy affects economic policy is a fundamental political development concern, the developmental literature has generally failed to address this question. Most of this literature has been concerned more with explaining social change and with investigating its influence on political and institutional development than with studying the effects of this development.[1] Developmental theory has characteristically focused on maximizing economic development on the one hand and political stability on the other. While such concerns are important, this developmental literature nevertheless neglects the effect of institutional change on policy outcomes.

A small number of works in the developmental literature do touch on this concern for the interplay between change and nonchange in economic and political structure. Barrington Moore, Holt and Turner, and Douglas North, for example, each include institutional structure as a fundamental variable in their analysis of economic and political development.[2] Their theoretical and often heavily historical analysis even includes regime change in its larger context of political and economic structural development and change. The fact remains, however, that most of the literature on the effects on institutional realignment and reorganization has not focused on transitions to democracy.[3] This literature has considered the question in terms of a democratic, mostly American setting. The "politics matters" debate, for example, has generally only addressed "politics" in a democratic context. Such a narrow definition of "politics" overlooks most nations of the world. One should consider "politics" in a much broader context—one that includes nondemocratic systems. We compare policy-making in both democratic and nondemocratic settings, with the advantage in design of making this comparison in the same country.

Furthermore, our thinking of political transitions has generally not questioned their effect on economic policy, with the possible exception of military spending and educational policy. The literature on political development, revolution, and colonialism has attempted to explain these changes without generally analyzing their policy consequences.[4] This research hopes to contribute to the policy literature by considering the consequences of regime change on policy. Furthermore, I shall do so by focusing on an issue that is of extreme importance in the contemporary era, and not only to systems experiencing institutional change. Energy policy and planning is an issue that is of paramount economic and political concern to all systems of the contemporary world. Energy planning has become a central component of macroeconomic planning in this era of energy scarcity. It is of particular importance to those economies that are struggling to survive at the margin. Third World nations have been greatly affected politically, economically, and psychologically by the energy crisis. Yet, it is these nations that are most likely to experience the political developmental sequence of moving from a military dictatorship to democracy. These nations often face both domestic and international pressures to institute more democratic processes and principles, despite a lack of democratic traditions, lesser economic development, and economies that are highly susceptible to the problems of an energy shortage.

The scope of this analysis is from the early days of the Franco regime until Spain's entry into the European Economic Community on 1 January 1986. Thus, this analysis does not consider any changes imposed on the Spanish economy from without by EEC membership. Spain's membership will undoubtedly force many changes in the structure of the Spanish economy. What is important to note here is that such change will come about as a consequence of changes in the economic structures, most of which will be imposed from without. Spain's transition to democracy obviously opened the doors to EEC membership. And, even though many of these reforms were desired by some Spanish policymakers, it is the rules of membership itself that will foster future economic changes and reform. While such changes and reforms are extremely important to the discussion presented here, particularly given that some change will occur in the area of energy, they nevertheless must remain the topic for future work. Economic changes produced by EEC membership will be slowly introduced. More time and other analysis will be needed to assess fully these changes.

# Acknowledgments

This project reflects a life-long interest in politics, democratic government, and the values and affairs of people in other countries. My early questioning, although not really about politics, was always strongly encouraged by my parents, John and Mary Jean Lancaster. A nascent interest in comparative politics began with the opportunity to spend a summer with a local family in Normandy, France, through an exchange program with the Lions International. My academic training in comparative politics began at Washington and Lee University. The late E. L. "Mike" Pinney of the Politics Department and S. J. Williams of the Department of Romance Languages both stimulated my interest and provided the training that ultimately led to this project. Lars Schoultz, now at the University of North Carolina, Chapel Hill, and Susan Kay took the time when I studied at Miami University (Ohio) to encourage my continued studies in comparative politics. Of course, everyone in the Department of Political Science at Washington University made my graduate education a challenging yet valuable experience. Special respect and esteem will always be held for James Alt and Kenneth Shepsle, both now at Harvard University. As director of my doctoral dissertation, Professor Alt gave invaluable guidance while simultaneously maintaining "free reigns," a method of teaching we both desired. I only wish I could have studied longer under him. Professor Shepsle has served as a very important intellectual role model for me and many other students. He possesses an incredible gift to formulate and carry out serious analysis. Equally important, he has the ability, and patience, to teach such skills to others. As a student and admirer, I know I will never be able to fully emulate such a great scholar and man of class. Finally, I wish to express my deep appreciation to Micheal W. Giles and the other members of the Department of Political Science at Emory University. As chairman of the department at Emory, Mike has been all that I could ask in a chair in my first academic appointment—encouraging, constructive, open, fair, and challenging. The entire department is characterized by a strong sense of openness and congeniality, something not always found in academic departments.

Washington University and Emory University both provided much needed financial support at critical times in this project's development. The Graduate School of Washington University and the Department of Political Science there provided support for the initial year of field research that served as the basis for this work. The Emory University Research Committee provided additional financial support with Summer Research Fellowships in 1983, 1984, and 1985. These grants provided necessary time in Spain for more interviews and the gathering of updated material.

This book could not have been written without the assistance of many people interested in Spain and its transition to democracy. In the United States, Juan J. Linz of Yale University initially suggested consideration and analysis of public policy issues during Spain's political transition. Richard Gunther of Ohio State University called to my attention obstacles in doing field research in Spain and provided some useful research strategy suggestions. Charles W. Anderson of the University of Wisconsin helped refine the original research proposal. Peter McDonough, Micheal Giles, and several anonymous reviewers read the manuscript and made excellent suggestions on how to improve it. The detailed letters I received from these scholars of Spanish politics were greatly appreciated. Many other people also encouraged this project at different points in its progress. These include Barry Ames, John Woolley, Samuel H. Barnes, Kenneth Maxwell, Eusebio Mujal-León, Robert E. Martínez, Robert Fishman, Gary Prevost, Michael S. Lewis-Beck, and James M. Markham. While some of these people have disagreed with certain parts of my analysis, the fact that they took the time to question it constructively and in open dialogue reflects their commitment to the enterprise in which we are collectively engaged—seeking to understand a perplexing world.

On the European side of the Atlantic, over the years many Spaniards have been kind enough to share their time, insights, and culture with me. To all of them I am forever grateful. Particularly important to me were the many state, business, and political leaders who freely submitted themselves to my barrage of questions during interviews. Related to this project, I especially wish to mention José Antonio Martínez Soler, Rafael Alberto Pérez, Javier Alvárez Vara, the late António Buitrago Moraleda, José Ingacio Gafo Fernández, José Rodríquez de Pablo, Julio Callesa González-Camino, José Luis Tora, Ramón Leonato Marsal, Angel Hernández, Javier Solana, Jeronimo Sánchez-Blanco, Carlos Davila, Paco Penalver, and Juan Tesora. On the nonscholarly front, I wish to extend my love and appreciation to María Carmen Bedmar Díaz and to the Barreneche family—Mari Carmen, Javier, Raquel, and Francisco—who, as my "Spanish family," made this an enjoyable endeavor.

Part of this book appeared in a volume I jointly edited with Gary Prevost entitled *Politics and Change in Spain* (Praeger, 1985). Some of chapter 1 appeared in that volume as "Introduction: A Coalitional Perspective on Politics and Change in Spain" and most of chapter 6 was also published in this edited volume as "Spanish Public Policy and Financial Power." I would like to thank Praeger Publishers and Gary Prevost for permission to use these materials in this book.

Finally, this book is dedicated to my maternal grandfather, Dr. H. D. Bollinger. "Pop," as he was affectionately called by his grandchildren, lived a life dedicated to world peace and justice. His social, cultural, and intellectual life touched many people in many ways. Through example, he unknowingly set the completion of this work as one of my academic goals. I only regret that I did not finish it in his lifetime.

# 1

## Issues in the Transition and Public Policy-Making

Spain's transition to democracy following the death of Francisco Franco in November 1975 is intriguing political history. A great deal of political maneuvering occurred in the years preceding the Generalisimo's death. Political groups jockeyed for position knowing that Franco's inevitable demise was imminent. Such activity took place both within and outside governmental circles. Within the government, the bureaucracy, the military, the business class, and the labor movement, among others, people began considering what form the Spanish system would take following the political vacuum created by Franco's death.

Franco himself had anticipated this state of affairs when, in 1967, he began transferring much of his power to Admiral Luis Carrero Blanco. In assuming the vice-presidency of the government, Carrero Blanco took over many of the day-to-day operations of government. His assassination in 1973 by Basque extremists served to keep open options for many aspirants of leadership in post-Franco Spain. Also central to the transition, Franco officially proclaimed Juan Carlos as his successor on 22 July 1969. Many in Franco's circle of leadership saw this as a provision to insure the continuation of the regime. Events proved differently. Juan Carlos, crowned King two days after the Generalisimo's death, moved slowly but pointedly. In June and July 1976, the King replaced the Francoist prime minister Arias Navarro with the young, unknown Adolfo Suárez through a brilliant series of institutional and political maneuvers. Events moved faster following this key governmental replacement. By October 1976, Suárez had pushed a reform project through the Francoist legislature that essentially saw the legislature voting itself out of existence. A nation referendum on political reform passed overwhelmingly on 15 December 1976. The process of democratization was then fully underway, with the legalization of political parties and the trade union movement, the conducting of elections, and a growing respect for civil liberties in line with other liberal democratic nations in Western Europe. The first elections held on 15 June 1977 chose a parliament which wrote a new liberal democratic constitution for Spain. This new governmental framework was approved in another national referendum on 6 December 1978. This nascent democracy nevertheless still faced many problems: terrorism in the Basque country, poor economic performance and high unemployment, questions about EEC and Nato membership, and the removal of the military from daily political life. Yet, the best indicator of the progress Spain made in its implementation of democracy is in the area of political participation. The Franco regime openly discouraged political participation. In contrast, Spain's new democratic regime has encouraged citizen participation and legitimated public conflict over alternative policies. After years of political quiescence, Spanish voters have been called to the polls for general elections in 1977, 1979, 1982, and 1986, for local elections in 1979, 1983, and 1987, and for three national referenda.

The trials and tribulations of this Mediterranean country's peaceful, and apparently successful, transition from an authoritarian regime to a liberal democratic one has received much journalistic and scholarly attention.[1] Curiosity about political parties,[2] the elections,[3] and the labor movement and the political Left[4] has tended to be satisfied first. Not as much attention has been paid to economic policy.[5] Yet, throughout the transition, government policy-making had to continue. The business of running the country did not stop despite the fact that a major political change was occurring. Particularly in the area of the economy, difficult decisions were postponed so as not to create additional conflict and tension. Economic conditions and issues generally took a political back seat to the consolidation of democracy itself.[6] The centrality of "politics" during the early stages of the transition often meant that difficult economic decisions simply were not made or were taken in a manner of "the path of least resistance." Foremost on the minds of Spain's active political leadership was the political transition and the seemingly impossible hurdles yet to be faced in the attempt at democratic reform.

Who made many of the central economic decisions during these times of political reform? Who controlled the agenda of economic policy-making during these difficult days in recent Spanish political history? Analysis has generally neglected what occurred economically during the transition to democracy. Nevertheless, some hints may be culled from this discussion. Del Campo, Tezanos, and Santin, for example, allude to one possibility in their discussion of Spain's political elite and economic elite when they state:

> The power of the economic oligarchy has manifested itself in its influence on political and social life, while at the same time certain high level bureaucratic elites have developed great power beyond the strictly political sphere, and particularly in the economy. In this manner, members of the political and bureaucratic elite have become outstanding members of the economic oligarchy, a fact that has reinforced the political power of the oligarchy. . . . The democratic transition has taken place in a period of economic crisis and has produced only a few changes in the intercommunication between politics, economy, and bureaucracy.[7]

This reference to a financial oligarchy also surfaces in other discussions of Spain's transition to democracy. In an excellent historical account of the transition, Paul Preston in *The Triumph of Democracy in Spain* refers directly to the existence of an economic oligarchy toward the end of the Franco regime when he states: "The violence of September 1975 underlined more than ever that the political obsolescence of the regime's structures had created a powerful coincidence of interest in change which spanned the democratic opposition and large areas of the economic oligarchy, the middle classes and the administration."[8] In another work, one focusing on the party system in the new Spanish democracy, Richard Gunther, Giacomo Sani, and Goldie Shabad also refer to evidence regarding the existence of a financial oligarchy in Spain.[9] They make several analytically undeveloped references to the activities and the role that the oligarchy played in Spain's transition to democracy. For example, they quote one interviewee who refers directly to "the great economic oligarchy." And, while preferring to refer to it as "the Spanish business class"[10], the authors themselves suggest a high degree of financial concentration in Spain, even if not an "oligarchy," when they state that one party's "economic program called for nationalization of the ten largest banks (which control 80 percent of total financial resources) and fifty of the largest industrial firms in a wide variety of sectors."[11]

These references to the existence of a "financial oligarchy" or "a Spanish business class" raises many questions about its position in Spain. What role did it play during the transition? Did it occupy a central place in policy-making during the highly politicized and critical years of Spain's democratic reform? The chapters that follow seek to advance and illustrate the argument that the existence of a financial oligarchy in Spain strongly determined the direction for one critical area of policy that involves important macroeconomic issues—energy.

Energy is a fundamental macroeconomic policy issue in Spain as well as much of the world. Energy policy-making heavily overlaps the domain of Spanish economic planning. Spain's national energy policy-making in general and the National Energy Plan (PEN) in particular permit direct comparison of the making of policy both before and during Spain's transition to democracy. The Spanish state played a central role in energy as it did in many other economic areas. The first PEN was written and approved by the Franco regime; the second PEN was caught up-in the politics of the transition, being written in 1977 but not approved by the Cortes (Parliament) until 1979, its revision published toward the end of 1981; and Felipe González's Socialist government issued a new PEN in 1983. Energy policy thus permits analysis of the changing influences and forces on policy-making in each of the distinctive periods of the Spanish transition. And to extend this line of reasoning, energy policy may be only one example of the lack of the Spanish regime change's influence on economic policy outcomes. Similar patterns may exist in other areas that are more generally characteristic of the effects of regime change on economic policy.

## The Central Argument

Why did Spain's transition to democracy not produce great changes in energy policy? Why, given a regime change, did "politics" take a back seat to "economics" in energy policy? How does this square intellectually with the "politics matters" assumptions and research findings that underscore so much of the political science literature?

One reason why the democratic reforms in Spain did not produce significant energy policy change is that the regime transition changed Spain's overall financial structure very little. More specifically, the transition to democracy had little effect on private vested financial interests in energy. Spain's transition to democracy was a political reform, one which left unaltered the country's fundamental economic structures housing financial interests that had become firmly institutionalized over a long period of time. The Spanish regime change could have, yet did not, include reform of the country's economic as well as governmental structures. These financial interests were in both the coalitions that supported the Franco regime during the 1960s and 1970s and the one that has supported the reforms that produced parliamentary democracy. The continuity and centrality of these financial interests in the coalition upon which the political leadership of both the Franco regime and the current democratic system ultimately rested provided an opportunity to perpetuate economic policies compatible with their needs and desires. These financial interests were central, particularly with regard to energy, primarily because of the capital intensive nature of energy production, the need for investment in energy development, and because energy underpins industrial and other economic development. And, industrial and economic development is a national concern in which all members of the nation have a stake. Financial interests in Spain, established before and during the Franco regime, penetrated the institutions of planning and thus were able to control energy policy during the early periods of democracy in Spain.

A second reason advanced for why Spain's transition to democracy did not produce significant energy policy change is that alternative sources of policy had little effect on policy decision-making. Nongovernmental political parties, labor unions, public opinion and other groups and organizations articulated differing policy preferences. These alternative preferences, therefore, did not significantly change Spain's energy policy outcomes. While these preferences possessed the potential to constrain policy, they remained nonbinding constraints. A more radical transition, one that transformed both political and economic institutions and processes, might have made these nonbinding constraints binding in nature. Or future political and economic reform may do so. But the Spanish democratic transition prevented such a "revolution." Once economic institutions radically change, either imposed from within Spain or from outside the country by such organizations as the EEC, other models will be required to explain energy policy direction.

## Coalitional Elites

A major realignment of a political system's decision-making coalition is central to a transition from authoritarianism to democracy.[12] The need for a stable coalition of policymakers brought a shuffling of the roles filled by various elite groups. The shift in Spain's policy-making coalition's composition and the degree to which this coalition initially remained unchanged in democratic Spain signal the extent to which the political transition affected energy policy outputs. The financial interests' "pivotal" nature in the coalitions supporting both regimes' governments is key to our explanation. Before this "pivotal" notion can be developed, however, some general comments are necessary concerning the critical interests in Spain competing for membership in such coalitions. Analytically, and somewhat overstated for the sake of clarity, three central political forces are central to our understanding of Spain's policy-making coalitions before and during the transition to democracy. These three groups are the military, business, and labor.

## The Spanish Military

The Spanish armed forces as a political participant comes from the same mold as those of many Latin American nations. Politically and culturally conservative, the Spanish armed forces have historically perceived themselves as the ultimate defenders of the Spanish nation. They see themselves as the protectors of God and country, always ready to come to the defense of the Spanish way of life. Defense of the church, the family, the monarchy and all centralized authority, and other traditional Spanish institutions are of utmost concern to them.[13] The Spanish military has principally been inward looking, seeing the potential danger from within Spain itself, not from foreign invasion. The military has viewed the political Left as the greatest threat to these institutions and thus to the military's own central role in politics and the nation's governmental decision-making. The military's active role in Spanish politics has a long history, until recently closely linked to that of the Spanish monarchy. The military coup, or the Spanish version known as a *pronunciamiento*, has been a regular feature of Spanish political life. The Spanish military traditionally plays the role of an arbitrator or overseer, stepping into politics to set the nation back on a "correct" course. It often quickly returns power to a civilian government. Francisco Franco's early hold on power, while an anomaly in terms of its bloody beginning and duration, should be viewed within this tradition.

## Spanish Business

In Spain, as in most other Western, capitalistic systems, the large business interests carry a great deal of political weight. Spanish scholars, analysts, and the citizenry itself generally refer to these business interests as oligarchical in nature.[14] This oligarchy includes the financial institutions, businesses, and capital-intensive industries. The incentive for these entities to be politically active is primarily economic. Large industry, the banking sector, business organizations, and similar groups often pursue special tax status, trade agreements, and other political-economic favors from policymakers. They attempt to obtain these directly by influencing the governmental policy-making processes via consultations, overlap of personnel on advisory bodies, and intense lobbying. On the one hand, their power over private investment often determines the nature and very success of Spanish state planning. On the other hand, competition for state capital in the nation's private enterprises creates a strong incentive to intervene or influence public economic decisions as a means of protecting their own interests.

The Spanish business community, of course, does not act at all times as a coherent political force. Economic interests in different companies and industries may diverge. While the Spanish business community's economic interests may differ at times, individual businesses, entrepreneurs, and the holders of capital have all sought to defend their interests in the political arena, both as individuals and as groups, associations, and corporations. Business's close association with partisan interest groups, political parties, and certain government industries provides a prominent platform from which to influence governmental economic policy. Furthermore, most members of the Spanish business community have a common economic necessity that links then in a fundamental way. The Spanish business community has a structural center that provides a great deal of influence-exertion cohesion. The Spanish financial system, and more specifically, the major Spanish banks, have an extremely strong hand in giving direction to the entire Spanish business community. This banking influence, as will be developed later, extends well beyond the business community. The Spanish banking system strongly influences Spain's macroeconomic performance, often charting the course for governmental economic planning.

## Organized Labor

A third major political actor is the Spanish labor movement. The economic and political associations representing the Spanish labor force possess the potential to affect the politics of macroeconomic decision-making. Free labor unions are the voice and, depending upon the numerical level of membership and placement within the economy, the muscle of the work force. Labor unions are interest groups with basic concerns—employment and compensation. Organized labor's cooperation often facilitates state economic planning that includes large construction or production efforts. Governmental planning, particularly in areas where choices between capital and labor-intensive economic decisions are to be made, is an area where labor organizations play a salient role. Jobs are often at stake in such capital-intensive undertakings, e.g., nuclear plants with their many construction jobs but few openings in relation to coal-burning facilities after the plant is complete. Labor organizations are well-organized monitors of the political processes that have an effect on their members' and the country's well-being. Their dissemination of information generally broadens the rank and file's awareness of relevant economic issues.

Leftist in political orientation, the labor movement has a long tradition in Spanish political history. The labor unions often work closely with leftist political parties, utilizing these as a political means of expression: the Workers Commissions (CCOO) with the Spanish Communist Party (PCE);[15] the General Workers' Union (UGT) with the Spanish Socialist Workers' Party (PSOE); and the National Confederation of Workers (CNT) linked to Spain's weak but persistent anarchist movement.[16] The fact that parties live day to day primarily with political realities and labor unions with economic realities does not, however, guarantee a harmonious relationship between the two. Differences are accentuated, given the demands of the milieu of political reform, without corresponding economic changes. The organized labor-union movement and the leftist-oriented political parties nevertheless parallel each other in many of their policy goals. These unions and parties, as will be discussed in detail in chapter 5, often speak with one voice. In this sense, they are analytically quite similar to the business community—not in the energy policy direction they advocate but in that they have the potential to give or deny important support to the government.

These three central political groups—military, business, and labor—have competed over the years to be part of Spain's policy-making coalition. The absence of significant change in Spanish energy policy outcomes following the country's recent transition to democracy is, in part, a consequence of business's centrality in Spain's decision-making coalitions.

## A Coalition Shift with a Pivotal Member

Business, labor, and the military are three of the major political forces that have contended for power in Spain since the end of the Civil War. General Franco led the Spanish State's decision-making apparatus following his 1939 military victory in the Spanish Civil War. The regime remained dominated by the Spanish military forces until the 1953 treaty with the United States. This end to international isolation began a process of economic revitalization. The 1959 Economic Stabilization Plan entrenched Spanish business alongside the military in the governing decision-making coalition.[17] This military-business coalition held together until Franco's death, although gradually business and the "rationalist" technocrats came to dominate the military within this informal coalition of support. Carlos Moya Valganon seemed to make a similar point when he stated:

> Spanish development under Franco was initially spearheaded not by a new and assertive bourgeois-entrepreneurial-bureaucratic elite, as most theorists have maintained, but rather by the Spanish government, relying first of all upon old-line military technicians who had risen to prominence during the Civil War and upon the traditional aristocracy whose fortunes rested on land and finance capitalism.

Only later, as the government sought to rationalize the economic structure, did the new bureaucratic management experts and entrepreneurs begin to attain power.[18]

The Spanish transition to democracy brought a shift to a new alignment in the policy-making coalition: a business-labor composition. King Juan Carlos I and Adolfo Suárez delicately orchestrated this regime change. The monarch kept the Spanish military at bay by fully utilizing his traditional role as head of the armed forces. He handpicked his governmental leaders and skillfully manipulated the Francoist Cortes to pave the legal way for the implementation of parliamentary democracy. This constitutional change formalized the military's earlier removal from political power, left the Spanish economic structures untouched, reasserted the legitimacy of the business-governmental linkages, and opened up political and economic representation to organized labor. Political parties were legalized, including the Socialist and Communist parties. Labor unions were deemed a legitimate part of the Spanish political-economic system. And these newly surfaced political groups immediately played a central role in the transitional process. Political agreements between business and labor openly demonstrated the shift in the composition of the ruling decision-making coalition. The Moncloa Pacts smoothed the transition in 1977 by exchanging, among other things, certain political reforms for restraints on wage increases. Later, the Interconfederal Outline Agreement, the National Employment Agreement, and the Social and Economic Pact extended this political and economic cooperation between business and labor. A center-right political party, the Union of the Democratic Center (UCD), controlled the government throughout this period of political reform. Organized labor and the political left remained staunch defenders of Spain's new democratic political regime.[19]

Spain's peaceful transition to democracy with business as a pivotal member of the policy-making coalition permitted business and other financial interests to constrain the scope and direction of economic policy changes. The central position of business is based on an essentially unaltered economic substructure. The position of major financial interests in Spain's economic structures provided a base for protection of their concerns. Personnel overlap, through mutual executive board memberships, and cozy public-private economic relationships permitted strong economic self-defense during the political transition. Such protection activities stemmed from and in turn produced significant influence in Spain's policy-making bodies. The interpenetration of private economic interests and matters of economic policy limited the amount of policy change. The actual composition of this policy-making coalition, its change during Spain's political development, and the political maneuvering both within and without it shed much light on the effect of a transition to democracy on economic policy and planning.[20]

The business class's pivotal position was reflected in the Spanish state bureaucracy. Governmental institutions with responsibility for formulating economic policy were closely tied to business. The bureaucratic arrangement encapsulated much of the economic substructure's struggle for influence within the policy-making apparatus. Certain key sectors of the nation's economic structure had close formal and informal relationships with relevant branches of the state bureaucracy, e.g., the banking system with the finance ministry, business with commerce, industry with industry, utilities with energy. This public-private relationship, and its evolution across regimes, directly affected policy direction. Administrative policy-making and planning were generally formulated in a way satisfactory to private economic interests.

It would be a mistake, however, to view a central bureaucracy as a coherent whole. Rather, in a period of political reform, the various parts of the bureaucratic structure compete against each other for administrative hegemony, protesting their realm of existence from encroachment by others. The formal ministerial division of powers, the informal "norms" and "standard operating procedures," and the relationships of outside interests to the state's administrative bodies were a product of continual determination of bureaucratic "turf." Each part of the state bureaucracy was concerned with maintaining and increasing its responsibility for the various plans it produced. Both authoritarian and democratic political systems possess elements of this bureaucratic competition. Transition from an authoritarian system to a democracy accentuated this struggle. The shifting composition of the policy-making coalition during this transition threatened some bureaucratic areas while strengthening others, e.g., the Spanish Ministry of Finance's influence in state macroeconomic and energy planning grew with a concomitant growth in the centrality of business interests in Spain, thus lessening the powers of other ministries such as Industry and Energy. Such transitions are undoubtedly very unsure periods for state bureaucracies, not only concerned about their own interests but reflecting attempts by members of the policy-making coalition to institutionally protect theirs. Policy direction is most certainly affected by this uncertainty.

While this work does not attempt to explain the reasons underlying Spain's transition to democracy (rather being concerned with its policy consequences), business support for the transition undoubtedly assisted in smoothing its path. Many members of the Franco regime called for democratic reform. Christian-Democrat high-level functionaries such as José María de Areilza and Manuel Fraga were motivated by the preference "to concede a little rather than lose everything."[21] Furthermore,

> Joaquin Garriques-Walker, one of the most significant figures in Spanish capitalism and one-time representative of several multi-

national corporations, led growing calls from the financial and industrial oligarchy for political change. He expressed the liberalizing position with great clarity: It is only by taking the risk of possible change . . . that one can control the change. Otherwise, the social forces which are bringing pressure to bear on the institutions of the state will end by triumphing as did Ho Chi Minh in Saigon.[22]

Stated differently, the Spanish political crisis and transition to democracy "created a coincidence of interest between part of the economic oligarchy and the opposition."[23] The transition to democracy came, in part, due to concessions that had to be made because of the economic crisis. "The prospect of increased unemployment and lower living standards heralded growing militance. Limited political reform seemed to be a reasonable concession to avoid a serious challenge to the entire structure of power in Spain."[24] Furthermore, many in the Spanish oligarchy had come to believe that the Franco regime constituted a major obstacle to further economic development, particularly with regard to EEC membership.[25] Many economists were "also convinced that the health of the economy necessitates an expansion of the public sector in order to finance a more adequate infrastructure. The necessary fiscal reform would only be possible within a democratic structure."[26] Thus both the working class and a significant fraction of industrialists and bankers possessed a need for democratic liberties.[27] A new political coalitional alliance came to the forefront with the death of Franco and his political regime. Particularly during the early stages, the political-economic interests created under the Franco regime remained at the center of the alliance.

## Instruments and Allocations

Did Spain's peaceful transition from an authoritarian system to a democratic one affect the choice of policy instruments? The instruments of policy implementation are the means by which the state, under the auspices of the policy-making coalition, chooses to carry out its policies. Economic regulation is such a policy instrument. Decisions to regulate or not to regulate various sectors of the economy, however, determine benefits for members of the policy-making circle. Similarly, the choices between a free market and a planned economy in certain sectors reflect a desire to maintain or alter one's prospects for benefits. Other policy instruments include taxation, state investment, spending, and different allocation schemes. What changes in policy outputs do we expect as a political system transforms itself from a military dictatorship to a parliamentary democracy? What differences do we expect to see in the Spanish energy officials' use of policy instruments? In the area of institutional reorganization, such reform generally contains policymakers' attempts at position solidification or desires for greater benefits. If a ministerial reorganization is proposed or implemented, for example, a member of the policy-making coalition likely perceives it as advantageous. (Given the argument that organized finance is the critical member of Spain's governing coalition, attempts at such institutional reorganization should reflects its members' two central motivating factors: profits and a desire to continue in a government policy-making role, i.e., to remain in power.) Similarly, it may be advantageous to block reorganization or reform. Reforms in the economic system or the economic-governmental relationship may likewise be implemented or blocked. Reform processes themselves and the political maneuvering behind them affects the nature and outcomes of policymaking, both by design and not.

Energy policy-making in a democratic political system, one might expect, should be more receptive to popular sentiment. More direct political accountability might partially serve to "check" oligarchical policy-making in energy policy. Democratic politics might foster demand-reducing energy policies in Spain. Electoral and parliamentary accountability might call the financial oligarchy to account for and justify any "windfall" or otherwise extraordinary high profits in the energy sector, particularly if such profits have an inflationary effect on the economy as a whole. More direct political accountability might also direct the government to use some stronger demand-reducing measures such as consumption rationing, especially if it is perceived as being more egalitarian and fair than the present market system. Greater citizen expression and direct policy accountability might influence policymakers to slow down such controversial energy programs as nuclear energy, as has been the case in some Scandinavian countries. Greater political accountability for policymakers, however, may encourage continuation of some past aspects of energy policy, instruments, and outputs. Central financial interests' push for low energy prices in order to maintain high volume sales would probably be reinforced by the general population's desire for low consumption prices. Energy-pricing policy may not change despite the transition to democracy. The potential for or absence of such policy change ultimately depends upon the degree and nature of this political accountability.

Our understanding of political transitions has generally not questioned its effect on public policy, with the possible exception of military spending and educational policy. Previous analysis of political development, revolution, and more moderate forms of political change have sought to explain such occurrences while neglecting their policy consequences.[28] This book seeks to contribute to the policy literature through consideration of the effects on policy of a political system's transition from an authoritarian regime to a representative democracy. And it seeks to do so through the consideration of an issue central to all contemporary political systems. Energy policy and planning have become a critical aspect of macroeconomic management during the 1970s and 80s. Energy is critical to the success of the economies of all political systems, especially the developing countries. Higher energy prices on the world's market have placed an even greater hurdle in the path to development for these nations. Because of more expensive energy, they face more serious challenges to successful economic development, yet their economies remain highly susceptible to the problems of energy scarcities. Nevertheless, given both domestic and international pressures, these are the very nations that most likely face a transition from a military dictatorship to a democracy. I thus believe the research reported in this book can assist as well in our understanding in other nations of the policy consequences of political change.

## Outline of the Book

I hope that the discussion of the effects of a transition to democracy on policy-making procedures and outcomes will lead our thinking beyond the Spanish case. I begin in chapter 2 by developing expectations about transitions to democracy and public policy based on the history of the relationship of business and finance to Spain's policy-making coalition. This chapter provides much of the historical context within which to assess the nature of the policy-making coalition during the Franco period. Chapter 3 narrows the discussion by focusing on energy as the specific policy issue under consideration. Spain's energy situation is placed in a cross-national perspective. The governmental and other institutional arrangements within which policy is articulated and made are then described. This chapter also analyzes the Spanish governments' formal policies on energy planning with a description of PEN, the National Energy Plan. Particular emphasis is paid to the economic and political setting in which the regime transition occurred. Chapter 3 also analyzes the actions and interactions of the various political participants during the formulation of the different national energy policies. Emphasis is placed on the participants within the ruling policy-making coalition. Chapter 4 gets into the politics of Spanish energy policy both before and after the transition to democracy by analyzing the governments' macroeconomic instruments in its implementation. After a discussion of the politically induced delay in Spain's macroeconomic policy responses to the energy crisis, I present a more detailed analysis of several basic instruments of energy policy, including such instruments as pricing policies, investment, and institutional coordination.

Chapter 5 then assesses the nature of governmental and extragovernmental opposition to PEN, Spain's overall energy program, and the specific instruments used in its implementation. Besides the policy positions by the major Spanish political parties, chapter 5 analyzes Spanish energy politics and the influences on energy policy through a cross-regime comparison of public opinion on the state's energy program and policy instruments. Chapter 6 explains why Spanish energy policy continued relatively unaltered despite the country's transition from authoritarianism to democracy, and analyzes the composition of the policy-making coalition before, during, and after Spain's transition to democracy. This chapter's argument is that the pivotal nature of the business-financial oligarchy in this policy-making coalition helps explain energy policy continuity. Chapter 7 then looks to the international context for pillars of support for Spanish energy policy continuation during the transition. The International Energy Agency is analyzed as a case in point. Chapter 8 focuses on Spanish energy policy during the early period following the PSOE's coming to power. This period is important because many analysts consider the smooth alternation of governments in 1982 as the end to Spain's transition period. This analysis of energy policy, however, continues up to 1 January 1986, when Spain officially became a member of the European Economic Community.[29] Finally, chapter 9 turns away from the particular Spanish case. It reconsiders this book's view that the composition of the ruling policy-making coalition determines the effects of a transition to democracy on economic policy, given our understanding of the Spanish case. This concluding chapter reassesses the general objective of this study—to better understand the consequences of a peaceful transition to democracy on policy related to economic issues. More specifically, it reassesses the problems inherent to energy policy-making during a political transition to democracy. Both understanding the consequences of peaceful transition to democracy on energy policy and considering the impediments the energy area may present to such transitions point to obstacles to be avoided by other political systems passing down this road in the future. This road is not, after all, one that will go untraveled.

# 2

---

# The Franco Regime's
# Economic Performance,
# Planning, and Policymakers

Following the Civil War, the Franco regime took extremely harsh measures to build and strengthen its political and economic institutions. The sternness of authoritarian rule was not unexpected following such a divisive and bloody civil war.[1] International economic isolation following the war's devastation created economic hardship. Autarkic economic policies were pursued. New state economic structures and governmental institutions sought to promote development. Economic lethargy resulted. Franco's dictatorial rule responded with economic reform in the late 1950s and early 1960s. The resulting prosperity strengthened the "inside position" of certain economic interests in government policy-making. Politics then returned to center stage. By the late 1960s, demands for political reform intensified as the regime and its leader aged. Calls for addressing the regional question and the rights of organized labor combined with Spaniards' desire for psychological and political acceptance in the European community of nations eroded support for the Franco regime's political institutions. Given these and other pressures, the government policy-making institutions could not survive the Caudillo's death in 1975. Support for public policy-making processes was fatally removed, despite the continuing presence of many of the key political participants. The political system underwent radical institutional change.

Spanish leaders both during and after the Franco regime sought stability through a process of institutional adaptability and reinstitutionalization. While it is true that "Francoist institutions were not as flexible and open as has been suggested by some," they were adaptable enough to insure the regime's existence until the Caudillo's death.[2] This adaptability continued through the regime change. Key economic interests positioned themselves to direct the system's policy-making during this institutional change, even in its most extreme form of regime change. The Franco regime's desire for survival led its leaders to institutionalize certain economic interests in its government policy-making processes. Many of these same economic interests were to remain in place following the transition to democracy.

The political powers in Francoist Spain, due to increased economic demands placed upon it, had to permit a new policy-making group into Spanish economic structures following the institutional easing of the corporatist ideology. The modified institutional structure and the new economic policy-making group it co-opted in turn served as the basis for stability during the reinstitutionalization caused by Spain's transition to democracy. These economic powers did not challenge the political reform in order to guarantee their own survival. The Franco regime's political survival necessitated changes in Spanish economic policy during the 1950s and 1960s. This regime institutionally situated a new "political business" class in the coalition which dominated Spanish economic decision-making. The governmental coalition co-opted this new economic elite. The emergence and institutional solidification of these new technocratic planners and policymakers stemmed from the interaction of roles and interests of economic and political decision-making. This group's linkage with the financial oligarchy during the Franco regime provided a stable foundation upon and around which political stability could more or less be peacefully maintained in Spain.

This chapter outlines the governmental organization of the Franco regime and the slow but significant shifts in the political coalition supporting it. It also describes the economic development and planning in post–Civil War Spain. Also, concerned over questions raised by Juan J. Linz,[3] we seek to understand the extent to which new economic power holders became integrated and co-opted into the existing economic structure, the degree to which they have become a channel of access for the most powerful groups and firms in the economy, and more generally, the extent to which political power can be transformed into economic power.

## The Francoist State

The Franco regime was an *étatist* right-wing dictatorship. The regime's institutional blueprint and early political and economic institutions were based on the Italian fascist-corporatist model.[4] The 1966 Organic Law of the State outlined the regime's formal governmental and political institutions.[5] This law updated and slightly revised the four Fundamental Laws: the Labor Charter of March 1938, the 1942 law establishing the Cortes as a quasi-corporatist national parliament, the Charter of the Spaniards in 1945, and the Law of Succession in 1948. The Organic Law of the State laid out the state's institutional arrangement with no separation of powers, based on "the principle of the unity of power and coordination of function" (Article 2).

General Franco, as chief of state, was the supreme political authority. All important state officials were responsible to and either directly or indirectly appointed by him. Franco appointed the president of the government, i.e., the prime minister, who chose the members of the Council of Ministers (synonymously termed the cabinet or government) in close consultation with the chief of state. Franco himself served as both chief of state and president of the government from 1 October 1936 to 9 June 1973.[6] Franco remained chief of state until his death on 20 November 1975. The Francoist Council of Ministers was responsible solely to the chief of state, despite a superficial resemblance to cabinets in Western European parliamentary democracies. The Council of Ministers consisted of the prime minister, fifteen ministerial department heads, and three ministers without portfolio. The departments included Foreign Affairs, Justice, Army, Navy, Air, Treasury (Hacienda), Interior (Gobernación), Public Works, Education and Science, Labor, Industry, Agriculture, Commerce, Housing, and Information and Tourism. Ministers without portfolio included the National Movement's secretary-general, the planning commissioner, and the minister of syndicalist relations. The Minister of the Interior, also in consultation with Franco, appointed the civil governors of the fifty-one provinces and the mayors of all major cities. The civil governor appointed the mayors of towns with fewer than 10,000 people.[7]

Imposition of authority from above also characterized the legislative structure. As chief of state, Franco appointed the president of the Cortes. This parliamentary head chose the presidents and members of the various committees.[8] The chief of state also determined Council of the Realm membership. This was primarily a consultative body. Franco thus dominated the system at the legislative level as well. Generally stated, the Franco regime was a personalistic, authoritarian, no-party political system despite the institutional trappings.[9] General policy emanated from Franco himself and his "inner circle." Franco's military cronies, relatives, and advisers comprised this group during the regime's early years, with the Caudillo having the last word.[10]

## Franco's Coalitional Support

The Franco regime's early political base carried over from its origins in the 1936 military uprising and Civil War against the Second Republic. The Franco regime co-opted such conservative social and ideological elements as the Carlists and Alfonsine monarchists, Catholics, Falangists, the Catholic church, and the military, and later added business and economic interests.[11] The regime's traditional-conservative orientation reflected a preference for rural values, which sat well with supporters who "argued vociferously in favor of agriculture as the firmest base upon which to construct the New State."[12]

Particularly in the regime's early years, Franco successfully managed partisan rivalries between his supporters despite his lack of political sophistication. Franco recognized the regime's coalitional nature by altering the composition of the Council of Ministers from time to time to include various coalitional components. Franco balanced the different groups supporting the regime by awarding ministerial posts through a variation of a spoils system. The timing of these rewards generally indicated the regime's need for the different groups' political support. Noteworthy groups involved in this institutional co-optation were the traditionalists, i.e., Carlists and clerical conservatives who had opposed Spanish liberalism since the 1830s, the Falangists, monarchists, the military, and Catholic organizations such as the National Catholic Association of Propagandists (ACN de P),[13] and Opus Dei.[14] Each of these groups defined its cabinet or ministerial domain over the years. The Minister of Justice and the presidency of the Cortes were controlled by the traditionalists. The Falangists dominated the Ministry of Labor, the Syndical Organization, and the National Movement. The ACN de P focused predominately on education and foreign affairs. And, most important for the analysis here, Opus Dei members monopolized economic affairs between 1957 and 1974. During this period, Opus Dei dominated the ministries of Finance, Industry, Commerce, and the Planning Subsecretariat. It also had a strong role, along with Catholic Action, in the Ministries of Foreign Affairs and Education. Opus Dei technocrats, who supported Franco's conservative political and social programs, were the force behind the economic liberalization policies of the early 1960s described below. Franco's institutional co-optation of these groups bought the stability necessary to address both domestic and international political concerns.[15]

The nineteenth and early twentieth centuries provided the nurturing period for the partnership between economic policymakers in government and private economic interests that was to carry the nation through its contemporary transition to democracy. The political weakness of the incipient industrial sector forced a merger of the entrepreneurial class with the interests of the traditional *latifundia* and the industrial oligarchy. Like the industrial sector, these *latifundia* interests were politically weak relative to other European countries. Napoleon's conquest and occupation of Spain in the early nineteenth century had facilitated a political revolution that dismantled the estate system. A powerful monarchy then further weakened Spanish feudalism. Furthermore,

> the sale of mortmain had created a new bourgeois land owning class whose interest was not in conflict with the aristocratic latifundia owners. These agrarian elites very often lived in the cities, had close ties with professionals, the administration, and even the military and the emerging industrialists.[16]

By the 1920s, the radicalization of organized labor challenged the industrial entrepreneurs. Their need for alleviating problems of capital accumulation became secondary to the containment of the labor challenge. This further strengthened the political alliance between the entrepreneurial class and the *latifundia* landlords. Spanish economic development forced a political alliance of the *latifundia* and the industrial entrepreneurs to face the alleged threat emerging from the industrial working class.[17]

In a manner similar to many other market economies during the same period, Spanish economic power had become concentrated in a few firms in the industrial sector. The demands of modern industry for capital left market entry open only to old Spanish wealth. The Primo de Rivera dictatorship encouraged this during the early twentieth century. The Franco regime initially also heavily depended on a large number of people who had strong links with the financial and industrial oligarchy. Much of Spain's business and professional elite, in addition to the large landowners, had supported the Nationalists' revolt against the Republic.[18]

The opening of the Spanish economy in the 1960s and the inclusion into government of the technocratic management group brought a change to the governing coalition. The Franco regime had maintained during its early stages the traditional alliance between the *latifundia* landlords and owners of industry. Decades of autarkic policies did not break this alliance. Following the economic reforms of the late 1950s, however, market forces were allowed to carry out "what politically could not be done within the context of traditional political power."[19] European tourism and the counterflow of Spanish labor economically weakened this alliance. The removal of the *latifundia* as a coalitional partner did not, however, go without some political soothing.

> The continuing alliance between industrial and latifundia interests required both atavistic rituals of political support as well as concrete financial payoffs in the form of price supports, subsidies, quotas, etc., in order to let the market do what economic planning devoid of political muscle could not do.[20]

The *latifundia* landlords continued to receive relatively high profits courtesy of the politically suppressed wage rate and the removal of the threat of agricultural or land reform.

Organized labor, on the other hand, was not a member of Franco's ruling coalition. The Franco regime simply shut labor out of the policy-making process.[21] The Labor Charter of March 1938 served as Franco's corporatist manifesto and the legal basis for labor's exclusion. The Law of Syndical Organization of 1940 institutionally structured the suppression of labor conflict. This law, which stated in its preamble that "syndicalization becomes the political form of the whole Spanish economy," created a national labor organization. This first major piece of Francoist legislation compelled most workers, technicians, and employers to join the government-controlled syndicates and prohibited strikes. The twenty-six vertical corporations corresponded to the country's major functional economic sectors.[22] The stated purpose of the *Sindicatos* was to facilitate communication between the worker and the state.

This corporatist structure institutionally divided collective working-class interests. The official syndicate representatives were regarded as illegitimate and frequently ignored despite the fact that they were to set wage and working conditions and to provide social services such as benefits and recreational and training programs.[23]

> [The] official representatives of working-class interests—sindicato officials—were not regarded as legitimate spokesmen for laboring interests by a large number of State Administration officials.[24]

Thus, in practice, the *Sindicatos* served to control rather than mobilize workers.[25] Medhurst correctly indicated their impotence:

> No *Sindicatos* have successfully pushed wage claims, sometimes to the embarrassment of their political opponents in charge of planning, but they lack the independence needed to secure a major reassessment of aims. The necessary freedom to organize, on both the industrial and political fronts, would imply the abandonment of con-

trol that the present regime has always regarded as an indispensable feature of its system of rule.[26]

The national labor syndicates even often "became organizations closely connected to the informal leaders of the business community and were at their service."[27] The Franco regime's labor-union structure simply did not give labor a voice in economic decision-making and planning. Even as late as December 1973, a group of labor leaders received long prison sentences for attempting to create a broadly based labor movement.[28] Motivated by political survival, the Franco regime's change in economic policy slowly required a slight easing on labor. During the regime's last years, collective bargaining did play a role in settling wage disputes between individual enterprises and their respective labor force. Strikes remained illegal, of course, but they were to become a part of the normal development of wage disputes.[29]

## Economic Policy-Making and Performance

With their coalition of support, Franco and his inner circle made policy decisions, including energy policy. Recent Spanish economic history provides the background for Francoist energy policy. Four periods can be distinguished in Spain's economic evolution since the Civil War and the establishment of the Franco regime.[30] Three of these will be discussed here, with the fourth being analyzed in chapter 3's discussion of Spain's energy situation. These four economic periods are:

1. 1939 to 1951—The end of the Civil War to the treaty with the United States. Economic policy during this period followed a corporatist model. Economic performance consisted of eleven years of virtual stagnation dominated by the instability of agricultural production.
2. 1951 to 1959—A period of slow economic development prodded by American aid and characterized by import substitution and continued heavy state regulation.
3. 1959 to 1973—The period begins with the Spanish Stabilization Plan in which a liberal economic policy was pursued. A realistic exchange rate was adopted and an open door policy to foreign capital was implemented. The twelve year Spanish "economic miracle" followed, financed by tourism and emigrant remittances.
4. 1973 to the present—The Spanish economy was pierced in its Achilles heel. The economy received two severe shocks due to its almost complete dependence on foreign petroleum; the first, in

1973, brought the Spanish economic miracle to an end; the second, in 1979, continued the balance-of-payments, inflation, and unemployment problems.

## Hardship During the Corporatist Years: 1939 to 1951

Autarky characterized Spanish economic policy between 1939 and 1951. The Franco regime's early economic policy was "taken as a means to achieve political and economic independence both as an expression of nationalism and as the necessary pre-condition for a war economy." [31] The regime's political and economic advisers enthusiastically embarked upon autarky, despite the fact that this economic policy direction was forced upon them. [32] The regime's economic goal quickly became survival through self-sufficiency.

The Spanish government strongly intervened in domestic industry during this period. It pursued an anti-liberal economic policy despite the quick taming of the Falangists' radical anti-capitalistic rhetoric following the Civil War. [33] State economic intervention was compatible with the ideological desire for unity and national integrity. Intervention and the desire for economic self-sufficiency were consistent with Spanish economic tradition. The state played a central role in industrial expansion, particularly through direct capital investment. During the 1940s, public investment reached about 40 percent of total investment. "The idea that the state through its bureaucracy should play a growing role in the development of the country by creating financial institutions . . . has its origin in the Primo de Rivera regime." [34] Protectionism, through high tariffs, had also been a central feature of Spanish economic policy during many previous governments and regimes. [35] No foreign goods could be purchased in Spain that were available from domestic manufacturing or production.

The creation of the Sindicatos, the industrial laws of 1939, and the creation of the National Institute of Industry (INI) in 1941 highlighted policy during this period. The two industrial laws of 1939 sought, in essence, to develop private capitalism by strengthening existing firms and encouraging the creation of new ones. The 24 October 1939 Law of Protection and Development of National Industry sought to give private enterprise the incentive to produce goods which had previously been imported. These incentives, for firms declared to be of "national interest," included: (1) a fifteen-year period of significant economic advantages; (2) tax reductions up to 50 percent; (3) the right to acquire land under eminent domain; (4) machinery and equipment imported under special customs treatment; and (5) a minimum 4 percent guaranteed return on capital investment, with returns over 7 percent being taxed 50 percent by the state.[36]

The second industrial law, the 24 November 1939 Law of Regulation and Defense of National Industry, required all firms receiving any type of governmental economic benefit to use domestically produced products in its production and distribution whenever possible. This meant, of course, higher than world market prices for these firms. Both 1939 laws introduced many other market inefficiencies. Governmental control of investments and the larger firms' advantages in obtaining quotas, importing licenses, and credits from both state and private banks during the early period of the Franco regime further encouraged an already strong tendency toward monopoly in almost all industrial sectors.[37] As Pedro Schwartz stated:

> Quantitative restrictions on imports, foreign exchange control, centralized regulation of foreign trade and direct state intervention in the economy became the main devices used by the government to help it achieve its objectives of rapid industrialization and economic self-sufficiency.[38]

Big business prospered during this period given the low taxes and strict protection for established companies.

Institutionally, the creation of the National Institute of Industry (INI) to channel the state's industrialization effort was part of Francoist Spain's interventionist economic policy. INI serves as a state holding company, developing state-owned companies and buying into other enterprises requiring capital stimulation. INI became the chief means for the vertical integration of Spain's large firms. Capital concentration was intensified through this new state institution and economic instrument. Even today, INI remains one of the state's prime instruments for maintaining general economic activity. Yet despite its defined objectives, "INI's policies have often seemed to reflect little more than the private whims of its directors. Consequently, it proved impossible to use the organization as a basis for economic planning."[39] One reason for this may be a lack of accountability. INI's decision-makers were initially responsible only to Franco, thus bypassing ministerial control.

Until 1962, the Spanish government pursued under the Labor Charter a full employment policy in line with its corporatist philosophy and Spanish economic tradition. Legislation prohibited the dismissal of redundant labor for "economic reasons."[40] This further hindered the industrial sector's economic efficiency, fueling an already high inflation rate, reflected in Table 2-1. The Franco regime obtained much of the money necessary to finance all aspects of economic development, including wages, through running government deficits. "For twenty years, the dictatorship operated at an almost constant deficit."[41] Until 1957 the public debt was automatically rediscountable in the Bank of Spain. Private banks as well as some state-controlled institutions "were legally compelled to devote a given proportion of their resources to the purchase of public debt. But because of its discountability, this debt could be immediately turned into cash, leaving the control of money supply in the hands of the private banks."[42] The government thus had little control over its own money supply. Public investment was thus financed through "forced" savings drawn mostly from working-class wage-earners by means of the inflation created by the public sector. In addition, a regressive taxation policy that the Franco regime inherited heavily taxed the lower classes.[43] The Franco government, however, made no effort to alter it.

Spain's uncontrolled inflation also priced Spanish goods out of the international market.[44] Table 2-2 shows that a balance-of-payments problem plagued the Spanish economy. Economic development meant the industrial sector required a high level of capital-goods imports. Yet Spanish imports had traditionally been agricultural. The rate of inflation increased the com-

Table 2-1  Spanish Price Index

| Year | Base Increase | Yearly Percentage Increase |
|------|---------------|---------------------------|
| 1940 | 100.0 | — |
| 1941 | 118.2 | 18.2 |
| 1942 | 130.0 | 10.0 |
| 1943 | 145.1 | 11.6 |
| 1944 | 156.1 | 7.6 |
| 1945 | 173.2 | 11.0 |
| 1946 | 207.8 | 20.0 |
| 1947 | 243.8 | 17.3 |
| 1948 | 261.1 | 7.1 |
| 1949 | 279.4 | 7.0 |
| 1950 | 329.7 | 18.0 |
| 1951 | 423.5 | 28.5 |
| 1952 | 427.1 | .1 |
| 1953 | 457.5 | 7.1 |
| 1954 | 459.8 | .5 |
| 1955 | 477.7 | 3.9 |
| 1956 | 521.3 | 9.1 |
| 1957 | 608.4 | 16.7 |
| 1958 | 668.2 | 9.8 |
| 1959 | 682.3 | 2.1 |

SOURCE: *Anuário Estadístico 1960*.

petitive gap between the industrial and agricultural sectors. Agriculture simply could not turn high enough profits to keep up with the nonagricultural sector's rate of inflation, thus blunting entrepreneurial desire to invest.

In sum, the first phase of post–Civil War economic development was a failure. Industrial production did not even reach its pre–Civil War level until about 1950. Neither civil-war destruction nor international ostracism is a plausible excuse. The consequences of Spain's autarkic policy were quite apparent. Raw materials were scarce, real income remained below pre–Civil War levels, and private capital accumulation remained low. "The subordination of economics to political ambitions had manifestly failed."[45] The desire for a powerful autarkic economy was quickly replaced by a less ambitious desire for simple economic survival.

## Slow Development: 1951 to 1959

The Franco regime took a first step toward ameliorating Spain's economic stagnation in 1951. The government dropped the unattained goal of economic self-sufficiency and turned toward a more open economy. Spain accepted the United States' offer of economic aid. Loans with private foreign banks were arranged. The mutual defense treaty of September 1953 with the United States sent $618.2 million in grants, $404 million in loans, and $436.8 million in military aid to Spain between 1953 and 1961.[46] This money enabled Spain to overcome production bottlenecks created by previous eco-

**Table 2-2**   International Trade Balance

| Year | Percentage: Imports Exceeding Exports |
|------|----------------------------------------|
| 1931–35 | 125.6 |
| 1941–45 | 97.0 |
| 1946–50 | 118.1 |
| 1951 | 83.2 |
| 1952 | 126.7 |
| 1953 | 126.4 |
| 1954 | 132.2 |
| 1955 | 138.3 |
| 1956 | 173.4 |
| 1957 | 181.2 |
| 1958 | 179.2 |
| 1959 | 158.1 |

SOURCE: Instituto Nacional de Estadística.

nomic policies by substantially increased imports of petroleum and heavy industrial machinery and products.[47] Although not a full return to a free-market economy, this policy shift marked the Spanish government's abandonment of its goal of economic self-sufficiency. More orthodox management of the public sector and private initiative, as opposed to étatism, was introduced into the system.[48] A shift from traditional agriculture to industry was backed by a new program of public investment. Imports were increased until domestic industrial output could rise. Domestic supply improved as imports of raw materials and semifinished and capital goods stimulated domestic production. Backed by long-suppressed demand, the economy grew significantly. Earlier investments in industry, transportation, and utilities began paying off in the 1950s. The Spanish economy experienced greater economic growth during this period.[49] And between 1951 and 1959, the price index rose more modestly, not experiencing its previous wide fluctuations.

This second period of the Franco regime's economic policies remained nevertheless plagued by many economic problems. Economic policy continued to be long on political ideology and short on economic analysis. Emulation of the economic and political practices of the Germans and Italians in the 1940s and nationalist pride continued to have a strong influence on economic policies. The government's desire to protect the traditional social and economic elite's interests also took its toll. In both 1954 and 1956 the government raised public-sector wages to stimulate domestic production, only to have inflationary pressure heighten Spain's balance-of-payments crisis and capital flight.[50] And underconsumption continued, given low levels of real income. Demand for manufactured goods did not rise as fast as expected. Industry had developed, but it remained cost-inefficient and uncompetitive on world markets. Product oversupply forced the government to remove restraints on wages in order to soak up the excess supply. The resulting inflation, and the fact that imports became more expensive, led to a balance-of-payments problem affecting the foreign-exchange rate.

By the late 1950s, the Spanish economy slowed down again. The rate of increase of industrial output slowed sharply. Inflation could push the economy no farther. Once again inflation had adversely affected foreign trade, restricting Spain's export capacity and foreign currency needed for import. The continued overvaluation of the peseta hindered exports. Neglect of agricultural development further weakened Spain's potential for traditional exports. The system of import-export licensing and Spain's bilateral agreements, which fixed both country and product quotas, also exaggerated the problem. All this, added on to the industrial inefficiency introduced by government protectionism and intervention, handicapped the Spanish economy. Even the beneficial effects of the relatively weak tourism trade and large-scale U.S. assistance could not keep the Spanish economy from becoming a victim of the continuing imbalance in foreign trade.[51] National bankruptcy loomed large by late 1958. Spain had only $10 million in reserves and a net deficit of $60 million. Labor problems and strikes plagued many parts of the country.[52] Something had to give.

# Liberalization and the Economic "Miracle": 1959 to 1973

The first move to address the country's economic problems came when Franco swore in a new government in February 1957. The General cleaned out his economic ministries and replaced them with a new team of technocrats with liberal economic views. Franco's near exhaustion of rightist-oriented economic policy led him to opt for these more market-oriented advisers. Franco furthermore received international encouragement to move in this direction. Spain joined the major international economic associations in 1958: the OEEC, the forerunner of the Organization for Economic Cooperation and Development (OECD); the International Monetary Fund (IMF); and the World Bank. Under new economic leadership, Spanish economic policy turned toward a neo-liberalism, free-trade orientation. This leadership's desire to introduce complete economic liberalization developed into the Spanish Stabilization Plan. This plan was approved in July and August 1959 with the assistance of Jacques Rueff, the architect of the 1958 French Stabilization Program, which the Spanish plan emulated. French "indicative planning" thus proved strongly influential.

The Spanish Stabilization Plan has been extensively analyzed.[53] Based on IMF recommendations, the plan sought to slow inflation, to restore the balance-of-payments equilibrium, and to implement greater economic liberalization. The Stabilization Plan cut public expenditure, raised taxes, and froze wages in its fight against inflation. The balance-of-payments and capital flight problems were attacked by an effective devaluation of the peseta. Foreign investment was encouraged. The liberalization program sought to create an institutional environment in line with Western European economies in all areas except the labor market. Over a five-year period this included establishing a new tariff system (1960), the nationalization of the Bank of Spain, the freeing of industrial investments (1963), a minimum size requirement for new industrial investment, free entry into banking (1963), the creation of an anti-monopoly court (1963), and a rationalizing of the tax system that left it highly regressive (1964). The Stabilization Plan also facilitated Spain's first emigration wave to Europe in that it made it considerably easier for Spanish workers to emigrate.[54] The effect was double—it lowered Spain's unemployment level, and emigrant remittances helped reduce the country's balance-of-payments deficit. The program stopped short, however, of a major liberalization of foreign trade, a fundamental change in the tax system, serious anti-monopoly action, the liberalization of the labor market, and the long-awaited reform in land ownership.[55] Stated differently, the plan introduced limited economic reforms while not challenging the existing economic interests in Spain.

Spain's "economic miracle" began after a slow start following the implementation of this plan. Spain's enormous economic growth and development occurred between 1961 and 1973. Between 1961 and 1970, the annual growth in per-capita income average 6.45 percent. "The real growth in Spain's GNP for the decade 1960–70 was 75.5 percent, the highest in all of Europe and surpassed in the world only by Japan with its increase of 110.5 percent."[56] The growth rate of real GNP averaged 7.4 percent during the 1950's, varying between 4.5 and 11.4 percent.[57] Increased tourism, as seen in Table 2-3, played a central role in this economic growth.[58]

Table 2-3   Spanish Tourism

| Year | Tourists (in thousands) | Foreign Currency Tourist Receipts ($ millions) | Balance-of-Trade Deficits ($ millions) |
|------|------|------|------|
| 1959 | 4,194 | 128.6 | 253 |
| 1960 | 6,113 | 297.0 | 57 |
| 1961 | 7,445 | 384.6 | 279 |
| 1962 | 8,668 | 512.6 | 634 |
| 1963 | 10,931 | 679.3 | 1,004 |
| 1964 | 14,102 | 918.6 | 1,056 |
| 1965 | 14,250 | 1,156.9 | 1,737 |
| 1966 | 17,251 | 1,292.5 | 1,964 |
| 1967 | 17,858 | 1,209.8 | 1,745 |
| 1968 | 19,183 | 1,212.7 | 1,548 |
| 1969 | 21,682 | 1,310.7 | 2,333 |
| 1970 | 24,105 | 1,680.8 | 2,360 |
| 1971 | 26,758 | 2,054.4 | 2,025 |
| 1972 | 32,506 | 2,486.3 | 2,911 |
| 1973 | 34,559 | 3,091.2 | 4,405 |
| 1974 | 30,343 | 3,187.9 | 8,340 |
| 1975 | 30,122 | 3,404.3 | 8,516 |
| 1976 | 30,014 | 3,083.3 | 8,723 |

SOURCE: Harrison (1978), 156.

# Economic Planning

As just mentioned, economic planning in Spain had its roots in the reforms of 1957, which brought technocratic economic planners into the government. These planners sought a more efficient economy. Institutionally, their initial attempts at economic planning came through the creation of the Office of Economic Coordination and Programming. This office coordinated capital investments by the various spending departments. An Investment Ordering Program initially coordinated investments during the 1959 and 1960 fiscal years.

The creation of the Development Planning Commission in 1962 led to the implementation in January 1964 of the first of three Economic and Social Development Plans. The purpose of these plans was to stimulate long-term economic growth through extensive capital investment and the coordination of public and private economic activity. The Spanish "economic miracle" occurred at the same time as the first two development plans. With these plans, the Development Planning Commission relied on World Bank advice, recommending greater liberalization, an introduction of greater rationality in public-investment project selection, greater orthodoxy in the public sector, and certain structural reforms.[59]

# The First Plan

The first Economic and Social Development Plan received government approval in December 1963 for the period 1964–67. Despite its title, this initial plan contained no "social" components.[60] Administered through the office of the prime minister, the plan included a set of macroeconomic forecasts, a compulsory plan for public investment and other major macroeconomic measures, and a set of recommendations to the private sector.[61] Its simple projections and forecasts generally reflected "events which would otherwise have taken place independently through the internal logic of the market forces in operation."[62] The plan's policy directives were mandatory for the public enterprises but served only as a guide for the private sector.

The plan focused primarily on tourism, the coordination of market forces activated by tourism, and related concerns.[63] Indicative of the plan's economic strategy were its investments: transportation received 24.58 percent of the total public investments; housing 19.54 percent; nationalized industries 17.09 percent; and irrigation 14.58 percent.[64] The building of Spanish highways, other road construction, and tourist facilities were a clear priority.

Freeway investment, for example, amounted to 1.14 percent of GNP during the plan's tenure. In the plan's final year, total investments in tourist facilities almost matched total state investments in agriculture. The first Spanish Economic Development Plan did not, however, attempt to radically reconstruct Spain's economic system. Spanish economic planners did not include in the plan any fundamental reorganization of the country's economic or political-economic institutions or structures.[65]

Spanish economic performance under the plan, whether attributable to it or not, was good. The economy grew during the first plan at a yearly rate of 6.4 percent, but the balance-of-payments problem persisted. "The problem was not only the lack of coordination between short-term and long-term economic policies, but the inability of the public sector to fulfill its own commitments. The public investment in some sectors did not reach 50 percent of the planned figure."[66] These problems led to a devaluation of the peseta and a tougher stabilization program in November 1967.

## The Second and Third Plans

The first plan was extended to February 1969, until the second Social and Economic Development Plan's publication date. The second plan covered 1967–71, making it half over by its publication date, something not atypical of Spanish economic planning. The second plan followed similar lines as the first, with slight modifications in growth rates, and continued the lack of coordination between short-run and long-run economic policies. Unlike the first, however, it also emphasized housing and the unequal interprovincial distribution of wealth, placed more importance on an area's developmental potential as a criterion for the "growth pole" program,[67] and gave local governments a greater voice in regional planning. Most important, the second plan strengthened state *dirigisme* in economic affairs.

The second plan was not, however, extremely successful.[68] In part due to its late start, public-sector investment did not meet its goals. The 1967 devaluation of sterling, which lowered the peseta, also seriously hurt the second plan. The second plan nevertheless continued to determine the total volume of the state's capital investments.[69]

The third Economic and Social Development Plan, covering 1972–75, introduced social issues such as housing and qualitative considerations in areas like quality of life and the environment.[70] This third plan was very short-lived, never being fully implemented. The 1973–74 oil embargo and the economic crisis which followed fatally wounded the third plan. The plan was abandoned in 1974 following the cabinet's dismissal and Prime Minister Carrero Blanco's assassination.

# A Politically Created Economic Elite

Despite all this economic planning, Franco had limited interest and expertise in economic concerns. Franco generally acquiesced in this area of policy-making. He rarely exercised his limitless authority to direct public economic policy. Throughout his tenure, most economic policies fell within Franco's "zone of indifference" and were formulated within a relative power vacuum.[71] The Council of Ministers as a collective body did not coordinate economic policy, generally being more interested in noneconomic issues. Franco's laissez-faire attitude toward economic policy encouraged others to formulate Spain's policy direction. This leadership style intensified as time passed and Franco's military friends died off; the contraction of the policy-making "inner circle" created an even larger policy-making vacuum.[72] Simultaneously, the demands for critical economic policy intensified as the Spanish economy "took off." Individuals with liberal economic views were eagerly sought to exercise such power. Franco left the coordination of economic planning to the ministerial hierarchy. He encouraged Opus Dei technocrats to occupy economic policy-making positions in government. The "inner circle's" contraction and a growing demand by many for better economic performance led Franco to permit the economic policy-making slack to be taken up by these liberal, technocratic decision-makers. Their common economic interests, which they also shared with the country's more traditional economic forces, e.g., the banking industry, eventually produced a "political business" elite.

In specific political terms, the different phases of Spanish economic development progressed "with the slow downfall of the quasi-fascist and xenophobic Falange and the emergence of a new breed of technocratic decision-makers."[73] "Instead of developing into a totalitarian single-party state (as some Falangists wished), the Franquist regime evolved into an authoritarian no-party system, within which a 'limited pluralism' flourished."[74] The Franco regime permitted limited pluralism only in the sense that certain economic and social interests which did not challenge the regime could be articulated by prominent individuals.[75] This limited pluralism, as it affected economic policy in the 1950s and 1960s, arose from different sectors of the Spanish business community.[76] Despite differences, these economic interests had enough in common and monopolized enough economic power that they quickly developed oligarchical tendencies. This elite exercise of, and influence over, economic policy-making grew as it itself developed.

As the Franco regime moved from a fascist-corporatist economic system toward a unique brand of state interventionalist capitalism, Spain's business class came to exert greater policy influence. The nature of private industrial ownership and monopolistic tendencies facilitated this. The concentration of economic power in Spain grew enormously under Franco, and the people vested with this power increasingly came to guide public economic planning. Stated differently, an economic oligarchy prospered under the Franco regime. The oligarchy's close link with the state's technocratic economic planners insured this prosperity.

Spain's large banks benefitted greatly under the Franco regime. Franco froze the establishment of new banks in 1939 in order to control wartime economic policy. Entry remained closed until 1963. The larger banks grew and absorbed or came to control smaller ones. The five largest banks—Bilbao, Vizcáya, Hispano Americano, Español de Crédito, and Central—grew phenomenally between 1940 and 1950, increasing their profits by 700 percent, or about 250 percent considering Table 2-1's inflation rate. During the 1950s, the "big five's" profits grew 430 percent, or about 208 percent in constant terms.[77] The banks gained absolute control over industrial finance during the 1950s through the existence of credit restrictions. This strength and privileged position soon led to the banks' penetration and control of most large Spanish firms. Major companies not linked to a major bank practically ceased to exist. Industrial companies were forced to attach themselves to banks. By 1956, "five of these Banks . . . controlled 51 percent of the capital in the country."[78] The directors of the large banks were members by law of the National Banking Council, the recommending body for monetary and fiscal policy. Twenty years of little government encouragement of competition permitted considerable industrial concentration, largely determined by these controlling banking groups.

The growth of oligopolistic firms not only centralized economic power but also reinforced institutional and social rigidity. The state discouraged all entrepreneurial activity counter to this system and its centralized economic policymakers. Normal competitive market pressures were largely contained or directed toward politically safe areas. Economic policy tended to protect existing businesses from competitive pressures of new firms and labor.

> Throughout the system the limitations of the market were a constraint not only to the opening of new lines of business activity; they were also considered to represent a guarantee against the emergence of competition on the part of the smaller firms. . . . The institutional setup and the postulated alliance between latifundia interests and entrepreneurial monopolistic firms precluded the sharing of economic (or political) power with the smaller marginal firms of the system.[79]

The oligopolistic structure of Spanish industry and finance moved toward a monopolistic status in such key areas as steel production, coal mining, electrical power, and banking. As early as 1953, nine of 338 coal-mining firms produced 55 percent of total coal production. In steel, ten of forty firms produced 82 percent. In electric production, fourteen of 511 companies produced 71 percent. And the five largest banks controlled from 45 to 60 percent of industrial investment in Spain.[80]

Besides facilitating the creation of monopolies, the state also helped develop this economic elite through "the generous inducements that government held out to those who would contribute their efforts to the country's modernization."[81] Leaders of industry had privileged access to, and control of, the rise in industrial wage rates, product prices, and the expansion of the money supply. Spanish industrialists received tax reductions and guaranteed returns on investment.[82] Public funds channeled through such institutions as INI, combined with private capital, created businesses that often passed into the hands of private capitalists. The state and INI

> presided over the induced birth of large scale Spanish industrial capitalism. The process led to the ultimate incorporation into the political power base of a new capitalist sector made up of the men who had taken fullest advantage of the favorable circumstances afforded by government.[83]

The Economic Development Plans tightened the knot between Spanish private business and the State in the form of "concerted action." A firm promised certain levels of productivity or other goals in exchange for governmental financial aid for a period of four to eight years. This aid generally was low-interest credit for up to 70 percent of a new plant's installation cost or an older plant's expansion and modernization.[84] Other aid included tax exemption, avoidance of import duties, speedier depreciation accounting, and the power of eminent domain. Such programs added another layer to public economic intervention and strengthened the nexus between the government and the private sector.

The Economic Stabilization Plan of 1959 and the different economic-development plans were a new twist in the direction of Spanish economic policy. Despite their economic language, these plans also had political motives. They reflected the Franco regime's attempts at economic reinstitutionalization in order to guarantee political survival. This planning "can be seen as a basis on which collaboration could be achieved between competing political forces, rather than a basis for allocating economic resources. Even in 1969, the Minister of Planning Laureano López Rodó, said of the first two plans that they served to provide continuity to the regime and that a development plan could be considered to have any real significance only in relation to politics."[85] In the final analysis, "the Spanish government opted neither for a free market economy nor for a rationally planned economy in the sense that indicative planning was an attempt to obtain greater economic efficiency throughout the economy. The government favored instead the establishment of a partnership between its economic managers and the representatives of important sectors of the private economy."[86] Francoist economic planning "served as an excuse for the refusal on the part of the regime to undertake even the most elementary structural reform which might have upset vested interests."[87]

Spanish business' source of strength in economic policy came from the fact that most large-scale economic undertakings required both public and private participation. This private-public coordination initially solidified during the implementation of the Economic and Social Development Plan. It continued in many other economic programs such as highway construction, many industrial projects, and energy planning. The government's need for the provision of such goods and services and the private sector's ability to negotiate for favorable terms combined to give Spanish business a central role in economic policy.[88]

The shift in economic policy in 1957 permitted a new elite with groups like Opus Dei to use

> its power and influence to gain access to positions of economic power or privilege by occupying seats on the board of directors of the newly created enterprises of the public sector under the holding of the Instituto Nacional de Industria (INI) and the boards of the public banks and private businesses, particularly the larger corporations and increasingly the banks.[89]

This accession to power provided innumerable possibilities for the enhancement of personal and company wealth and influence. Always strongly linked with economic interests, Opus Dei used its political power during the 1960s economic boom

> to create a large number of enterprises and banks that its members staffed and that provided influence and opportunities for that elite, which also occupied key positions in the public sector and the economically powerful savings banks.[90]

It was common knowledge, for example, that Opus Dei controlled the Banco Popular. Furthermore, Opus Dei solidified its position within the Spanish business community in the areas of economic education and information. The University of Navarra is essentially Opus Dei's own university, having one of the nation's best business schools, and Opus Dei controls many newspapers and magazines, including many influential economic publications.[91]

While it cannot be definitively concluded that Opus Dei, as an organization, controlled economic policy in Francoist Spain or during the transition to democracy, its membership characterized the basis of economic policy during the transition: a hand-in-glove relationship between Spanish government and business. Suffice to say Opus Dei and the ACN de P were staunch supporters of the governing coalition during the 1960s and early 1970s.[92] They also served as "a nursery of elites" for the system.[93] Furthermore:

> Unless Opus Dei lifts the veil surrounding all its business, one has to conclude on the evidence available, that it has become one of the most powerful individual groups in Spanish life, and that although in the ministerial reshuffle of January 1974 the last of its membership in the government, López Rodó, was dismissed, Opus Dei—or at least the politically active faction of its membership—remains a force to be reckoned with.[94]

Less specifically, recruitment patterns into the Spanish bureaucracy also maintained business' tie to policy-making. Allegations frequently surfaced to illustrate this relationship, e.g., the Banco Popular and the support of its vice-chairman, Luis Valls-Taberner, were direct paths to high administrative posts in government.[95] The fact that public administration consisted predominately of persons with middle- and upper-middle-class social backgrounds also strengthened business' tie to the Franco regime.[96] Officials in the Francoist bureaucracy, consciously or not, favored the interests of groups and individuals who had similar social, economic, and educational backgrounds:

> Most functionaries at present responsible for the day-to-day management of economic affairs are, by virtue of their backgrounds and general attitudes, well disposed to the business community and more accessible to its spokesmen than to the official spokesmen for labor.[97]

Of equal note were the elite administrative bodies known as "cuerpos." They wielded great influence in the recruitment process. They were not reluctant to make use of their power in recruitment or administrative lobbying, or to serve as significant obstacles to policy change in order to protect their own administrative and economic interests. The state's heavy intervention in the economy, despite Franco's general disinterest in the nonphilosophical, day-to-day activities of managing the economy, gave these administrators a fairly unconstrained hand. The power vacuum in economic policy-making "led to a systematic bias in public policy outputs—a bias in favor of upper- and upper-middle-class economic interests."[98]

The relationship between Francoist policymakers and Spanish business goes well beyond social background. Extensive personal ties existed between governmental policymakers and business interests. At the ministerial level, for example, 64 percent of the eighty-seven Francoist ministers and ex-ministers living one year before the regime's end were members of the boards of directors of one or more large businesses between 1961 and 1974.[99] The fact that about 15 percent of the ministers were career military officers, thus not normally associated with business interests, strengthens this linkage. Each minister was generally

> closely affiliated with firms directly involved in the activities of his ministry. The widespread practice of pantoulage, then, had a profound impact not only on the articulation of demands by private sector lobbyists, but on the social outlooks and policy predispositions of governmental officials.[100]

More important, the Franco regime tolerated a "system of interactions which rewarded ministry officials for maintaining cozy personal relations with private firms and for carefully looking after the interests of their respective cuerpos."[101] Spanish administrative law strictly dictated authority in economic policy, making the process highly compartmentalized. Policy jurisdictions were rigidly defined, with each minister having full authority to set policy falling within his department's jurisdiction.[102] Given Franco's disinterest in economic policy, the Ministry of Finance became a superministry in charge of coordinating economic policy. The minister of finance inherited this coordination task mainly because his jurisdiction overlapped those of many other departments. This included energy policy.[103]

## Concluding Comments

Spain's economic growth and increased economic demands led Franco to promote a new group to the forefront of policy-making. This cadre of economic policymakers, who gained additional influence due to Franco's personal acquiescence in economic matters, had strong linkages with both established and nascent powers in the Spanish financial world. The growth of this policymaker/financial oligarchy institutionalized a new "political business" class, which provided a stable foundation for political stability. This political business class quickly found itself situated in the center of the regime's economic policy-making structures. Once in place, as will be seen in chapters 3 and 4, this cadre of economic policymakers rationally directed Spain toward policies that generated financial benefits for themselves and their associated interests. Franco's institutionalization of these economic policymakers to ensure his regime's stability also proved to moderate economic policy change during the regime transition.

The Franco regime's attempts at technocratic economic planning during the 1960s greatly improved the country's economic performance. Such economic planning, however, never reached a level of precision and efficiency similar to other European systems. Furthermore, the Franco regime, despite all its attempts at economic development, did not address many of the Spanish economy's central weaknesses, such as energy. Energy as an example of policy, planning, and decision-making central to national economic health permits a more in-depth analysis of the nature of the financial oligarchy's constraining influence on economic policy outcomes. Chapter 3 focuses on Spain's energy situation on both sides of the regime change, implicitly contrasting democratic governmental and institutional policy-making context with that of the Franco regime just presented.

# 3

# Spain's Energy Resources and Government Policies

Spain's national energy program permits a useful comparison of policy in two different regimes. Through the National Energy Plan (PEN), the Spanish state played a central role in this fundamental economically related policy issue. The Franco regime wrote and approved the first national energy plan, PEN-75. The second, PEN-79, got caught in the politics of the transition, written in 1977 but not approved by the national parliament, the Cortes, until 1979. Toward the end of 1981, Spain's Union of the Democratic Center (UCD) government revised PEN and Parliament approved it in 1982—thus PEN-82. The Socialists' version of the national energy plan (PEN-83) continued government planning in this important policy issue. Spain's energy program may thus serve as a indicator of political and economic influences on macroeconomic policy in each of the distinctive periods of the Spanish transition.

This chapter describes the context of Spanish energy planning. Initially, the Spanish energy situation and its dependence on foreign petroleum and domestic production in this and other energy sources is presented. Spanish officials have often cited this petroleum dependence as the reason given for Spain's strong nuclear program. Second, the central public and private institutions, companies, and structures of the Spanish energy system are outlined. This discussion introduces the public and private structures through which the political-business elite directed energy planning in Spain. Third,

PEN is considered in its distinct parts. Here, the various versions of PEN are described. Continuity and change in Spain's energy program of both the Franco regime and the current democratic system reflects a protection of the political-business elite's interests.

## Spain's Energy Situation

Like most other European nations, Spain's energy needs have ballooned during the last quarter century. Spain's total energy requirements, pushed by very strong economic growth during the 1960s, grew at a faster rate than Europe as a whole over the past two decades. While Europe's total energy requirements grew by 107 percent between 1960 and 1979, Spain's energy needs increased by 271 percent.[1] Spain's "economic miracle" pushed the country's energy demand much harder than that experienced by either Italy, with a 188 percent growth, or France, with a 121 percent increase. Figure 3-1 compares Spain's increase in energy consumption with other European countries. Spain's energy consumption clearly reflects the fact that it had a much more industrialized and consumption-based economy than either Greece or Portugal but much less than the United Kingdom, France, and Italy. Spain can thus be categorized in the "middle range" of overall energy consumption in Western Europe.

Figure 3-1 also highlights another point. The 1973–74 oil embargo and the resultant energy crisis clearly had severe repercussions for the energy-consuming habits of industrial nations. Britain's, France's, and Italy's growth in energy consumption changed significantly following the crisis. Spain's constant growth in energy consumption suggests this "shock" did not have even a temporary stifling effect on Spanish energy consumption. Unlike the more developed Western European countries, the "energy crisis" did not significantly alter Spain's total energy requirements. Nor did Spain's, Greece's, or Portugal's transitions to democracy in the mid-1970s alter, at this level of aggregate consumption, the economic habits of energy consumption.

Spanish energy requirements grew faster than those of its two industrialized neighbors—Italy and France—at the time of the 1973–74 oil embargo. More important, Spain rapidly lost energy self-sufficiency in the 1960s.[2] This energy dependence is directly attributable to Spain's increased importation of petroleum, driven by its rapid economic growth. Table 3-1 depicts Spain's growth in crude oil demand since 1960. Spain's petroleum needs grew by 661 percent between 1960 and 1985, compared to 293 percent by OECD Europe. This growth occurred even though Spain imports practically all of its crude

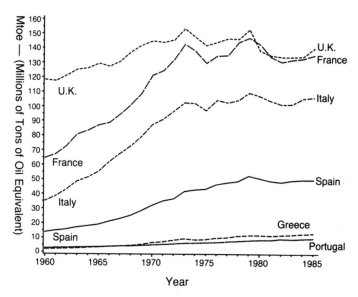

**Figure 3-1.**    Total Final Energy Consumption
Source: *Energy Balances of OECD Countries, 1970–1985*

oil. However, Spain was quite similar to the other European countries in its near total dependence on foreign oil.

While similar to many other European countries in its dependence on foreign oil, Spain's levels of petroleum imports increased more rapidly. Spain's economy expanded at the expense of a larger energy umbilical cord. As a matter of fact, demand for petroleum grew at a faster rate than that of the country's economic growth. Figure 3-2 shows the ratio of total energy requirements to gross domestic product in Spain and four other European countries. This comparison interestingly reveals that while Spain's energy requirements steadily grew, energy usage relative to GDP declined in the United Kingdom and the United States, and France and Italy's declined slightly during the 1970s. Spain's energy/economic growth ratio, however, steadily increased after 1964. Furthermore, this growth was apparently not affected by the 1973–74 energy crisis nor by the political crisis and regime change following Franco's death in late 1975. In contrast, repercussions from the oil crunch can be seen in the patterns of France, Britain, and the U.S.

Italy's pattern of energy requirements most clearly resembles the Spanish case. This similarity suggests a look at other southern European countries that economically, politically, and culturally share much in common with

**Table 3-1**    Total Energy Requirements, Oil (in millions of tons of oil)

| Year | Spain | OECD Europe | Italy | France | Portugal | Greece |
|------|-------|-------------|-------|--------|----------|--------|
| 1960 | 5.9   | 186.1 | 20.3 | 28.4  | 1.5 | 2.1  |
| 1961 | 6.6   | 209.0 | 24.9 | 30.5  | 1.7 | 2.4  |
| 1962 | 8.0   | 241.8 | 30.3 | 34.3  | 1.7 | 2.6  |
| 1963 | 8.4   | 279.4 | 35.5 | 40.5  | 1.9 | 2.6  |
| 1964 | 11.0  | 319.2 | 41.9 | 46.9  | 2.1 | 3.2  |
| 1965 | 11.8  | 357.0 | 45.9 | 51.9  | 2.2 | 3.4  |
| 1966 | 14.6  | 394.5 | 51.0 | 55.7  | 2.4 | 3.9  |
| 1967 | 18.1  | 428.9 | 56.5 | 63.2  | 2.7 | 4.6  |
| 1968 | 21.7  | 476.1 | 64.0 | 70.0  | 2.9 | 5.0  |
| 1969 | 23.2  | 527.7 | 71.0 | 78.6  | 3.5 | 5.5  |
| 1970 | 26.1  | 590.8 | 62.3 | 91.7  | 4.0 | 6.0  |
| 1971 | 30.0  | 619.0 | 65.5 | 100.9 | 4.7 | 6.8  |
| 1972 | 30.7  | 661.2 | 69.1 | 111.2 | 5.0 | 8.0  |
| 1973 | 37.6  | 705.6 | 72.5 | 122.6 | 5.4 | 9.4  |
| 1974 | 41.7  | 663.5 | 69.8 | 115.9 | 5.7 | 8.6  |
| 1975 | 42.6  | 622.0 | 64.2 | 106.1 | 6.3 | 8.6  |
| 1976 | 47.0  | 668.0 | 67.8 | 114.3 | 6.8 | 9.1  |
| 1977 | 44.1  | 653.9 | 65.4 | 106.9 | 6.4 | 10.1 |
| 1978 | 48.2  | 679.4 | 66.2 | 114.9 | 6.9 | 11.3 |
| 1979 | 48.2  | 691.6 | 69.9 | 115.8 | 7.7 | 11.6 |
| 1980 | 49.8  | 645.9 | 66.7 | 109.3 | 8.2 | 11.7 |
| 1981 | 46.5  | 592.5 | 63.6 | 97.4  | 8.3 | 11.0 |
| 1982 | 43.7  | 566.4 | 61.4 | 91.8  | 9.4 | 11.0 |
| 1983 | 43.0  | 552.5 | 62.2 | 89.5  | 9.3 | 10.7 |
| 1984 | 40.4  | 556.0 | 62.8 | 85.5  | 9.2 | 10.9 |
| 1985 | 39.0  | 546.6 | 61.6 | 84.5  | 8.5 | 11.1 |

SOURCE: OECD, *Energy Balances of OECD Countries 1970–1985*. Paris: OECD.

Spain. Figure 3-3 indeed reveals that Spain's growth in total energy usage characterized that followed by other southern European nations. This pattern suggests that economic growth in its early stages requires a proportionately higher utilization of energy than growth at a more advanced stage. Spain, Greece, and Portugal all witnessed a rapid increase in the ratio of total energy requirements to gross domestic product. The more developed economies of the United Kingdom, the United States, and Italy experienced a drop in this ratio while France held constant. Despite the similarities in southern Europe, differences nevertheless occurred. One difference is that

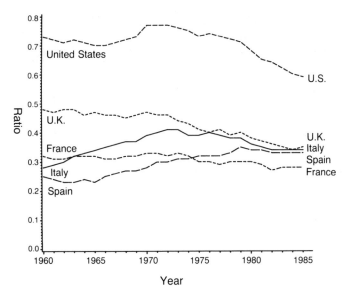

**Figure 3-2.**   Ratio, Energy Requirements, and GDP
Source: Calculated from *Energy Balances of OECD Countries,*
*1970–1985*

Greece responded sharply to the 1973–74 petroleum shortage while Spain did not. Why did Spain fail to respond adequately? Before turning to this question, Spain's domestic energy resources should be described.

## Domestic Energy Situation

Spain possesses two relatively abundant energy sources. One is hydroelectricity. Despite the generally held impression, Spain is not a totally arid country. The northern sections of Spain receive ample rainfall. This, in addition to mountainous terrain, facilitated hydroelectric production in the twentieth century. Hydroelectricity has been a primary energy source in Spain throughout this century. Since the 1960s, however, hydroelectricity has been increasingly unable to meet growing energy demands. Additional hydroelectricity supplies are practically exhausted, with most economically feasible sites already in use. Unfortunately, the marginal return on new hydroelectric production reached zero at approximately the same time Spain's modern economic development began requiring new energy supplies.

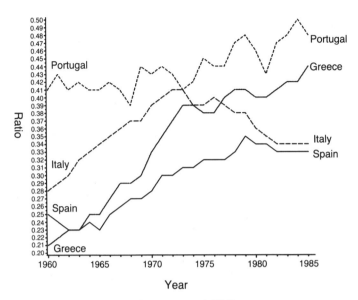

**Figure 3-3.**   Ratio, Energy Requirements, and GDP
Source: Calculated from *Energy Balances of OECD Countries,*
*1970–1985*

The other potential source of energy in Spain is, of course, the sun. Southern Spain is abundant in this natural resource, with approximately three hun-
dred days of sunshine a year. Solar energy thus appealed to many groups
during the transition as an alternative energy source. Politically, the cry for a
"solar path" to energy independence could be heard in Spain. Students, environmentalists, and some leftists pushed for such alternative energy policies. They remained, nevertheless, off the political agenda for several reasons. An energy policy heavily focused on solar energy appeared popular
only to politically marginal groups. The policymakers in a position to guide
Spanish energy policy argued that solar energy was not technically feasible
for large-scale energy production.

Much of the political intensity on the question of solar energy stemmed
from the fact that Spain has an extreme shortage of traditional domestic
sources for energy production. Spain has only small quantities of coal, petroleum, and natural gas. Yet coal, petroleum, and natural gas remain central
features in Spain's overall energy-policy picture. Domestically, Spain possesses approximately only four billion tons of coal reserves. In 1980 alone,
12.1 million tons of bituminous and anthracite coal and 26.6 million tons of
black and brown lignite were produced. Seventy percent of all Spanish coal

is found in the northern Spanish regions of Asturias and Leon, with Asturias accounting for 50 percent of all coal and Leon producing 70 percent of the nation's anthracite coal.

Spanish coal has numerous problems. The nation's coal mines are old and rapidly being depleted. The Asturian mines, for example, have been mined since the fifteenth century, with modern exploration beginning in 1828. Furthermore, Spanish coal is of poor quality.[3] Its caloric potential is low and the ash and sulfur content is high. It is also expensive to mine. Three factors account for high production costs.[4] First, the veins are narrow—fifty to sixty centimeters—and slant. This makes the use of large extracting machines practically impossible. Second, it is not "clean" coal. Most must be washed. Third, high production costs reflect the coal's brittleness. Sixty percent of the coal mined in Spain possesses this quality. The fact that Spanish domestic coal is of low quality, near exhaustion, and expensive to mine leads to heavy importation.

Spanish petroleum production is even more limited than coal. Its domestic supply of crude oil accounted for only 2 percent of the nation's petroleum demand in 1978 and 5.6 percent in 1985. Table 3-2 presents Spain's 1985 domestic petroleum production. The little petroleum Spain possesses tends to be in the Mediterranean, with Dorada and Casablanco situated on the Tarragona coast. Seventy-five percent of all exploratory investment is directed toward offshore sites. It is also noteworthy that well over half the investment in petroleum prospecting and drilling has come from foreign sources. Spain's public sector accounted for less than one-third of investment, with the private sector providing less than 12 percent. Spanish governments have not felt it economically feasible, even when fiscally possible, to spearhead domestic petroleum exploration. Despite some exploratory activity, the fact remains that exploration efforts are minimal in Spain. Spanish territory is simply not a likely source for future oil reserves.

Low natural-gas utilization is also a central part of Spain's energy structure.[5] Natural gas accounts for only about 2 percent of Spain's primary energy consumption. Like petroleum, Spain simply does not have much domestic natural gas. The country has approximately twenty million TEP (Tons Equivalent of Petroleum). The largest site is in Bermeo (Vizcaya) with twelve million TEP. Other sites are found in Sabinanigo, Cádiz, and San Carlos, Tarragona. Potential finds have also been discovered in Pairineo de Huesca, between Jaca and Sabinanigo, but chances of finding additional natural gas on Spanish territory are not good.

Spain's limited domestic petroleum and natural gas supply has not curtailed domestic energy consumption. Demand for petroleum in Spain increased throughout the period of rapid economic development. Figure 3-4 reflects the growing use of petroleum in overall energy consumption. In

**Table 3-2**   Spanish Crude Oil Production, 1983–1985 (in tons)

| Site | 1978 Percent Production | 1983 | 1984 | 1985 | 1985 Percent Operation | Year Production Began |
|---|---|---|---|---|---|---|
| Amposta | 39.1 | 85 | 44 | 80 | 3.7 | 1973 |
| Ayoluengo | 6.2 | 79 | 81 | 86 | 3.9 | 1966 |
| Casablanca | 10.7 | 2170 | 1623 | 1489 | 68.2 | 1978 |
| Castellón | 27.3 | 277 | 695 | 172 | 7.9 | 1978 |
| Dorada | 16.7 | 367 | 202 | 279 | 12.8 | 1978 |
| Salmonete | — | — | 71 | 72 | 3.3 | 1984 |
| Angula | — | — | — | 6 | .3 | 1985 |
| Total | 100.0 | 2978 | 2316 | 2184 | 100.0 | |

SOURCE: Adapted from Fundación Juan March, *Boletín Informativo* 87 (November 1979), 17, and Ramón Tamames *Estructura económica de España* 17. (Madrid: Alianza Editorial, 1986), 250.

1960, for example, petroleum represented 30 percent of Spain's primary energy consumption. By 1979 this had soared to above 70 percent. Petroleum increasingly became the centerpiece of the Spanish energy picture, and increased demand simply could not be supplied domestically.

As seen in Figure 3-5, Spain's dependency on petroleum and the loss of energy self-sufficiency occurred because the growing total energy requirements were increasingly met by the burning of fuel oil to generate electricity. The scarcity of "clean" coal, the unavailability of additional reservoir sites, and the low worldwide price of petroleum encouraged use of fuel-burning generators. Industry wished to insulate electrical production from the capriciousness of rainfall: A higher percentage of electricity had to be generated by burning petroleum in dry years, e.g., 1970, 1976, and 1980. As considered later, concern for short-term profits by the private electricity industry also motivated this shift. Growing consumption of petroleum meant greater energy dependency on foreign suppliers.

In sum, Spain's energy situation before and during its transition to democracy was bleak. Domestically, it possessed few energy sources such as petroleum, coal, and natural gas. Hydroelectricity had reached its potential, and solar energy remained a resource for the distant future. Despite these limited energy sources, the Spanish economy grew by leaps and bounds during the 1960s. This growth relied heavily on the attachment of an energy umbilical cord to foreign petroleum suppliers. This dependency produced few economic problems until that supply line suddenly became more expensive and undependable.

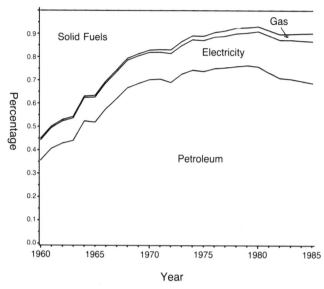

**Figure 3-4.** Spanish Energy Consumption, by Type
Source: *Energy Balances of OECD Countries, 1970–1985*

# Economic Impact and Energy Usage

As seen in Table 3-3, Spain paid dearly for its economic growth with the large increase in petroleum imports. The sudden surge in the price of petroleum severely affected Spain's balance of payments. Spain also indirectly suffered from the oil-crisis-induced economic slowdown. The European recession hit the two main sources of Spanish foreign income particularly hard: tourism and remittances from emigrant workers.[6] These factors attributed to high unemployment and inflation. The balance-of-payments problem stems from the fact that by 1978 petroleum accounted for almost 34 percent of imports—double that of five years earlier.

The energy consumption habits of different economic subsectors in Spain also strongly affected economic performance. In the 1960s, Spain moved from a primarily agrarian system to an industrial and service-oriented economy. The energy crisis, when it came, directly affected various subsectors quite harshly. The Spanish economy's severe reaction may be traced in part to the fact that the Spanish industrial sector is an extremely large consumer. Figure 3-6 compares industrial energy use as a percentage of the country's final energy consumption to that of other European countries. Industrial consumption of energy was higher in Spain than in the more industrially ad-

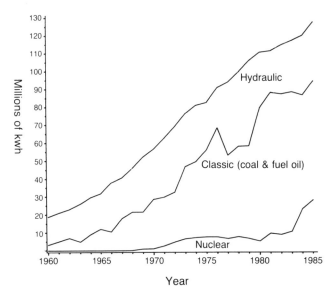

**Figure 3-5.**    Spanish Electrical Production, by Type
Source: UNESA

vanced western European nations and quite different than her southern European neighbors of Portugal and Greece. Industry's demand for electricity increased during the growth years of the 1960s at the same time that electricity increasingly became petroleum-generated. High energy use by industry suggests its interest in the continuation of a supply-oriented energy policy. Suffice to say at this point that increased dependency on petroleum after 1973 forced Spain to send money abroad in pursuit of more expensive petroleum and that a decline in tourism and worker remittances simultaneously occurred. The inevitable result was an economic downturn in this highly service-oriented economy.

High rates of unemployment and inflation were another consequence of high consumption of energy in other economic subsectors. Figure 3-7 shows that in Spain transportation absorbed a comparatively large amount of energy. The Spanish economy, and business profits, depended heavily on the transportation of goods. Yet in Spain, most of these goods were transported over land by petroleum-burning trucks. The Spanish rail and river transportation systems were permitted to deteriorate when gasoline became relatively cheap worldwide during the 1950s and 1960s. During Spain's political transition, Spanish business kept the trucks rolling by supplying the necessary petroleum.

**Table 3-3**  Spanish Economic Performance

| Year | Consumer Prices | Unemployed (as percent of total labor force) | Balance of Payments (net trade billion pesetas) |
|------|------|------|------|
| 1961 | .9 | | |
| 1962 | 5.4 | | |
| 1963 | 7.9 | | |
| 1964 | 6.4 | 1.8 | |
| 1965 | 11.8 | 1.6 | |
| 1966 | 5.8 | .9 | |
| 1967 | 6.2 | 1.1 | |
| 1968 | 4.6 | 1.1 | |
| 1969 | 2.2 | 1.0 | − 147.9 |
| 1970 | 5.3 | 1.1 | − 131.9 |
| 1971 | 7.7 | 1.5 | − 127.0 |
| 1972 | 7.5 | 2.1 | − 161.7 |
| 1973 | 10.3 | 2.3 | − 214.1 |
| 1974 | 13.6 | 2.6 | − 433.0 |
| 1975 | 14.5 | 4.0 | − 415.0 |
| 1976 | 15.0 | 5.0 | − 490.5 |
| 1977 | 19.7 | 5.7 | − 524.9 |
| 1978 | 16.5 | 7.5 | − 312.0 |
| 1979 | 13.6 | 9.2 | − 500.1 |
| 1980 | 13.4 | 11.8 | − 915.3 |
| 1981 | 12.8 | 14.4 | − 1041.6 |
| 1982 | 11.3 | 15.9 | − 1097.7 |

SOURCE: Adapted from OECD, *Main Economic Indicators*, yearly.

In many countries, transportation's part of total energy consumption appears to be highly correlated with economic development. Spain certainly exemplifies this relationship. Once the energy crisis halted Spain's overall economic development, transportation's energy dependency increased. With the economic downturn, Spanish business interests were not in a position to cut their own energy requirements, needs that included maintaining the transportation so vital to their businesses. Transportation's continued heavy energy usage thus added to the desire of business for no significant conservation initiatives in energy policy.

A comparison of Figures 3-6 and 3-7 also suggests that, to a general degree, countries on the higher end of energy usage in transportation are at the lower end of industrial consumption. (The reverse also appears generally true, with consumption in the more developed economies of Italy, France,

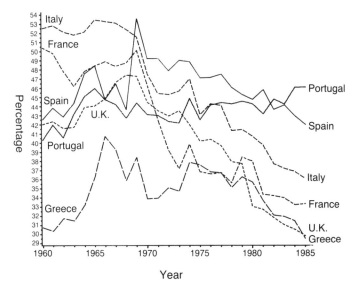

**Figure 3-6.**   Industrial Energy Consumption (Percentage of Total Consumption)
Source: Calculated from *Energy Balances of OECD Countries,*
*1970–1985*

and the U.K. being low in Figure 3-7 but toward the upper end of Figure 3-6.) Except for Portugal's sharp rise in percentage of industrial energy consumption after 1973, Spain is the anomaly. Spain's propensity for relatively high energy usage in *both* the industrial and the transportation sectors makes its energy consumption habits over time quite different than her other western and southern European neighbors.

## Institutional Arrangements

Energy planning in Spain is formalized within state institutional, bureaucratic, and organizational structures. The State produces and implements energy policy through these structures. A brief description of these organizational and institutional arrangements sets the stage for later analysis on how the political-business elite intervened in energy policy.

Figure 3-8 presents a flow chart for energy policy-making in Spain. This rather complex schema reflects many of the central components and institutional arrangements within which Spanish energy policy was made and implemented. Beginning at the ministerial level, this chart depicts most orga-

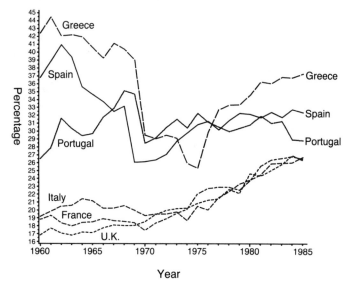

**Figure 3-7.**    Transportation Energy Consumption (Percentage of Total Consumption)
Source: Calculated from *Energy Balances of OECD Countries, 1970–1985*

nizational relationships. Discussion of only the more central institutions and relationships is appropriate. We thus begin the brief description at the organizational top, with the cabinet, or Council of Ministers. Next, the ministers directly involved in energy policy-making and policy management are discussed. Discussion of the Ministries of Industry and Energy, Finance, and Commerce is then followed by a summary of several central state institutions such as the Center for Energy Studies and the Nuclear Energy Commission. The analysis then considers the private sector.

## The Government

Spain is a constitutional monarchy with a parliamentary form of government.[7] Consistent with most other continental-style parliamentary systems, the Spanish cabinet—the Council of Ministers—has ultimate responsibility for political decisions. The Spanish Council of Ministers, following the classic parliamentary model with a fusion of legislative and executive powers, not only is the highest policy-making organ but also is responsible for the administration and implementation of all policy. The cabinet is collectively responsible to the lower house of the Spanish parliament—the Congress of Deputies—for its policy decisions. In turn, each individual cabinet member with portfolio heads a ministry which administers the different areas of policy. Each minister is, of course, politically accountable both individually and politically for all activities within his department.

The cabinet's policy accountability obviously took a much different form during the Franco regime. Franco made all cabinet appointments as well as many to the Cortes. Francoist cabinets followed the pattern of "a group of administrative assistants."[8] Francoist cabinets administered economic policy decisions made by the Caudillo or the cabinet itself which, because of Franco's lack of interest in economic policy, increased in frequency during the later years of the regime.[9] As the Franco regime developed, the cabinet's centrality in policy-making grew. Similar to democratic Spain, Franco placed individuals at the head of specific ministries who had the responsibility to make and execute policy. These cabinet-to-ministry relationships changed very little during the transition to democracy. Of course, ultimate accountability for policy did shift from Franco to a democratically elected parliament. Ministerial control of economic policy issues like energy remained relatively unaltered. While the Council of Ministers had the final word on energy policy during the transition, the different ministries each controlled a separate area of bureaucratic "turf" related to energy.

## The Ministry of Industry and Energy

The Ministry of Industry and Energy is the center for public policy on energy. The Franco regime originally included concerns of energy-related policy in the Ministry of Industry. This inclusion of energy policy in a well-established department focused on industrial policy meant that energy and industrial planning became tied, leaving other areas of energy consumption difficult to coordinate. Energy policy remained, in this sense, a "stepchild" to industrial policy.[10]

The Ministry's internal organization can be briefly outlined, highlighting several areas of Figure 3-8. One step below the minister in the hierarchy is the commissioner of energy and mineral resources. As the head of the Energy Commission, he is the senior official responsible for all public policy in energy.[11] The commissioner of energy, as second-in-command at the Ministry of Industry and Energy, has a counterpart concerned with industrial policy. The commissioner of energy, through the minister of Industry and Energy and the full Spanish cabinet, authorizes price increases, the installation of nuclear plants, and all other energy policy decisions. The commissioner of

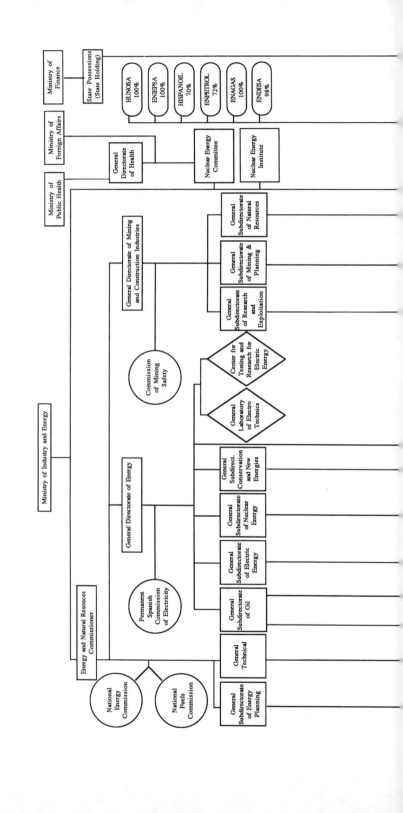

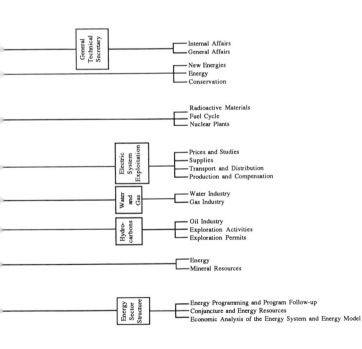

ENHER 79%
ENECO 60%
GESA 97%
ENUSA 60%
BUTANO 50%
CAMPSA 50%

REMOLQUE MARITIMOS 65%
PROAS 25%
APLESA 100%
PETRONOR 33%
AESA 50%

Center for Energy Studies

Institute of Mining and Geology

I.N.I. (National Industry Institute) (State Holding)

Coals and Radioactive Minerals
— Social Programs of Energetic Resources
— Energetic Resources
— Mining Promotion
— Non-metallic minerals and industrial rocks

Mining Rights Registry
— Undergrown Hydrology
— Mining Permits Transfers
— States Reserves
— Mining Registry and Rights

Explosives and Mining Safety
— Fineness Determination
— Geological Resources Exploitation and Research
— Safety, Mining Police and Explosives
— Mining Exploitation

General Technical Secretary
— Internal Affairs
— General Affairs
— New Energies
— Energy
— Conservation

Radioactive Materials
Fuel Cycle
Nuclear Plants

Electric System Exploitation
— Prices and Studies
— Supplies
— Transport and Distribution
— Production and Compensation

Water and Gas
— Water Industry
— Gas Industry

Hydro-carbons
— Oil Industry
— Exploration Activities
— Exploration Permits

Energy
Mineral Resources

Energy Sector Structure
— Energy Programming and Program Follow-up
— Conjuncture and Energy Resources
— Economic Analysis of the Energy System and Energy Model

**Figure 3-8.** The Spanish State's Energy Structure, 1984

energy coordinates energy policies made by the directors of different energy-related administrative bodies both within and outside the Ministry of Industry and Energy. The commissioner of energy's cabinet, the National Energy Commission, includes the general director of mining, the general director of energy, the general subdirector of energy planning, and, among others, representatives from the Ministries of Finance, Public Works, and Commerce.

Entirely within the Ministry of Industry and Energy, and organizationally one step below, is the general director of energy. The general director oversees state affairs in energy, primarily nuclear and hydroelectric, as well as petroleum, coal, and new energies. As head of the Commission of Electricity, the general director works closely with the private electricity industry.

With the Ministry of Industry and Energy, the general director of mining serves parallel to the General Director of Energy. The general director of mining has policy responsibility for all mining activities, ranging from exploration to research to mine safety. Activity revolving around mining, particularly coal, made this a politically sensitive position at times during the transition. Organized labor often stressed its concern with issues of miners' employment, wages, and safety to the general director of mining.

For our concerns here, the subdirector general of energy planning is the other position within the Ministry of Industry and Energy that needs mention.[12] This subdirector general directs all public planning in energy. Because he reports directly to the commissioner of energy, his responsibilities include coordinating energy planning for all departments within the ministry. His membership on the National Energy Commission institutionally attempts to include and coordinate medium- and long-range planning for all energy policy. The work of the subdirector general is highly technical. Mathematical modeling of Spain's energy needs are widely used as an instrument of policymaking.

During the Franco period, energy planning was included in the Ministry of Industry because of the department's relationship to the National Institute of Industry (INI). INI, as the industrial state-holding company, provided the Ministry of Industry and Energy the institutional mechanism through which to pursue energy administration. As previously mentioned, INI was formed in 1941 to give the Francoist state a strong instrument for industrial policy.[13] Initially, INI was institutionally quite autonomous. Juan Antonio Suanzes, the director of INI from 1941 to 1963, was responsible only to Franco as president of the government. Since March 1963, however, the Ministry of Industry has been responsible for most INI activities. This shift in responsibilities gave the Ministry of Industry and Energy greater leverage in the administration of energy policy. The Commission of Energy within the Ministry of Industry and Energy was ultimately politically and administratively accountable for INI's energy-related policies. The same applies to the new state holding company in energy—the National Institute of Hydrocarbons (INH).

Through INI, the Ministry of Industry and Energy held 100 percent of HUNOSA, a coal company, 70 percent of HISPANOIL, the overseas petroleum company, 100 percent of the gas company ENAGAS, and 50 percent of the gas company Butano. Many other energy-related enterprises were also controlled by INI. Figure 3-9 outlines in greater detail these and other relationships. INI, however, was clearly part of the reason why the Ministry of Industry and Energy held so much power in making public policy in energy during Spain's transition to democracy.

INI, and now INH, served as a conduit for huge sums of investment, having the capacity to allocate financial resources not held by traditional financial institutions. Most INI investments in the 1940s were in the areas of

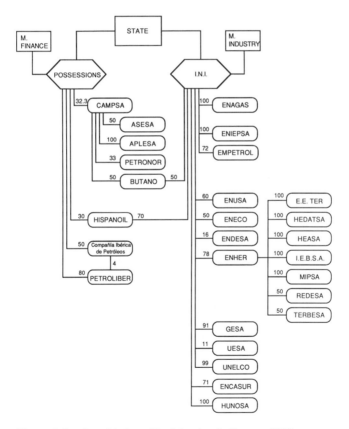

**Figure 3-9.** Spanish State Participation in Energy, 1984

fuels, fertilizers, and electrical power. In 1944, INI established ENDESA to construct thermoelectric plants to burn Spain's low quality coal. At this time, INI and the general Spanish economy also needed more reliable and extensive sources of electrical power for substantial industrial development. In 1946, ENHER was founded to develop electrical power from the Noguera-Ribagorzana River in the Catalan Pyrenees. These two companies helped meet Spanish demand for electricity and thereby facilitated Spanish industrial development.[14] INI also created the National Enterprise Calvo Sotelo in 1942, which quickly submitted to the government a detailed study on the location of refineries, methods of production, and market demand. The Francoist Cortes implemented this study as law as "a plan for the national production of liquid fuels, lubricants, and connected industries," authorizing credit to finance these works. This plan included four large industrial complexes, the handling of such energy-related production as the treatment of bituminous shale, an electrical generating plant in the Ebro area and Puentes de Garcia Rodriquez, and an oil refinery in the Levante.[15] From these beginnings, INI, as a holding company, served as the chief public instrument of industrial policy for almost half a century.

## The Ministry of Finance

Industry and Energy is not the only ministry that directed Spain's energy policy. As seen in Figure 3-9, the Ministry of Finance, now combined with the Ministry of Commerce, plays a central role in the financial well-being—and thus the influence—of numerous energy companies. The Ministry of Finance's primary role in energy policy during the transition emanated from its relationship to the Compañía Arrendataria del Monopolio de Petróleos, S.A. Always referred to by its acronym, CAMPSA is the fiscal monopoly which controls and manages the domestic distribution of petroleum.[16] Established in 1927 as part of the Primo de Rivera's "grand design" for the Spanish economy, CAMPSA extended public financial and commercial activities to facilitate government control of national economic development.[17] CAMPSA's creation aimed to derive fiscal benefit for the State from the distribution of petroleum products. Furthermore, CAMPSA was placed under the administration of a consortium of Spanish banks in order to allow the government to appropriate most of the profits made by the two companies that dominated Spain's distribution market at that time—Standard Oil and Shell. CAMPSA diverted the profits and stopped the fiscal evasion these companies were accused of engaging in. Oil prospection, the construction of a tanker fleet, and the development of a refining industry were also initial assignments for CAMPSA in this early attempt to reduce Spain's dependence on foreign oil. CAMPSA survived the fall of the Primo de Rivera regime and the Second Republic. Despite its longevity, CAMPSA failed in its attempt to create an economically efficient Spanish petroleum industry, both in the Franco regime and during the transition to democracy.[18]

Analysis of CAMPSA is critical for a full understanding of the Spanish petroleum industry.[19] This centrality stems from CAMPSA's management of the petroleum distribution monopoly on the peninsula. An extremely important but subtle point must, however, be made clear—something most Spaniards tend to overlook. There exists a fundamental difference between the Petroleum Monopoly and CAMPSA. The Monopoly is a creation of the state, linked to the treasury through the Ministry of Finance. This Monopoly held exclusive rights to import, distribute, and sell petroleum products on the peninsula. The government set the prices and authorized refining. On the other hand, until recently, CAMPSA was a privately owned company that ran the Monopoly. CAMPSA was not a nationalized company. It was a private enterprise that had been granted sole management of the Petroleum Monopoly. It functioned as a private company although the government's delegation in CAMPSA, which is responsible to the Ministry of Finance, had the right to veto the board's decisions. For its management of the Monopoly, CAMPSA received 4 percent of profits and .25 percent of the money collected in taxes. In sum, the patrimony, whose title corresponds to a monopoly, was an organism of the state managed by a corporation of mixed capital, CAMPSA.

The key here is that CAMPSA was, until 1985, a private company. Profits were its bottom-line motivation, not necessarily some "national interest." Throughout the Francoist period and most of the transition to democracy, the Monopoly greatly benefitted the large financial interests tied either directly or indirectly to international capital. These financial interests used their participation in CAMPSA to guarantee the large international oil companies access to the Spanish market and exploited the refineries whose products CAMPSA ultimately distributed.[20] Politically and administratively, the subsecretary of Finance directly controlled all petroleum concerns. The decisions of CAMPSA's board could be vetoed by a delegate of the Ministry of Finance. The state permitted CAMPSA to run the Monopoly but maintained a strong delegation physically situated in CAMPSA's offices. The Ministry of Finance also maintained direct influence in energy-policy management in that the Finance Ministry directly held in 1980, via the state's patrimony, 80 percent of Petroliber, 51 percent of CAMPSA, 30 percent of HISPANOIL, 66 percent of REMOLQUES Maritimos indirectly, through CAMPSA, 50 percent of Butano, 50 percent of Petronor and Asesa, and 25 percent of Proas.[21]

## Ministry of Commerce and the Quota

The Spanish State has directly intervened in the foreign purchase of petroleum since June 1927, when it established the petroleum monopoly. The Monopoly covered the importation of liquid fuels and their derivatives. However, the Monopoly granted an exemption to the refineries for crude purchases and sales of petroleum derivatives. The Spanish refining industry was thus left in private hands. State coordination, but not ownership, of the refining industry did not begin for another forty years.

Initially, the Ministry of Commerce instructed all private refineries on the quantity of crude petroleum they were permitted to acquire and stated each refinery's participation percentage in all joint foreign-purchase contracts. Since 1969, however, HISPANOIL—which INI originally created solely for the purpose of foreign petroleum prospection—has taken the refineries' place in foreign purchasing. HISPANOIL took charge, on behalf of the Ministry of Commerce and specifically the Office of Tariffs and Import Policy, of negotiating crude purchases. On 9 March 1968 the state decreed to the refineries the free importation of crude, up to the percentage of total consumption equal to the amount of foreign capital in the venture. The remaining crude was to be allocated through an annual National Combustible Plan which determined the petroleum's derivation and origin. This is the origin of the Commerce Ministry's quota. Originally 20 percent of the refineries' petroleum was covered by this quota. It was raised to 30 percent in 1969, 45 percent in 1975, and, officially, to 50 percent in the early 1980s.

Although the state controlled about 50 percent of petroleum purchases, in practice approximately 60 percent of Spain's supply of crude oil was provided through this quota system of the Ministry of Commerce. It may have actually come closer to 70 percent of national consumption.[22] This "Commerce quota" was carried out by HISPANOIL and accounted for by the Ministry of Commerce. HISPANOIL obtained these supplies and later distributed them to the different refineries, which are a mixture of public and private companies. The remaining 40 percent formed part of a free quota. Here each company, both public and private, obtained supplies in the free market. The crude purchasing committee was an interministerial committee having rather systematic and specialized roles. Its job was to approve the proposals for the purchase of crude oil of the quota. This committee was presided over by the subsecretary of Commerce.

"Commerce's quota" was initially advantageous to Spanish exports because of the coordinated contracting of crude purchases. This coordination was especially needed when supply dominated the international crude market, holding prices low—both the case in the late 1980s and prior to the energy crisis of 1973–74. When demand dominated the market, the quota became less of a commercial advantage and more of an instrument for securing stable crude imports. The "Commerce quota," however, was not without its controversial elements. These political and economic debates focused on the business and economic relationships of a *public* department allocating petroleum to *private* refineries to be, in turn, sold back to the *public* distribution monopoly.

## Other State Agencies

The dispersion of policy-making into various ministries, departments, and companies impeded governmental coordination. It also accounted for other problems: few successes in crude purchases, excessive refining capacity, the irrational distribution of the refineries, the wastes in transportation costs. As we have seen, three ministries, Finance via the Patrimony, Industry and Energy through INI, and Commerce through the quota, each controlled a central part of the public petroleum sector. (Following PSOE's 1982 election, Finance and Commerce have been combined.) The Ministry of Transportation, the Ministry of Public Works, and the Ministry of Foreign Affairs also had a direct interest in energy policy. Tensions existed between these ministries over control of petroleum policy specifically, but also concerned other areas of energy.

Throughout the Franco regime and the period of the transition, the general *governmental* solution to these *administrative* problems was to create new interministerial commissions or agencies. Several independent or quasi-independent state agencies play a role in Spanish energy policy. Many of these appear in Figure 3-8. Two of these agencies, the Center for Energy Studies and the Nuclear Energy Commission, were the center of much criticism.

The Franco regime created the Center for Energy Studies (CEE) on 9 December 1974 as an institutional response to the energy crisis. The CEE's mandate was to provide general, nontechnical assistance to industry and other consumers in the area of energy conservation. The Ministry of Industry decreed that the CEE's goals were "to carry out studies for the possible reduction of energy consumption, the proposal of measures necessary for such conservation, assistance to the administration in the area of energy planning, and research in the development of new energy sources and better utilization of existing ones."[23] Three years after its creation, in December 1977, the CEE was transformed into an autonomous organ, removing it from direct responsibility to the Ministry of Industry. The CEE remains today, however, tied to the Ministry of Industry and Energy, other ministries, and several autonomous agencies.[24] Later the Socialists replaced the CEE with the Institution for the Diversification and Savings of Energy (IDAE).

Despite its goals, the CEE remained powerless throughout the transition to democracy. It generally remained outside the deliberations that produced Spain's national energy plans. Its legal jurisdiction did not cover the administration of national energy plans. Significant studies on energy conservation were not undertaken or ignored by policymakers. Political opponents often criticized the CEE for producing no more than public relations campaigns to "turn out the lights." The CEE's activities reflected preferences of other policymakers and the imposition of budget constraints. On the other hand, the CEE did give some direction to Spain's collection of data—an important feature in making effective policy.[25] In sum, however, the CEE, and the IDAE as its reformed version, was an autonomous public institute on energy that did not significantly contribute to the formation of energy policy in Spain.

The Nuclear Energy Committee (JEN) is one of the oldest public energy-related organizations in Spain.[26] It reflects a longstanding commitment to the development of nuclear energy. For many years, JEN conducted significant research of a highly technical nature, generally under subcontract to the United States Atomic Energy Commission. In general, JEN attempted to stay out of the politics surrounding energy policy. Aside from giving technical direction to the makers of energy policy, JEN tried to remain above controversies. JEN's very raison d'être nevertheless made it quite political. Its strong public funding, its international connections, and the very nature of its undertaking did not permit JEN to escape these controversies.

## The Private Sector

Spain's public sector did not possess a monopoly on the making of energy policy. A heavy interspersion of public and private affairs dominated Spanish energy. Important private-sector actors included the petroleum refining industry, the electrical industry, and the gas industry. Of these, the refining and electrical industries were the most powerful and involved in Spanish energy planning and administration. These were also the energy companies in which Spanish finance had huge holdings.

## Refineries

As previously mentioned, the Spanish state reserved for itself the buying of imported petroleum through the Ministry of Commerce's quota and the management of the public company, HISPANOIL. However, a heavily private, although mixed, capital system refined the petroleum. Compañía Española de Petróleos, S.A.—known as CEPSA—a company of the financial group of Banco Central, built the first refinery in Spain in 1929. It refined crude from Venezuela in Santa Cruz de Tenerife. From this start, CEPSA became one of the healthiest businesses in Spain, distributing all petroleum products where the Monopoly did not apply (the Canary Islands, the Balearic Islands, and the Spanish enclaves in North Africa) and lubricants on the peninsula itself. The Calvo Sotelo National Company constructed the second refinery in 1942 in Escombreras near Cartagena. Due to World War II, it was reorganized in 1949 as a mixed company through the creation of REPESA, which INI underwrote by 52 percent and Caltex and CEPSA 24 percent each. The new company's main function was to expand the country's supply of petroleum products. The American participation helped REPESA achieve its goals quickly.

Since its birth, then, the Spanish refining industry has been a mixture of public and private ownership. As of the early 1980s, six of the ten Spanish refineries were entirely Spanish owned, with the other four having U.S. participation of 40 percent or less by Exxon, Texaco, Marathon, and Gulf.[27] Four of the refineries were private: Aleciras (CAMPSA); Tenerife (CEPSA); Huelva (Explosivos Riotinto); and Castellón (Petromed). Bilbao (participation by Petronor) was predominantly public. In the public sector, the 1973 merger of the three INI-owned refining companies, REPESA, Calvo Sotelo, and ENPTASA, created ENPETROL. As seen in Table 3-4, its sheer size, with the sixth largest refining capacity in Europe, made it the most important in Spain. Seventy-two percent of ENPETROL was owned by INI, 22 percent by Chevron/Texaco, and the rest by banks and industrial groups.

The Spanish refining industry unquestionably overreached itself in terms of capacity. It grew steadily during the 1960s and 1970s, reaching a capacity of fifty-eight million metric tons in 1975. With domestic production of only two million metric tons in 1975 and Spanish imports around forty-one million metric tons, the Spanish refining industry faced a capacity utilization problem. The volume of refined products in 1975 reached forty-five million tons, leaving 22.5 percent of its capacity idle. Supply-oriented public policy in energy encouraged this large capacity. Energy policy before and during the transition to democracy, however, failed to respond to the crisis. One reason for this was that financial interests could clearly see that there were no profits generated if refining was curtailed.[28]

# UNESA

While Spain's refining industry was highly concentrated, small companies characterized the electrical industry. The electrical industry contained close

**Table 3-4**    Spanish Refining Industry

| Company Acronym | Full Company Name | Location | Capacity (millions of tons) | Percent Total Capacity |
|---|---|---|---|---|
| CEPSA | Compañia Española de Petroleos S.A. | Tenerife Algeciras | 16 | 21 |
| ENPETROL | Empresa Nacional de Petróleo S.A. | Escombreras Puertollano Tarragona | 26 | 36.8 |
| PETROLIBER | Compania Ibérica Refinadora de Petróleos S.A. | La Coruña* | 7 | 9.2 |
| PETROMED | Petróleos del Mediterraneo S.A. | Castellón | 8 | 10.5 |
| E.R.T. | Union Explosivios Rio Tinto S.A. | Huelva | 6 | 7.9 |
| PETRONOR | Refineria de Petróleos del Norte S.A. | Bilboa | 10 | 13.2 |
| ASESA | Asfaltos Españoles S.A. | Tarragona | 1.1 | 1.4 |
| Totals | | | 76.1 | 100 |

*La Coruña absorbed by EMP/Enpetrol in 1985.
SOURCE: CAMPSA, *Memoria, 1985*. Ministerio de Economía y Hacienda.

to 170 separate companies. Most of these were privately owned, with many small ones controlled by a single family. They were scattered throughout the peninsula, serving particular but often overlapping areas. These companies generally possessed small generating capacities. As such, they were survivors of early twentieth-century Spanish electrical structures. Table 3-5 shows the evolution of the Spanish electrical industry in terms of the decreasing number of these smaller companies. Economies of scale have slowly forced many of these companies out of business or made them merge with larger companies. Despite this consolidation, the electrical industry contained many smaller, and increasingly economically inefficient, companies.

Table 3-5 also suggests that a few electrical companies increasingly controlled a larger share of overall Spanish capital expenditures. This hints at the electrical industry's role in the politics of Spanish energy policy. Despite the appearance of diversification, the Spanish electrical industry was in fact dominated by a small group of companies. These companies were either well-established and private, with long histories, or newer state-owned companies

**Table 3-5**   Evolution of the Spanish Electrical Industry

| Year | Number of Companies | Percentage of Spanish Companies | Percentage of Total Spanish Capital Expenditure |
|---|---|---|---|
| 1922 | 477 | 13.6 | 14.2 |
| 1940 | 411 | 10.2 | 17.0 |
| 1959 | 313 | 2.6 | 18.1 |
| 1966 | 278 | 1.7 | 19.0 |
| 1970 | 243 | 1.2 | 19.1 |
| 1977 | 171 | 0.7 | 20.2 |

SOURCE: Serrano and Muñóz, 1979.

**Table 3-6**   The Spanish Electrical Industry, 1977

| Company | Location Headquarters | Year Founded | National Capacity (percent) | National Production (percent) |
|---|---|---|---|---|
| Iberduero | Bilbao | 1901 | 18.01 | 16.87 |
| Hidrola | Madrid | 1907 | 15.97 | 13.44 |
| Sevillana | Seville | 1907 | 9.09 | 8.77 |
| FECSA | Barcelona | 1951 | 8.85 | 7.39 |
| ENDESA (INI) | Madrid | 1944 | 6.15 | 8.02 |
| Union Eléctria | Madrid | 1912 | 5.68 | 5.76 |
| FENOSA | La Coruña | 1943 | 5.74 | 4.86 |
| ENHER (INI) | Barcelona | 1946 | 3.53 | 4.11 |
| 51 other electric-producing companies | — | — | 22.69 | 26.48 |
| 41 other self-producing companies | — | — | 4.30 | 4.30 |

SOURCE OF PRODUCTION FIGURES: *Estadística de Energía Eléctrica, 1977*. Ministerio de Industria.

controlled by INI. Table 3-6 lists these large Spanish electrical companies and their production share.

This small group of companies became the elite of the Spanish electrical industry. They were also the industry's political voice, placing them in the center of Spanish energy policy-making. We later analyze in detail the electrical industry's links to Spain's policy and the political criticisms directed toward the industry. At this point, we need only mention that these companies were well integrated into UNESA, the Spanish Electrical Institute.[29] This umbrella organization coordinates the electrical industries' activities, protects its interests, and preserves monopolistic behavior in the electrical industry.

UNESA was created in 1944 by seventeen of Spain's principal electric companies in an attempt to avoid strong consumption restrictions imposed by the government.[30] At the time, these seventeen companies controlled more than half of all national electrical production. Toward the end of Spain's transition to democracy, UNESA's twenty-four member companies produced 96 percent of Spain's electricity from 97 percent of the country's installed capacity.[31] UNESA's self-defined objective is "to coordinate production according to programs, energy utilization, construction of interconnections for regional systems, and promotion of electric consumption in urban areas."[32] UNESA has argued that "it doesn't seek any business benefits but rather the optimization of resources by the various plants in the country's different regions."[33] Indeed, UNESA quite efficiently coordinated most industry activities. Nevertheless, UNESA's activities went beyond purely technical areas. Economically, UNESA created a system of dividing the industry's responsibilities and benefits. Politically, from its headquarters in Madrid, it served as the defender of electrical interests regarding prices, tax problems, statistics, investments, etc. UNESA's coordination of policy for the electrical industry was so complete that it was often critically viewed as behaving as a single company with strong oligarchical tendencies.

One more point about UNESA. It is an additional example of where the Franco regime's lack of effectiveness in dealing with monopolies carried over into Spain's democratic system. As previously mentioned, the founding of INI sought, among other things, to create public enterprises to compete with established firms. The supply of electricity was to be made more competitive in this manner. Several public electric companies did manage to enter the market, ultimately accounting for 30 percent of UNESA's supply. This did not, in practice, produce an open market in electricity. After their creation, a tendency rapidly emerged in which these public companies openly cooperated with their private counterparts in maintaining restrictive practices.[34] Membership in UNESA by public—specifically INI—electric companies reinforced the oligarchical tendencies in the industry. Such membership facilitated successful lobbying efforts for higher tariffs and public-investment decisions which greatly benefitted these companies.[35]

# Gas Industry

During the Franco period and the transition to democracy, the Spanish gas industry was of mixed capital in a manner similar to the petroleum refining industry. Unlike the refining and electrical industries, however, the structure of the Spanish gas industry was dispersed and lacked cohesion.

Petroleum-derived and manufactured gases such as propane and butane have been used in Spain since 1934. These gases, sold in the ubiquitous orange canisters found throughout the country, were the prime energy source for domestic cooking and hot water. Initially CAMPSA imported the bottles from France. In 1953, CEPSA's Tenerife refinery began producing these gases. REPESA's Cartagena plant initiated production toward the end of 1956. Since natural gas was not readily available during these times, propane and butane consumption generally remained limited to this domestic market.

The distribution of these gases during this time was part of the Monopoly. Francoist policymakers nevertheless considered CAMPSA's management of this part of the Monopoly inadequate. They decided to create a separate company to manage this gas distribution. Fifty percent of the capital was provided by CAMPSA as a private company, and the other 50 percent by REPESA, which at that time represented all other public and private petroleum interests in Spain—INI, CEPSA, Texaco, and Standard Oil of California. On 27 September 1957 BUTANO, S.A., began selling these gases throughout the Monopoly's area. BUTANO's distribution of these gases continued throughout the period of this study, that is, until 1 January 1986 when Spain joined the EEC.

The introduction of natural gas into Spain was more recent. Significant amounts of this energy source were not imported until 1970, although the area of Alava began using it in 1963 following a small domestic find in 1960. Spaniards never had much luck in their search for domestic natural gas. Furthermore, Spanish capital failed to take advantage of the growing international natural gas business, thus not only missing out on the large profits other European and American companies were making but also impeding Spain's access to overseas gas supplies. It was 1966 before the Catalunya Gas Company, along with a group of Spanish banks and Exxon, formed Gas Natural, S.A. This company imported liquified natural gas from Exxon's Libyan fields. Since Exxon's expulsion from Libya, these imports have come mostly from Algeria.

Spain's natural gas and petroleum-based industries thus remain small in comparison to other energy-related industries. This is due primarily to Spain's low natural-gas consumption. Gas consumption is nevertheless increasing.[36]

# Energy Planning

Up to this point, we have considered Spain's energy situation, resources, and usage and both the public and private structures involved in managing the country's energy needs. In many ways Spain was not all that different from other countries: It was highly dependent on foreign energy. We have also discussed, however, that Spain did possess public structures for making energy policy uniquely related to the private sector. A full elaboration of this nexus follows in later chapters. However, the analysis now turns to the heart of Spain's public policy on energy.

Energy has been a component of Spanish economic planning for some time. Several energy issues were included in the first Social and Economic Development Plan, published in November 1962 and covering the period 1964–67. The second Development Plan (1968–71) had an energy commission. The third Development Plan (1972–75) set the precedent for later energy planning.[37] The policymakers behind the third Development Plan did not foresee the energy crisis of the 1970s. They predicted only negligible change in the prices of imported petroleum in 1972–75. Spanish national planning specifically focused on energy, however, is best summarized in five stages.[38] Each revolves around a major policy document.

## The National Electrical Plan

A product of the Franco period, the National Electrical Plan was formally approved by the Council of Ministers on 31 July 1969. It was the first of Spain's national plans concerning energy.[39] This initial public attempt to co-ordinate on the national level activities of the numerous small and regionally situated private electrical companies had the full cooperation of the electrical industry. UNESA actually proposed the plan to the Ministry of Industry. The plan ended a long period of speculation and confusion about the future of the development of electricity in the country. It fixed directives for locations, minimum size of electrical generating plants, national industrial participation, and technological contribution, and determined priority for the functioning of UNESA's companies. This UNESA-elaborated plan heavily favored the large companies by financing and providing government grants on a proportional basis.

The National Electrical Plan also contained projections for the demand of electricity, installed generation potential, and utilization over a period of ten years. The plan's most important revision appeared in December 1973, projecting the country's electrical needs for 1976–85. However, neither quantitative projections of the original plan for the period 1972–81 nor those of the revision were ever realized. The events of 1973 changed this. Nevertheless, the National Electrical Plan is noteworthy not only for its pioneering character under the Franco regime but also because it was elaborated *before* the energy crisis.

## The National Energy Plan

In response to the 1973–74 oil embargo and the energy crisis it produced, the Franco government broadened its planning to include all areas of energy, especially petroleum. This resulted in the first National Energy Plan, appearing toward the end of 1974. The Plan was largely the work of the Director General of Energy—José Luis Díaz Fernández, who played a key part in much of Spain's contemporary energy planning. The government formally approved PEN-75 on 24 January 1975. The Committee on Industry of the Francoist Cortes (Parliament) received this plan in June of that year. Like its predecessor, PEN-75 considered the period between 1976 and 1985. PEN-75 established the core of future energy planning in Spain: to guarantee continuing supplies; to diversify energy resources so that no single energy source would be susceptible to world pricing and supply instability; to reduce supply costs to a minimum; to reduce the importation of primary energy in order to achieve a better equilibrium in the balance of payments; to promote the rational use of energy with the object of moderating the growth rate of demand without effecting economic development; to reduce to a minimum, economics permitting, the environmental impact of energy installations; and to contribute to the technological development of the country and promote energy-related research. However, PEN-75's fundamental goal was to progressively reduce Spain's heavy petroleum dependency by substituting coal, hydroelectricity, and nuclear energy.

However, PEN-75 projections were unrealistic. PEN-75 heavily overestimated demand: it assumed Spain's GNP would grow between 5 and 6 percent annually and energy consumption between 6 and 7 percent. PEN-75 projected electrical demand at an annual increase of 10 percent, with nuclear power providing 56 percent of 1985s electrical supplies. As seen in Table 3–6, the fact that nuclear generation produced only 9 percent of Spain's electrical supply at its peak in 1975 suggests that extreme optimism prevailed. PEN-75 estimated that nuclear energy would permit Spain to provide 22 percent of its own primary energy needs in 1985, compared to only 3.2 percent in 1975. PEN-75 scheduled twenty-three nuclear plants to be added to the three already in operation by channelling 44.5 percent of its investment in this direction. As a coherent program conceived in the authoritarian framework of the Franco regime, PEN-75 failed to consider the political and economic arrangements or policy instruments necessary to realize most of its goals.

While political opposition to PEN-75 could have easily been suppressed under Franco's rule, Spain's first attempt at a comprehensive energy program came to be severely challenged by the economic reality of the times. PEN-75's premises of sustained economic growth prevented its general acceptance on technical grounds. After a short period of discussion within public structures involved with energy policy, the State bureaucracy, and Franco's government, PEN-75 was abandoned in mid-1975.[40] This left Spain with an energy policy void throughout 1976, 1977, 1978, and much of 1979. Spanish energy-policy formulation simply did not meet the country's needs during these critical years of energy scarcity. Furthermore, this policy stagnation was passed on. Democratic Spain followed the same aimless energy-policy direction characteristic of the Franco regime for the next several years.

## Energy in the Moncloa Pact

Following Franco's death in November 1975 and the subsequent transition to democracy, Spanish governments reconsidered many policies. Energy was one of these. The Moncloa Pacts signed in October 1977 by representatives of business, labor, and the state contained a passage on energy policy. Much of the Moncloa Pacts, including the section on energy, took the form of a very rough outline of programs to be elaborated at a later date. This vagueness was rooted in the political needs for negotiated settlements between the government, business, and labor. Energy policy as outlined in the Moncloa Pacts had many general objectives similar to PEN-75: a realistic pricing policy, encouragement of the rational use of energy, expansion of technological investigation, and diversification of energy supplies. In other ways, the Moncloa Pacts' section on energy was more specific than PEN-75. It called for a reduction of petroleum's participation in Spanish energy needs to 50 percent (compare Figure 3-4), the coordination and maximal openness in the administration of business in energy, special consideration for the environment and the rights of energy consumers, and periodic revision of the plan's projections.[41] The Moncloa Pacts also continued to push the development of new sources, especially nuclear energy.

Participants in the negotiations agreed that before the year's end a new energy plan would be submitted to the Spanish parliament. This revision, written by the Ministry of Industry, considered Spanish energy needs for 1977 to 1987. It more realistically projected energy needs, basing them on a growth in GNP of 1.2 percent in 1978 and 4 percent annually until 1987. Primary energy consumption was estimated at 122.9 million TEC (Tons Equivalent of Coal) in 1982 and 153.8 million TEC for 1987, compared to

PEN-75's 196.7 million TEC estimate for 1985. The revision lowered projections for electrical demand from PEN-75's 10 percent annual increase to between 6 and 7.5 percent. It also reduced estimates for nuclear energy to 14.2 percent of the total energy supply, with only fifteen nuclear plants. This revision of PEN-75, following some modifications and corrections, eventually emerged as PEN-79.

## The Second National Energy Plan

Spain's Council of Ministers, under the leadership of Adolfo Suárez, approved the second National Energy Plan on 3 May 1978. The Spanish Parliament did not debate and approve PEN-79, however, until 27–28 July 1979. Politics caused this fourteen-month delay. The agenda for completing Spain's transition to democracy contained other items that took precedent.[42] Energy policy received low priority on the government's agenda because PEN-79 itself was politically hot. Opponents raised strong criticisms against PEN-79 during these months.

The Spanish left and other political groups argued during this time that PEN-79 was an expansionist energy policy with excessive demand projections, that its goal of doubling coal production by 1987 could not be realistically achieved, that natural gas's future potential was underplayed, and that PEN-79 barely mentioned alternative sources such as solar, wind, or geothermal energy, giving no plan of action for their development or implementation. These critics went on to maintain that PEN-79 excessively emphasized nuclear energy while failing to acknowledge its problems, e.g., nuclear wastes, worker safety, and high construction and dismantling costs. They contended that foreign energy dependency would not be lessened with nuclear energy because most of the technical know-how required importation, because PEN-79 did not contain a coherent energy-conservation policy, and because it did not treat the important but delicate topic of restructuring the electrical industry. Other criticisms focused on the lack of a clear rural electrification program, a pricing system to rectify regional disequilibrium, and the absence of discussion on the possible intervention of the new autonomous regions in the nuclear area, or PEN as a whole.

Given these criticisms, the Suárez Government decided not to bring PEN before the full Parliament until after the March 1979 elections. When the parliament finally approved PEN-79, the opposition Socialists and Communists added ten resolutions. These amendments were not, however, legally binding. They included many of the criticisms stated above. While democratic politics appear to have slowed down the planning process, they did not significantly alter the direction of energy policy.

As stated earlier, during its negotiated settlement finalized in the Moncloa

Pacts, PEN-79 emerged as a broad statement of legislation for later implementation. Several of these legislative steps were taken in the early 1980s. While in legislative opposition, the PSOE and the PCE initially proposed many of these. Ley 15/22 April 1980 created a Nuclear Security Council, and its members were nominated on 6 March 1981 by Royal Decree 386. The Nuclear Security Council is the state body concerned with nuclear security and radiation protection.[43] Other legislation included a modification of the Mining Law (Ley 54/5 November 1980), a change in the Electrical Production Statute (Ley 7/25 March 1981) that regulated interprovincial electrical prices, an Energy Conservation Law (Ley 82/30 December 1980), and the creation of the National Institute of Hydrocarbons (INH). The Socialists raised objections about the ultimate form that these last two took. They claimed the conservation law only cosmetically treated the government's lack of an energy conservation program. The creation of INH, many Socialists argued, compromised away to the traditional power holders in the electrical industry the real purposes for creating this national holding company.[44] Despite such political criticism, the UCD government slowly filled in some of the legislative framework provided by PEN-79.

PEN's basic objective was, of course, substitution for petroleum. By October 1980, fifteen months after PEN-79's implementation, Spain's energy authorities continued the emphasis on coal generation and the installation of nuclear plants in order to replace petroleum as the prime material for the generation of electricity.[45]

On 17 October 1980 the Council of Ministers reviewed PEN-79's first yearly status report.[46] Ignácio Bayón, the Minister of Industry and Energy, pushed for the acceleration of PEN. Bayon presented a full report. He detailed the status of energy consumption. He informed the cabinet that as a consequence of a bad year in hydroelectric production, petroleum dependence in the structure of primary energy consumption would increase in 1980 by 5.8 percent over the previous year, besides the large increases (around 28 percent) in the consumption of coal and natural gas, whose imports in the past year had been considerably increased.[47] In 1980 coal consumption rose to 30 million tons, 6 million tons over the previous year. Natural gas consumption also increased 40 percent over the previous year. With this rise, natural gas went from 1.7 to 3 percent of the primary energy consumed. Despite these figures, the report from the Ministry of Industry and Energy optimistically concluded that PEN-79 was accomplishing its goals, particularly in the essential investment program.[48] The accelerated program for the construction of seven coal-generating plants presented to the government in May 1980 was quickly contracted out.[49]

The Suárez government also accelerated the construction of Spain's nuclear plants. The entry of Almaraz placed on line a plant whose generating potential was equivalent to almost 6 percent of national consumption, saving almost 1.5 million tons of fuel (TEP). Three coal-generating plants soon began operations: Meriama (La Coruña), ENECO's plant in Córdoba, and Lada (Asturias). Their combined potential of 1,150 megawatts equalled about 1.5 million TEP needed to produce the same quantity of energy. The problem for Spain's energy authorities remained that coal-generating plants had an installation period of four years while nuclear plants require significantly more.

This progressive substitution of coal and nuclear energy for petroleum produced a need to restructure Spain's refineries. They had to shift from the refining of heavy crudes, which could be burned in these electrical generating plants, to lighter products. This meant that their 50-percent capacity for heavy crude had to be altered. The plans for this reconversion crystallized in 1981 with the beginning of "cracking" operations of Petroliber in La Coruña, followed by those of Petromed in Castellón and Enpetrol's Puertollano in 1983.

## PEN-82

By law, the National Energy Plan had to be revised and updated every two years. This mandatory revision occurred in the fall and early winter of 1981 but was not approved in parliament until the following year.[50] PEN-82's projections are summarized in Table 3-7. The modifications in these projections are contrasted with earlier ones in Table 3-8. PEN-82's estimates incorporated the 1979 petroleum price increases and the supply problems stemming from the Iranian revolution and the Iran-Iraq conflict. In this document, the government claimed it reduced Spain's dependency on imported petroleum and primary energy production by almost eight percentage points by the end of 1981, two years after the implementation of PEN.[51] PEN-82 realistically acknowledged the technical and political delays in nuclear construction. It modified the projections for nuclear-generated electricity, stressing imported coal as a petroleum substitution. This revision of PEN nevertheless did not significantly alter the strong nuclear direction of Spain's energy policy. PEN-82's projections for nuclear energy only pushed implementation farther back in time. PEN's basic direction and its call for reliance on nuclear energy were slightly modified, not abandoned.

Luis Magaña, UCD's last Energy Commissioner, stated that the centerpiece of this revision consisted of coal resources, increased investigation of alternative energy, and exploration and use of conventional resources. He emphasized that the use of domestic coal would play a major role, highlighting that the production of domestic coal had grown 47 percent between 1979 and 1981. He noted this was a response to market forces. Magaña also ana-

**Table 3-7**    Projections of PEN-82 (percent)

| Source | 1981 | 1985 | 1990 |
|---|---|---|---|
| Hydroelectricity | 11.3 | 10.0 | 9.2 |
| Natural gas | 2.6 | 5.4 | 6.1 |
| Coal | 21.3 | 24.3 | 22.8 |
| Nuclear energy | 3.4 | 10.6 | 15.1 |
| Petroleum | 61.4 | 49.3 | 45.2 |
| Other | — | .4 | 1.6 |
| Totals | 100 | 100 | 100 |
| (Thousands of TEC) | 105.1 | 124.2 | 152.1 |

SOURCE: *El País*, 6 December 1981, 53.

**Table 3-8**    Projections for Spanish Primary Energy Consumption

| Source | PEN-75 (1985) | PEN-79 (1987) | PEN-82 (1985) |
|---|---|---|---|
| Hydroelectricity | 9.2% | 9.4% | 10.0% |
| | (15.9) | (13.6) | (12.5) |
| Natural Gas | 11.1% | 5.3% | 5.4% |
| | (19.1) | (7.7) | (6.7) |
| Coal | 14.7% | 16.2% | 24.3% |
| | (25.5) | (23.5) | (30.1) |
| Nuclear Energy | 22.0% | 14.8% | 10.6% |
| | (38.1) | (21.5) | (13.1) |
| Petroleum | 43.0% | 54.3% | 49.3% |
| | (74.4) | (78.7) | (61.3) |
| Other | — | — | .4% |
| | | | (.5) |
| Totals | 100% | 100% | 100% |
| (Thousands of TEC) | (173) | (145) | (124.2) |

SOURCES: PEN-75: Ministerio de Industria, 1975, 3. PEN-79: Ministerio de Industria, 1978, 44. PEN-82: *El País*, 6 December 1981, 53.

lyzed the different investment policies in alternative energy and anticipated that in 1990 it should be possible to expect 2.5 percent of Spanish energy to be supplied from alternative sources, basically solar and biomass. The solar platform in Tabernas (Almeria) has become one of the most important centers of investigation not only of Europe but also for the member states of the IEA.[52]

Spain is similar to many other European nations in that it achieved economic development at the expense of energy self-sufficiency. Spain's energy dependency is great because few domestic energy sources exist. It has little petroleum or natural gas resources and its coal is dirty, difficult to mine, and rapidly becoming exhausted. Unlike its European neighbors, however, Spain's energy-consumption reaction to the 1973–74 oil embargo and crude price increases were virtually nonexistent.

The energy crisis did have a strong economic impact in this southern European country. Spain's "economic miracle" of the 1960s and early 1970s ended, with growth in GDP slowing considerably. Drops in tourism and remittances from emigrant workers combined with the more expensive crude-oil payments to affect Spain's balance of payments situation quite harshly. High inflation and unemployment rates were, in part, the price Spain paid for an inadequate governmental response to this new energy predicament. Unfortunately, this economic downturn corresponded with the country's transition to democracy.

Spain's institutional arrangements within which energy policy was formulated did not facilitate a strong policy response to the changing economic climate. The new democracy in Spain inherited such structures as the Council of Ministers, the Ministries of Industry and Energy, Finance, and Commerce, and two other state agencies that were central to the formulation of a governmental response. Each of these organizations exercised its defined role in the making of energy policy. These roles greatly overlap with many private interests, e.g., the refineries, the electric companies, and the gas industry. Public policy in Spain for energy heavily depended on the tacit approval of key institutions and companies in the private sector. Energy policy in Spain has been articulated in a series of official plans. These plans permit comparison of energy policy in Spain during the later stages of the Franco regime and in the country's period of transition to democracy. Different Spanish governments produced specific programs such as the National Electrical Plan and three separate versions of the National Energy Plan. Indications are that the policy decisions contained in these energy plans were a product of a political-business class that strongly influenced public policy in energy. This influence is a product of this elite group's pivotal position both during the Franco regime and the early period of parliamentary democracy. Chapter 4 will discuss the nature of this influence and the specific components of Spain's energy policy.

# 4

---

# Policy Instruments

The use of macroeconomic instruments to pursue Spain's energy program is central to any substantive understanding of this policy during the transition to democracy. Spain's macroeconomic policy responses to the rise in the world oil prices in the areas of monetary policy, incomes, and price measures reflect a fundamental lack of change in policy direction. The following analysis covers three distinct periods in the regime change: the last two years of the Franco regime, the early stage of the political transition, and the current democratic system. A more detailed analysis of several instruments of Spanish energy policy follows this general macroeconomic discussion. These instruments include pricing, investment, and institutional coordination. This leaves for chapter 5 much of the political analysis of these energy policy instruments and Spanish energy policy in general. First, however, comes analysis of the policy instruments themselves. The following discussion of the government's use of specific policy instruments serves several analytical purposes. First, it demonstrates a general absence of policy change in these more specific policy outputs despite the occasional appearances of change. Second, this analysis indirectly underscores the pivotal nature of the Spanish political-business elite that accounts for Spanish energy-policy continuity. This analysis of public policy instruments in energy suggests the means by which this pivotal elite generated an energy program beneficial to its interests. Third, discussion of these energy-policy instruments raises questions about the *political* controversies resulting from the state's continued use of these policy instruments and the overall direction of Spanish energy policy.

# Franco's Macroeconomic Policy

Franco's policy response to the problems caused by the 1973 oil crisis was negligible. The only direct policy relied solely on monetary instruments. Between 1970 and the early stages of the energy crisis, government officials had regulated short-term economic trends through short-term control of bank liquidity, i.e., regulation of the money supply. Initially, the main objective of the Bank of Spain and other monetary authorities was to bring down gradually the growth rate of liquid assets in order to control oil-imported inflation. The authorities continued these restrictive monetary policies through a raising of the liquidity rate well into 1974 in a vain attempt to offset the continuing effects of the oil crisis. During the first half of 1974, they fixed on a 20 percent growth in liquid assets (M3) as a main economic target (compared to a 17.7 percent average in 1961 and 23.7 percent for 1971–73). They targeted 18 percent in the second half of the year.[1]

The Franco regime also pursued wage and price policies during this time. The central economic policy, outlined in November 1973, was to combat inflation. Wage increases were not to exceed cost-of-living rises, with exceptions for productivity. Similar to the monetary authorities' temporary change, this policy was abandoned in 1974 only to be reinstituted in April 1975. In 1975, wage increases were not to exceed cost-of-living rises of the past 12 months, with room for an additional 3 percent increase in exceptional circumstances.

In price policy, the November 1973 provisions created three categories: free market prices, prices subject to surveillance, and prices subject to prior authorization. The only increases permitted in the two controlled categories were those that reflected higher costs as a result of more expensive raw materials and authorized wage rises.[2] The list of authorized price items was later increased and the rules for surveillance were clarified and strengthened.

One relevant example of the Franco regime's myopic view of the consequences of the oil crisis was in pricing policies. On 1 March 1974, in the midst of the early stages of the energy crisis, the Spanish authorities moved exactly opposite to the nation's long-term energy-related interests: they *reduced* taxes—and thus prices—on petroleum products. This tax decrease came at a time when many other European nations were beginning to *raise* taxes in order to lower consumption. This move underscores the Spanish government's belief that the crisis was to be short-lived.[3] The Francoist policymakers hoped to modify the effect of higher prices on petroleum sales: more sales meant higher profits for CAMPSA and larger tax receipts for the state despite the lower tax rate. This proved a particularly painful burden to carry since democratic policymakers did not for some time possess the necessary political strength to correct this and other decisions.

# Macroeconomic Policy During the Transition's Early Stages

The period following Franco's death proved to be both politically and economically difficult. The energy crisis deteriorated the Spanish economy, yet the governments of Arias Navarro, Adolfo Suárez, and Leopoldo Calvo-Sotelo had limited room for political maneuvering. Many Francoist officials clung to their positions after the Caudillo's death. Some business leaders feared rapid change that might have produced instability. The political Left, on the other hand, resurfaced following Franco's death and was intent on improving the workers' conditions after thirty-nine years of his rule. Both the Left and the Right had legitimate economic concerns. Inflation was high. Unemployment was at 6 percent and continuing to climb. The trade deficit was at $3 billion, the total foreign debt at $11.8 billion, and GNP rose not more than 2 percent annually between 1973 and 1977. The peseta was in severe trouble on the international markets. In sum, the reformists supported by King Juan Carlos I were not only struggling to keep Spain's political Left from moving too quickly but also had to address these economic problems without turning their backs on the more conservative elements within the government itself.

The transitional government of Arias Navarro made its first significant macroeconomic decision in February 1976. The peseta was suddenly devalued by 11 percent. This move ended a period of several weeks in which the Bank of Spain had been spending up to $30 million a day to support the peseta. Other effective policies, however, did not follow this devaluation. An emergency program announced in October 1976, for example, included the following:[4]

1. A temporary freeze on all prices with selected price controls thereafter.
2. Progressive wage ceilings: cost-of-living plus two points for those under $5000; cost-of-living only for those earning $5000-$10,000; incomes above $10,000 were frozen.
3. To lower the external oil bill, a surcharge of up to 50% for industrial diesel fuel, fuel oil, and electricity consumption in excess of 95% of last year's level.
4. Twenty percent increase in customs duties on imports, excluding some raw materials and food products.
5. Suspension for one year of article 35 of the labor relations law, which prohibits companies from declaring redundancies except in financial emergencies.

Following the announcement of these proposals, however, Suárez's appointed government learned quickly of their political impracticality. Opposition came from several sides. Labor opposed them because prior to this, Article 35 of the Francoist constitution had made it virtually impossible to fire workers covered by contracts. Suárez's proposal to permit layoffs came at a time when unemployment was already high. The unions did not treat this proposal or the controls placed on wages kindly. They considered these economic measures as "tantamount to a declaration of war on the workers."[5]

Many businessmen were equally alienated. Cries came for a coherent package of stern austerity measures instead of these proposals. Business viewed these measures with skepticism because previous price freezes had proved unenforceable. Finance leaders, in effect, saw the program as full of stopgap measures. They called for a long-term social pact between labor and management to insure both political and economic stability. This pact would include a modest wage increase of 10 percent to 12 percent and a coherent incomes policy in exchange for trade-union freedom. Most businessmen, in addition, urged steps to curb imports.[6] This combination of labor and business opposition assured the failure of these measures. Energy-induced economic problems were destined to continue.

Monetary policy during the early period of the transition did not differ much from that of the last years of the Franco regime. For example, in early 1976, monetary authorities set a target of 16 percent to 17 percent annual growth in M3. The Bank of Spain, in order to achieve this target, determined a compatible growth rate of bank deposits and bank liquidity. Authorities also decided to support some hard-pressed sectors. Credit rose on the whole by 23.4 percent during this easing period. This acceleration continued through 1977—a target of a 21 percent growth in M3 was met during the first half of 1977. This renewed monetary expansion, of course, increased inflationary pressures. Control of bank liquidity therefore continued to be very important to the policymakers in Spain as a means of managing the economy during the early transition.[7] Political pressures, however, prevented forceful adherence. Energy-induced economic problems thus continued to be addressed in a manner similar to the past. Economic policy continued under the influence of a certain policy inertia.

Spain's energy-induced economic problems continued without the adoption of more comprehensive measures. The inflation rate continued to rise. Energy consumption did not substantially taper off. Oil imports officially pushed foreign debt to $11 billion ($14–$16 billion by unofficial accounts). The trade deficit worsened in 1976. This deficit was covered only by dipping deeper into reserves and by borrowing heavily abroad. Spain's debt-service repayments on existing loans reached nearly $2 billion. Exports declined, partly due to an overevaluation of the peseta. Unemployment increased, further swelled by Spanish workers returning from layoffs elsewhere in Europe. Strong policy remedies to these economic problems had to wait.

## Democratic Macroeconomic Policy

During the June 1977 election campaign, Adolfo Suárez openly stated that the first move in economic policy of his new UCD government would be a large devaluation of the peseta. He knew that he had to wait until after the election to devalue because that action and the accompanying austerity needed to make it work would generate intense political pressures.[8] True to his word, immediately after the election Suárez's UCD government introduced an economic package based on the austerity measures and economic reforms recommended by the IMF and foreign bankers.[9] The Bank of Spain announced on 12 July, just one week after the new government took office, the first part of the program—a 25 percent devaluation of the peseta. This devaluation, whose purpose was to restore the balance-of-payments equilibrium tilted by the energy crisis, was timed to attract an August tourist boom.

The devaluation was quickly followed by sweeping fiscal reforms included in a rather vague economic package announced on 24 July. The government hoped this package would avoid the mistake of the February 1976 devaluation which lacked concomitant austerity measures. The new reform program included the following features:[10]

1. Reform of the taxation system, giving powers to the tax inspectors (including public disclosure) and, for the first time, making tax fraud an offense punishable by imprisonment.
2. A progressive tax on net wealth . . . applied with a 5 percent surcharge on an annual taxable income of over 2 million pesetas, and increases in inheritance and luxury taxes.
3. Tax incentive[s] for companies increasing their labor forces and a fund . . . to create jobs in areas of high unemployment; a public debt bond issue of 20 billion pesetas . . . floated and the proceeds invested in low-cost housing projects.
4. Expansion of the money supply . . . moderated and the Bank of Spain rediscount rate raised. Interest rates . . . progressively freed from official controls by 1978 and the credit system stimulated and enlarged; banks . . . [no] longer have to deposit with the Bank of Spain the full counterpart of any increases in foreign-held accounts denominated in pesetas.
5. Selective price controls . . . established until 30 September, and limits on wage increases . . . foreseen, with flat-rate increases;

increases based on proportions of present salary levels . . . forbidden.

6. The 20 percent import surcharge established in October 1976 . . . removed and the prices of petroleum products, coffee, soya oil, and transport services increased.

Of particular importance here is the conspicuous absence of energy-related policies even though the energy crisis had fueled many of the country's economic problems. The pivotal members of the regime's coalition support were obviously aware of Spain's energy problems. The fact remained that labor and business' different interests relating to energy policy forced the postponement of such policy compromise.

Political constraints made full adoption and implementation of these reforms problematic. Organized labor had gained strength through the dismantling of the government-run labor syndicates. This provided enough political muscle to contest official attempts to limit wage increases. The limit on wage increases of between 17 and 22 percent, while not binding by statute, meant that labor would not be able to keep ahead of inflation as it had in 1976. On the other hand, some segments of the business community believed these wage increases were behind the high 1977 inflation rate. They argued that Spain's "stagflation" was a result of strong wage-push, resulting in a decline in profits. Some believed the Madrid authorities had previously sought labor peace by acquiescing to wage increases that exceeded government ceilings. Two facts gave credence to this argument: Spain's ratio of personal income to GNP was higher than in all other OECD countries except Portugal; and Spain led all OECD countries in the percentage by which the increase in wages exceeded the rise in the cost of living. While many leftist-oriented Spaniards saw these new wage restrictions as preventing them from keeping pace with inflation, others felt wage-push needed to be curtailed. Political pressures once again threatened to delay the long-overdue policy responses to Spain's oil-induced economic problems.

In economic policy-making, the Suárez government thus needed to soften its internal political constraints. No program to control the economy was possible without appealing to the key interest supporting the regime: business and organized labor. The ruling UCD acknowledged this support in October 1977 when it arranged the Moncloa Pacts. This agreement with the opposition—PSOE, PCE, and organized labor—gave Suárez's economic policies a two-year grace period. A group of Franco's ex-ministers, led by José-María de Areilza and Manuel Fraga, lent support to this social-economic contract. These pacts were a clear indicator of the support of the post-Franco system by business, the political center and other moderate representatives of business interests, and organized labor. The Moncloa Pacts formalized the coalitional composition of the new democratic political system.

The Moncloa Pacts exchanged political reforms for economic austerity measures. The Left agreed to the pact because the government promised to reform drastically the highly regressive taxation structure and to pursue social-security reforms. More specially, the Communist-led Workers Commissions (CC.OO.) and the socialist General Workers Union (UGT) both gave their grudging approval to the program after the government sweetened it 1) by cutting employees contributions to social security from 28 percent of wages to 25 percent; 2) by increasing public spending by injecting approximately \$235–250 million into the unemployment fund, which was to be used to build roads and housing, providing employment to about 800,000 unemployed; and 3) by extending the period of eligibility for benefits from eighteen months to two years.[11] For its part, labor agreed to the restraints on wage increases.

The Suárez government's austerity package thus included wage restraints and a credit squeeze to tighten the money supply. It sought to reduce the M3 growth rate to 17 percent at the end of 1977 and to maintain this rate throughout 1978.[12] Suárez also threatened that if the unions proved unable to deliver their members on the "economic realities" of the Moncloa Pacts, his government would rely solely on monetary controls.

Suárez's economic policy achieved some immediate results. The 25 percent devaluation of the peseta in July 1977 produced some short-term improvements. By January 1978, the foreign-currency reserves had climbed \$2.5 billion to a healthy \$5.8 billion. Exports in September 1977 were more than \$200 million above the previous year, despite a slump in industrial output, and the \$4,238,000,000 foreign investment for January-October 1977 was 75 percent higher than for the same period in 1976. This economic rally, stimulated by the July 1977 devaluation and coupled with the ceiling on wage boosts, continued throughout 1978. At year's end, the balance of payments showed a \$1 billion surplus, reversing 1977s \$2.1 billion deficit. The unions held average wage increases to one point below the stipulated ceiling, which brought down inflation to 16 percent in 1978 from the 27 percent rate during 1977. Spain's 1978 GNP was also up 3 percent, bettering the Moncloa Pact's 1 percent estimate.

The results, however, were not all positive. Tight money policy forced some businesses to go under while pushing others to the brink of bankruptcy.[13] Day-to-day business in Spain had traditionally been covered by credit to a much greater extent than in the rest of Europe.[14] The cutback on credit helped push interest rates to nearly 20 percent by the end of 1977, up from a July 1977 level of 12 percent. Large banks and corporations were still able to tap the vast resources of the international banking community. These remained, however, beyond the reach of the smaller businesses. The policy of a 22 percent ceiling on wage increases but a 17 percent limit on monetary growth also pinched most businesses. According to CEPYME, the Spanish Confederation of Small and Medium Businesses, some 10,000 firms went bankrupt in 1978.[15]

This tight monetary and credit policy eventually cracked the political solidarity supporting the Moncloa Pacts. Business delivered the fatal blows, complaining of the virtual impossibility of obtaining credit even at prohibitive rates. The banking community also found that these money-supply restrictions posed serious difficulties for it.[16] After "five months of bombardment by business," Prime Minister Suárez was forced by the Right, and probably also influenced by his trailing of the Socialists' Felipe González in most opinion polls, to redraft his economic policies and shake up his austerity-minded cabinet.[17] On 22 February 1978 Suárez reluctantly accepted the resignation of his economic minister, Enrique Fuentes Quintana—the architect of the austerity program—and four other cabinet members involved in economic planning.[18] Interestingly enough, however, Fuentes's tight-credit, price-limiting austerity program was not the only problem. His proposal to nationalize the unprofitable steel industry and most of the nation's utilities, and to dismantle CAMPSA, led to a long series of clashes with the Right, especially businessmen who had held privileged positions under Francoist economic policies. When Fernando Abril, Fuentes's replacement at the Economic Ministry, proposed a 13 percent wage ceiling in 1978, it was rejected by both business and labor. The unions wanted a 16 percent wage ceiling, and the 1.5 million-member Spanish Confederation of Business Organizations called for a 10 percent limit. Political survival took precedence over forceful economic policy.

Following the March 1979 election, yet another economic minister, José Luís Leal, revealed that he intended to make only a few adjustments to previous economic policies. This vagueness about medium- or long-term plans satisfied none of the pressing political groups, for example, business, banking, and labor. The adjustments made were aimed at liberalizing the economy: to stem the flood of foreign currency into Spain and to stimulate private investment.[19] A decision to float the rising peseta also alarmed exporters. Given the political infeasibility of introducing a new comprehensive economic package, small adjustments in the Bank of Spain's day-to-day control of liquidity remained the UCD government's only available option until its defeat in October 1982. UCD's internal political problems, with the factional infighting that ultimately destroyed it following the October 1982 elections, prevented any stringent economic measures. The December 1979 crude oil price increases only added to Spain's economic problems. Spain's price for crude oil went up about $11.6 billion in 1980. Balance-of-payments and trade deficits continued to rise.

Thus the Spanish authorities' use of macroeconomic policy instruments did not appear to change significantly during this time. Franco initially failed to forcefully address Spain's energy-induced economic problems through such instruments. The politics of the early transition prevented the use of many macroeconomic instruments. This politically created indecision meant that the policy status quo prevailed. Policy continued as in the past. The energy situation aggravated Spain's economic problems, even if it was not the only cause. Energy's effect on the economy remained strong, in part, because of an absence of effective policy. A policy of low energy prices exemplifies this.

## Policy Instruments: Pricing

Three types of petroleum markets existed during this time in Western Europe: a free market in which each company freely fixed its prices, e.g., West Germany; a monitored market in which the government, in consultation with the companies, determined the basic criteria for the elaboration of prices submitted weekly or monthly, e.g., Belgium and Holland; and a controlled market in which the government exclusively set the prices, e.g., Italy. After the 1920s and the Primo de Rivera dictatorship, Spain also maintained a controlled market of petroleum at fixed prices.

Energy pricing exemplifies Spain's economic policy "drift" during the Franco regime and the transition to democracy. One of the reasons Spain continued to have balance-of-payments problems due to high crude costs was that the rise in oil prices was not passed on to consumers as rapidly as in other European countries. CAMPSA, the state petroleum monopoly, controlled, ran, and operated the country's petroleum distribution. The government, nevertheless, set prices. For close to four decades, Spanish authorities habitually set low prices for domestic energy. This pattern continued during the transition to democracy. Policymakers did not use price as an instrument to help achieve low demand for energy.

Figure 4-1 depicts changes in fuel prices in Spain, three other southern European nations, the United Kingdom, and the United States. This figure permits an across-timed comparison of the changes in the price of fuel in these six countries for the period 1960 to 1986. The figures represent the price with respect to 1975 prices, i.e., 1975 = 100, and are controlled for the effects of inflation. Such a cross-national comparison shows that fuel prices in Spain did rise somewhat following the energy crises of 1973–74 and 1979. Nevertheless, fuel is Spain remained much cheaper than in the other countries presented here. Spanish authorities regulated the price of fuel in such a way as to keep fuel comparatively cheap. Stated differently, in constant terms fuel consumption in Spain remained a bargain. The government in Spain failed to use higher fuel prices as a disincentive for energy consumption.

The effect of this policy in energy economics was that the authorities actually encouraged the purchase of energy at a time when higher consumption harshly affected most Western economies. Such a lack of creation of disincentives for fuel consumption was similar to the pattern followed by other nations prior to 1973. Spain stood out, however, in that its public leaders minimized for consumers the magnitude of the 1974 "shock." Incredibly, policymakers appeared to return to the policies of the past—fuel prices continued their downward trend. Other countries seemed to have learned from this petroleum shock. Spain did not. Authorities in Spain widened the gap between its fuel prices and those of other countries. Thus the 1973–74 oil crisis only temporarily altered a pattern characteristic of both authoritarian and democratic Spain: declining real fuel prices.

Figure 4-1 includes all petroleum-derived fuels. Another comparative analysis of Spain's pricing policies for gasoline and motor oil further substantiates this point. Table 4-1 presents the total price of the regular gasoline and motor oil in thirteen Western European countries in 1976 and 1985. These coun-

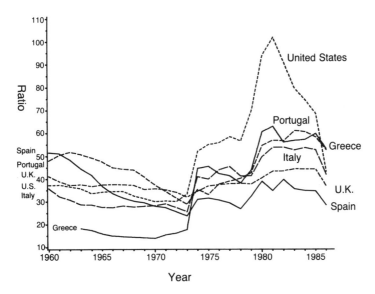

**Figure 4-1.**    Ratio, Fuel Prices to Consumer Prices (Prices Indexed)
Source: Calculated from *Energy Balances of OECD Countries, 1970–1985*

tries are listed according to the price of regular gasoline in pesetas per liter in 1976. In 1976, Spain was eleventh of thirteen in Europe in the price of gasoline. It was trailed only by Luxembourg and the United Kingdom in terms of providing relatively inexpensive gasoline. Gasoline purchases at the pump in 1976 were thus much less expensive in Spain than in most other European nations. By 1985, not much had changed. Well after the transition, Spain stilled ranked eleventh of thirteen in Western Europe in the price of regular gasoline, trailed only by Luxembourg and Germany.

**Table 4-1**   Petroleum Prices, November 1976 and October 1985 (pesetas per liter, taxation percentage in parentheses)

| Country | 1976 Regular | 1976 Motor Oil | 1985 Regular | 1985 Motor Oil |
|---|---|---|---|---|
| Italy | 65.294 | 15.797 | 114.300 | 66.060 |
| | (41.92%) | (24.99%) | (65.6%) | (31.1%) |
| Portugal | 56.532 | 14.427 | 103.215 | 64.878 |
| | (42.26%) | (9.50%) | (40.0%) | (8.2%) |
| Denmark | 48.716 | 14.084 | 104.035 | 63.614 |
| | (37.20%) | (11.47%) | (54.7%) | (18.1%) |
| Holland | 46.201 | 20.939 | 91.818 | 64.489 |
| | (37.43%) | (27.10%) | (58.5%) | (32.5%) |
| France | 45.907 | 27.285 | 107.050 | 84.082 |
| | (37.85%) | (33.38%) | (46.5%) | (31.4%) |
| Belgium | 43.085 | 24.002 | 94.658 | 73.923 |
| | (36.51%) | (30.08%) | (55.6%) | (41.3%) |
| Switzerland | 42.826 | 45.346 | 91.233 | 94.941 |
| | (36.60%) | (37.04%) | (50.5%) | (53.9%) |
| Germany | 40.412 | 39.281 | 82.208 | 80.990 |
| | (37.06%) | (35.97%) | (51.9%) | (45.9%) |
| Sweden | 39.856 | 11.360 | 89.964 | 62.346 |
| | (33.60%) | (9.09%) | (52.6%) | (17.3%) |
| Austria | 38.974 | 35.112 | 94.459 | 90.126 |
| | (32.58%) | (30.84%) | (48.6%) | (49.6%) |
| Spain | 30.250 | 16.750 | — | — |
| | (24.79%) | (16.42%) | | |
| Spain (including | 35.870 | 20.280 | 87.000 | 62.000 |
| Monopoly's revenue) | (36.58%) | (30.97%) | (54.5%) | (30.2%) |
| Luxembourg | 33.322 | 15.473 | 76.027 | 64.608 |
| | (32.78%) | (17.50%) | (46.1%) | (30.7%) |
| United Kingdom | 28.861 | 27.303 | 95.220 | 95.449 |
| | (33.16%) | (32.15%) | (56.2%) | (49.4%) |

SOURCE: Adapted from *Memoria*, CAMPSA, 1976 and 1985.

Two points about gasoline prices are important here. The first concerns taxes. Besides direct control of gasoline prices as in Italy and Spain, governments also affect prices through taxation. The amount of taxes levied on gasoline may serve as an indicator of the perceived of price as an instrument to discourage consumption by policymakers. Using this indicator for energy policy, in 1976 Spanish authorities were one of Europe's least committed to the use of high prices as a means of lowering energy consumption. By 1985, this had changed somewhat for regular gasoline, moving up to sixth of thirteen in Europe in terms of the percentage of the price collected for taxes. However, this was very different with respect to motor oil. Motor oil, which is distributed by private companies in Spain, was taxed at a level that ranked Spain tenth of the thirteen European countries reported here.

There exists a slight problem in directly comparing these figures on taxation in Europe. In most European countries, there are two different taxes on gasoline—a direct tax and an indirect tax, the Value Added Tax. Table 4-1's percentages include both taxes, yet not all countries imposed VAT in 1976. Nevertheless, these figures do indicate that energy policymakers in Spain did not use gasoline prices as an instrument of energy management despite the fact that petroleum accounted for 75 percent of Spain's final energy consumption. This had not changed by 1985. Also, the use of taxation as a means of raising the prices of energy and thus pushing conservation was average by European standards in terms of gasoline. Motor oil, however, was a totally different matter.

A second point about Table 4-1 concerns the two separate figures for Spain. Comparison of the Spanish price for gasoline in 1976 with that of the other European nations must not only include the original cost and taxes. The figure for Spain also includes CAMPSA's per liter receipts for administering the Monopoly. The total "at-the-pump" price was the sum of the gasoline's original price, the direct tax, and the Monopoly's revenue. It is significant to note that in 1976 this did not surpass the total price of those nations whose gasoline supplies were provided without the benefit of a private monopoly. Spanish leaders not only failed to use price as an economic instrument for energy management, but also deprived their own treasury of the revenues from higher taxes in a deregulated market. Private investments in CAMPSA and finance's pivotal position in the ruling coalition that permitted them to block such deregulation hints at a possible explanation as to why.

Table 4-1 clearly indicates that Spain provided energy consumers with relatively inexpensive gasoline. Do democratic policymakers perform any differently with regard to petroleum pricing? These data suggest that even after ten years of democracy and four general elections, policymakers in Spain use of the price of gasoline as an instrument of energy management had not changed much. Gasoline continued to be relatively inexpensive in Spain. Between 1976 and 1985, pricing as an instrument of energy policy was pursued with about the same amount of commitment.

No significant raises in energy prices, in effect, meant that the state subsidized energy consumption in that it absorbed the major portion of increased crude-oil costs. Gasoline in Spain, including agricultural and fishing fuel, remained highly subsidized.[20] CAMPSA's per-ton selling price in 1980, for example, was between 14,200 and 16,000 pesetas compared to the 18,000 to 19,000 pesetas per ton of imported crude.[21] Suárez's nondecision thus not only exacerbated the government's budget deficit but negated any effects on energy consumption.[22] Even when the Suárez government finally addressed the economic situation with some stronger measures in July 1977, neither a new energy nor a pricing policy was adopted. Instead the government stayed with a gradualist pricing policy that entailed only a periodic reconsideration of small—generally three pesetas per liter—increases in the price of gasoline, other petroleum fuels, and gas. Such increases simply did not increase the price to the consumer as fast as real cost, and were generally ineffectual steps toward the reduction of gasoline subsidies and the passing of increased costs to the consumer. Incremental price increases appeared better for proportionately reducing subsidies than increasing the selling price of gasoline during a time of projected high deficits in the state's budget.

These subsidies are especially significant given the peseta's long decline in relation to the dollar between 1976 and 1985. The second petroleum crisis of 1979 particularly affected the exchange rate and Spain's inflation rate. Despite the slow and incremental increases in the price of gasoline by the Council of Ministers, government officials continued to contend that such small price increases recouped the cost increases of importation, refining, and distribution.[23] Fuel consumption, as opposed to gasoline, represented 50 percent of all derivatives of petroleum. No coherent energy policy could promote petroleum savings while subsidies were simultaneously maintained to protect hard-pressed industries such as cement factories from increased energy costs.[24] Nevertheless, energy-pricing policy could still have been used as a critical instrument to diversify consumption. Pricing policy could have been used to wean the country away from its heavy dependence on petroleum. But only about 8 percent of Spain's energy demand was substitutable.[25] Nevertheless, in a country in which industry consumed 60 percent of the energy, it was industry, and the business community in particular, that received the greatest benefits from the consumption-subsidized energy policy.

## Electricity Costs

Price policy for electricity was troubled by many of the same problems as petroleum.[26] Periodically, the government made decisions to raise electricity prices in a manner similar to petroleum prices. Such price decisions normally came at UNESA's request. An initial glance at the history of these price increases gives the impression that adjustments were constant and regular. Figure 4-2, however, contradicts this. The nominal price of electricity in Spain increased steadily after 1959. The real price of electricity, however, has steadily declined since that time. Electricity prices thus actually went down despite the negative economic impact of increased energy consumption. Maintenance of low electricity prices was the policy of both authoritarian and democratic Spain. Electricity prices, like petroleum prices, were kept low.

In addition to maintaining low prices, another peculiarity existed in Spain regarding electricity:

> [This] peculiarity is that the legislation language is intertwined with an administrative procedure for inter-compensation behind which there are Government subsidies to the sector; the companies transfer part of their revenues to a fictitious account from which they sup-

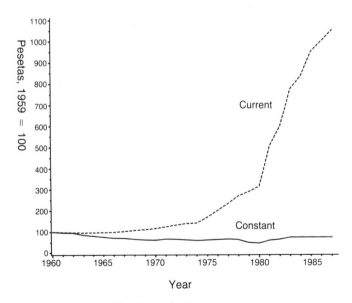

**Figure 4-2.**    Electricity Prices in Spain
Source: *Memoria Estadística Eléctrica UNESA, 1986*

posedly return to the companies as investment incentives, if there are deficits in this "account" the Government is expected to finance them.[27]

The electrical industry, like the petroleum industry, was thus often directly or indirectly subsidized even after the energy crisis. The government did not use price as an instrument of energy management. On the contrary, it subsidized the private companies who supplied energy. Explanation of this behavior in Spain rests with the relationship of the electrical companies, the state, and the banking industry as we will see later.

With regard to coal prices, PEN-79 called for a "parametric formula" for the automatic revision of prices. This formula would have automatically revised coal prices utilizing regionalized studies on production costs, price implementation, and rises in quantity. This formula, however, was never really fully implemented. As pricing policy, it was indefinitely suspended in 1980. Despite that, for over a year cost per ton exceeded price by more than 1.5 pesetas. By the end of 1980, when the formula was to be first implemented, the government had not produced any studies on the effects this price mechanism would have on the mining industry.

The abandonment of the pricing formula reflects continued policy guidance by business interests. In relinquishing this pricing technique, policymaking returned to practices of the past: politically determined prices individually negotiated between private companies and the administration. These time-tried negotiations began afresh in November 1980 when the large, private company Carbunion formally petitioned both the Ministry of Industry and Energy and the general director of mines for a 22.06 percent price increase, fully aware the government would settle for a 15–20 percent increase. Spain's medium and smaller coal firms, however, had to petition for a 32 percent price increase in the face of the operating deficits of 1.5 pesetas per ton. This negotiation scheme for pricing policy was clearly advantageous to the larger coal companies due to economies of scale.[28] Such a practice would have been economically rational except that most coal in Spain would have been unprofitable to mine if left unprotected. A nonregulated price structure would probably have shut down most Spanish mining operations. Many large firms were kept open at this time in the name of energy self-sufficiency. The negotiated price, however, was set at a level particularly harmful to their smaller competitors.

In sum, policymakers before and during Spain's transition to democracy did not rely on price as an instrument of energy conservation. Petroleum, electricity, and coal prices did not significantly change in real terms despite the change in economic conditions and political contexts. This pricing policy, however, was not the only macroeconomic instrument available to authorities. Investment was another.

## Investment

Budgets are generally clear indicators of policy goals and the means of obtaining them. In addition, financial investment serves as an instrument of policy implementation. Spain's energy program and its investment program were no exception. The ambitious energy policy outlined in the different versions of PEN necessitated enormous sums of money to turn these programs into reality. The capital required to convert existing oil-burning electrical generating plants, to build new nuclear plants, and to maintain the quality of other parts of the energy industry were discussed in each of the plans. Table 4-2 presents PEN-75's investment program. Parts of these investments were earmarked for each area of the energy industry. These investment projection figures reveal a great deal of information about the program's emphasis and direction. Nevertheless, several key points should be emphasized.

The first point focuses on the size of these investment projections. Spain's economic policymakers sought to channel considerable financial resources toward energy development and management. PEN-75 projected a large capital investment, despite the fact that Spain's overall investment rate of 0.3 percent of GNP was extremely low.[29] Table 4-3 suggests that the policymakers saw PEN's investments as a significant part of the country's entire gross capital formation. It is little surprise, then, that the authorities' rationale was that such investment would provide a stimulus for other investment.[30]

Second, PEN's projections for investment directed a huge amount of money toward the electrical industry. PEN-75 projected over 84 percent of all investments in energy for the 1975–85 period toward the electrical industry. The high percentage added credence to statements made by some opponents of PEN-75 that it entailed little more than an extension of previous electrical-energy plans and that the electrical industry produced, if not actually wrote it. Without doubt, PEN-75 benefitted the electrical industry over others. The financial community's link to electricity meant enormous profits from this public investment, particularly when the banks behind these companies also owned the construction firms.

Third, the policy emphasis of PEN-75 sought development of Spain's capacity to generate electricity with nuclear power. PEN-75's investment projections failed to consider numerous economic, technical, and political obstacles to construction of such plants.[31] PEN-79's investment projections, as seen in Table 4-4, significantly modified some of these nuclear investment

**Table 4-2**    PEN-75's Investment Programs* (in billions of 1974 pesetas)

|  | 1975 | 1980 | 1985 | Totals | Percentage |
|---|---|---|---|---|---|
| Coal mining | 5.2 | 4.8 | — | 30.8 | 1.76 |
| Petroleum and uranium exploration | 7.1 | 9.0 | 6.7 | 96.5 | 5.51 |
| Domestic petroleum refining and transport | 6.5 | 6.9 | 7.6 | 78.2 | 4.46 |
| Natural gas | 7.4 | 7.3 | 5.5 | 71.5 | 4.08 |
| Electrical production |  |  |  |  |  |
|   Coal generating | 9.0 | 1.7 | — | 64.5 | 3.68 |
|   Hydroelectric | 12.4 | 22.0 | 2.3 | 174.5 | 9.96 |
|   Nuclear plants | 39.0 | 87.0 | 90.0 | 780.0 | 44.52 |
|   Extra peninsular plants | 4.0 | 1.0 | 0.5 | 20.0 | 1.14 |
| Transportation and distribution (including rural electrification) | 30.0 | 40.0 | 40.0 | 410.0 | 23.40 |
| Nuclear fuel-enrichment | 0.5 | 3.5 | 2.4 | 26.0 | 1.48 |
| Total | 120.2 | 182.4 | 156.0 | 1,752.0 | 100% |

SOURCE: Plan Energético Nacional 1975–1985.
*Assuming 6 percent growth rate.

**Table 4-3**    PEN-75's Investments and Gross Capital Formation (billion of 1974 pesetas)

| Year | Gross Capital | PEN-75 Investment | PEN/GCF |
|---|---|---|---|
| 1975 | 1,062.9 | 120.2 | 11.3 |
| 1977 | 1,194.7 | 130.8 | 11.0 |
| 1978 | 1,422.4 | 182.4 | 12.8 |
| 1985 | 1,903.5 | 156.0 | 8.2 |

SOURCE: Plan Energético Nacional 1975–85.

projections. By 1979, policymakers themselves readily admitted the unrealistic nature of PEN-75's projections for nuclear energy, figures presented by the electricity industry itself. PEN-79 pared down investments to nuclear plants to about eighteen percent of the total, in part due to recommendations of the International Energy Agency. Nevertheless, the figure remained high considering PEN-79's investment figures were only for the first four years of the decade-long plan. PEN-79 did drop the construction of several nuclear plants. But, with such construction more long-term oriented, these short-term investment projections remained heavily oriented to nuclear power. Thus, during the transition to democracy, Spain had one of the strongest nuclear energy programs in the world. Democratic Spain implemented policies originally formulated in the Franco regime. Investment projections clearly reflected this.

PEN-79 continued PEN-75's emphasis on the electrical industry. This industry was to receive about 66 percent of PEN-79 investments. Continued orientation on the *supply* of electricity meant the predominantly private electricity companies had lost little influence on policy. Some minor concessions were made, such as the allocation of some funds for conservation and research on alternative energy sources. But the only significant changes in investment between PEN-75 and PEN-79 reflected policymakers' beliefs that movement away from the existing supply structure would take longer than initially hoped.

Finally, the financing of PEN-75's grandiose investment plans proved the most serious weakness of the entire investment program. This critical area was left extremely cryptic. The vagueness, however, was consistent with earlier planning in Spain. Yet this blueprint for energy policy was more than symbolic. Such vagueness in financial planning later proved to provide many benefits to the political-business class. It assumed that financing would be provided in part by the long-term capital market. The energy sector had, after all, placed in circulation approximately half of all fixed income bonds issued annually in Spain in the late 1960s.[32] The issuing of such bonds, often insured by the state, was very profitable for the financial community. Such profits, combined with the banks' ownership of many electric companies, were a strong incentive for the financial community's penetration into government policy-making in energy.

Policymakers also readily admitted a disparity in PEN-75's financing for the different subsectors in energy. The public sector was primarily to finance petroleum, natural gas, and uranium exploration. Coal development plans were to be financed up to 70 percent with official credit—with the companies themselves to provide 10 billion pesetas of the 30.8 billion projected for investment. Refining and domestic petroleum transportation would be self-financing, as would natural gas. Such self-financing was dubious in many of these industries. For example, the Spanish coal industry was racked by economic inefficiencies, charges of mismanagement, and labor problems. And the refining industry had seriously miscalculated previous investment undertakings.

The key to understanding the politics of the financing of energy lies in electricity. The fundamental problem of PEN rested with the electrical sector since it represented much of PEN's total investment.[33] Policymakers believed the electrical industry could rely heavily on stocks and bonds sold on the

**Table 4-4**    PEN-79's Investment Plans (in millions of constant pesetas and
September 1977 economic conditions)

| | 1978 | 1979 | 1980 | 1981 | 1978–81 | Percentage of total |
|---|---|---|---|---|---|---|
| Coal: mining and exploration (National Investment Plan) | 7,968 | 8,115 | 7,943 | 11,200 | 35,226 | 5.56 |
| Petroleum: National Exploration Plan | 11,063 | 15,563 | 16,063 | 18,300 | 60,989 | 9.63 |
| Domestic refining transport and distribution | 11,670 | 12,590 | 14,965 | 15,420 | 54,645 | 8.63 |
| Natural and other gases | 13,600 | 13,200 | 10,800 | 10,300 | 47,900 | 8.63 |
| Electric production | | | | | | |
| Coal generating | 15,830 | 14,869 | 11,558 | 12,535 | 54,792 | 8.65 |
| Hydroelectric | 9,184 | 16,361 | 17,741 | 15,343 | 58,629 | 9.26 |
| Fuel-oil plants | 3,464 | 2,659 | 2,735 | 2,457 | 11,315 | 1.79 |
| Nuclear plants | 27,543 | 24,938 | 27,631 | 32,797 | 112,909 | 17.83 |
| Transportation and distribution | 34,417 | 37,977 | 38,894 | 40,274 | 151,562 | 23.93 |
| Nuclear fuel cycle | 5,560 | 5,188 | 6,841 | 8,428 | 26,017 | 4.11 |
| Conservation and alternative research | 1,835 | 3,825 | 6,025 | 7,680 | 19,365 | 3.06 |
| Total | 142,134 | 155,285 | 161,196 | 174,734 | 633,349 | 100 |

SOURCE: Plan Energético Nacional 1978–87.

open market. They assumed that these financial markets would return to their expansive trends of the 1960s and early 1970s. They conjectured that this market could absorb the electrical industry's increased capital requirements without negatively affecting the overall economy. They also proposed that *foreign* credit would account for only one-quarter of the capital required for each nuclear plant—the most capital intensive and heaviest emphasized of all PEN's developmental plans. Domestic capital, of course, eventually had to finance most of these projects. Yet, it was more than just a coincidence that the capital raised through such bonds was primarily issued by or through Spain's private banks. The financial community benefitted enormously from the direction of domestic energy policy.

Besides bonds, this quotation reveals another aspect of PEN-75's financing:

> Conventional electrical energy production, which currently represents more than 60 percent, will be considerably reduced, in relative terms, in favor of nuclear energy. This will make production cost per KWH in 1985 approximately half the current cost, assuming fuel-oil prices will progressively increase in relation to current petroleum prices. As a counterpart, amortizations should increase considerably, given the strong investments that are currently being carried out, principally in nuclear plants, whose average life span is some 20 years. As a consequence, self-financing through wholesale accumulation of sinking funds and reserves will constitute an important means of financing, that will cover an appreciable percentage of the electrical sector's future needs.[34]

Such reasoning assumes away the most significant financial hurdles for electricity. Authorities simply ignored possible political, technical, and environmental obstacles to the building of nuclear plants, the cheapness of nuclear energy, and the continued increase in world petroleum prices. The assumptions they made simply were not plausible at the time. Each assumption proved to be false, yet these three points were necessary for the proposed financing to work.[35]

Despite a modified emphasis on nuclear energy, this logic dominated financial planning in Spain's National Energy Plan throughout the early transition to democracy. Table 4-5 outlines PEN-79's anticipated revenue sources for investment purposes. Almost 53 percent of capital investment was to come from self-financing. Policymakers continued to conjecture in PEN-79 that the profit margin of the electrical industry would increase, thus permitting this self-financing.[36] Table 4-6 reflects the policymakers' assumptions about self-financing and a continued growth in capital expansion and the bond market.

The state also had a role in the financial plans of PEN-79. Institutionally, the chief investment executor for public funds in PEN remained the National Institute of Industry (INI) until the creation of the National Institute of Hydrocarbons (INH). Before INH split from it, INI's investments in energy, like the National Energy Plan in general, represented more than half of total investments. These funds were very strongly directed toward electricity and INI's own companies like ENDESA, ENHER, and ENPETROL. The bulk of the investment went to the electrical industry for construction of nuclear plants and the conversion of refineries. Pressured by its terrible track record at long-term investment planning, INI's strategic plan for the period 1981–85 was approved by the state holding company's administrative council in late 1980 after eight months of development.[37] The central foci of this investment plan were energy, a structuring of companies in trouble, promotion of new activities, improvement of Spain's economic competitiveness before entry into the Common Market, and some regional economic developments.

## Institutional Reorganization as a Policy Instrument: INH

One major energy-related institutional reorganization occurred during the transition to democracy. PEN-79 included the creation of an "entity"—later to be known as the National Institute of Hydrocarbons (INH). This proposal sought to facilitate institutional coordination by grouping all public petroleum companies, much like the Italian National Hydorcarburates Corporation.[38] This created a controversy, with the central conflict being between the Ministry of Industry and Energy and the Ministry of Finance. Within a few months after its proposal, this "entity" had been compromised and diluted to such a point that when PEN-79 was submitted to parliament in June 1978, the recommendation had been dropped.

The need for institutional coordination in the petroleum sector, however, remained strong. Thus, on 24 April 1981 a decree-law established the National Institute of Hydrocarbons.[39] The preamble of the decree-law recognized the absence of coordination, reliability, and efficiency in the petroleum sector. These problems stemmed from the diverse character of public participation in the finances of hydrocarbon-related energy companies. INH's creation reflected a general desire to improve the coordination and management of public policy-making in bringing together the seven national companies in petroleum. This vertical integration of the public petroleum industry did not, however, directly affect the private sector.

Table 4-5  PEN-79's Projections for Total Investment in Energy Industries, 1978–1981 (millions of current pesetas)

| | Coal | Petroleum | Gases | Electric Energy* | Nuclear Fuel Cycle | Conservation and New Energy | Total |
|---|---|---|---|---|---|---|---|
| Self-financing | 13,990 | 30,026 | 17,000 | 262,630 | 700 | 3,028 | 510,188 |
| Capital expansion | 1,560 | 12,085 | 16,000 | 109,786 | 4,000 | 3,028 | — |
| Bonds | 850 | 4,724 | 8,000 | 124,062 | 6,500 | — | 144,136 |
| Credits: | 20,500 | 52,211 | 15,632 | 54,790 | 1,300 | 7,570 | 152,003 |
| Official | 18,000 | — | — | 33,026 | — | 4,542 | 55,568 |
| Private domestic | 2,500 | 14,550 | — | — | — | 3,028 | — |
| Foreign | — | 37,661 | 15,632 | 21,764 | 1,300 | — | 96,435 |
| Other sources | 8,042 | 5,455 | 6,000 | 73,374 | 12,855 | 10,176 | 115,902 |
| State Budget | 19,500 | 19,500 | — | — | 13,708 | 5,546 | 42,454 |
| Total | 47,082 | 161,916 | 62,632 | 624,642 | 39,063 | 29,348 | 964,683 |
| (Constant 1977 pesetas) | 35,226 | 115,634 | 47,900 | 389,207 | 26,017 | 19,365 | 633,349 |

SOURCE: Plan Energético Nacional 1978–87.
*Hypothesis 2.

**Table 4-6**   Electrical Industry: PEN-79's Different Hypotheses for Investment
(percent)

| Method | 1 | 2 | 3 | 4 |
|---|---|---|---|---|
| Self-financing | 25.4 | 42.0 | 42.4 | 49.8 |
| Capital expansion | 17.6 | 17.6 | 17.6 | 17.6 |
| Bonds | 30.7 | 19.9 | 19.6 | 15.6 |
| Official credit | 5.3 | 5.3 | 5.3 | 5.3 |
| Domestic private credit | — | — | — | — |
| Foreign credit | 9.3 | 3.5 | 3.4 | 0 |
| Other sources | 11.7 | 11.7 | 11.7 | 11.7 |

SOURCE: Calculated from Plan Energético Nacional 1978–87.

How much changed in energy policy-making through such institutional reorganization? It is noteworthy that democratic Spain's first significant institutional reorganization in energy occurred in much the same way as reorganization during the Franco regime. The INH was created through a decree-law, *not* an act of parliament. By the time the parliament considered INH, it was organized, had its directors appointed, and was physically situated and operating. This resemblance in decision-making to the past regime's style did not go unnoticed. Numerous members of the parliamentary opposition criticized this reorganization by executive fiat. The UCD government even sought to minimize debate by carefully timing the decree-law's introduction to parliament. The delay until late summer 1981 produced more criticism. This timing, critics argued, prevented a full airing of the issues because by then "all the body politic (was) ready for summer vacation."[40] Similar tactics undoubtedly occur in other parliamentary democracies and have been seen since the PSOE came to power in late 1982. Nevertheless, the leadership style did remind many of the past regime.[41]

INH's creation separated from INI all the financial holdings related to hydrocarbons. INH integrated the stocks and rights formerly held by INI, in addition to those held by CAMPSA, the Patrimony's head office in the Ministry of Finance, and the Bank of Spain. The Bank of Spain served as the vehicle for transferring CAMPSA's stock to the INH. This financially complicated transfer initially capitalized INH with approximately 40,000 million pesetas. While in retrospect it did not occur, some questions were raised that the removal from INI of the companies related to hydrocarbons might create a strong financial disequilibrium. Hydrocarbons were, after all, one of the few areas in which this "graveyard of unprofitable state companies" consistently turned a profit.[42] Nevertheless, neither this questioning nor parliamentary criticism impeded INH's creation.

INH took the following organizational form: an administrative council that meets twice a month; a five-member executive commission, initially comprised of Claudio Boada, José María Amusategui, Luís Ducasse, Luís Magaña, and Juan Alegre Marcet, with decision power over the institute's management; and a seven-member directive team.[43] In terms of executive control, royal decree 8/1981 stated that "the National Institute of Hydrocarbons is assigned to the Ministry of Industry and Energy" in the same manner as INI. The administrative council operates within the policy framework of the government's petroleum policy, raises proposals requiring State approval, and controls the management of all INH companies. The Ministry of Industry and Energy nominates INH Council members, even when confirmed by royal decree as in the case of the president and vice-president. Furthermore, INH's creators anticipated it would be self-financing. Its investment comes through a Finance, Investment, and Performance Plan (PAIF) which, if necessary, permits INH to sell bonds in the domestic and international financial market.

INH's creation did not address all problems in the public management of energy policy. Two fundamental weaknesses were left from its creation: the bicephalous power structure and the exclusion of the petroleum monopoly from INH. INH was created in part to arbitrate the conflicting interests among different "cuerpos" within the central administration, particularly those within the Ministry of Finance and the Ministry of Industry and Energy. Groups within the public bureaucracy managed to protect their administrative "turf" during this reorganization. The organizational structure reflected their political-administrative victories. INH did not eliminate the two-headed direction of the public petroleum sector. As mentioned above, INH was responsible to the Ministry of Industry and Energy. The Ministry of Finance, however, continued to direct CAMPSA, which remained *outside* INH. The Ministry of Finance did not relinquish control of CAMPSA to INH despite a potential for greater efficiency for energy and economic policies.[44] The continuation of CAMPSA's status quo was the most significant lack of institutional reorganization during the creation of INH. CAMPSA continued to hold the monopoly on the distribution and sale of petroleum and petroleum products on the peninsula, at least until 1992 as specified in the terms of Spain's entry into the EEC. During the transition to democracy, the major and most important part of the Patrimony remained outside the control of the National Institute of Hydrocarbons.

The state was thus hurt in its attempt to vertically integrate the public petroleum sector from investigation and exploration to commercialization. The Ministry of Finance was left the sole guide of the Monopoly except in the necessary joint approval with the Ministry of Industry and Energy to fix the selling price and with other ministries and commissions that help determine the purchase price of refinery products, investments in the monopoly, and approval of the annual program of the monopoly's product deliveries. CAMPSA's continued hegemonic role in certain activities of petroleum importation, distribution, and sales meant that a bicephalous structure persisted, directed as much by INH and the Ministry of Industry and Energy as by CAMPSA and the Ministry of Finance. Limitations on institutional reorganization left this part of Spain's public energy sector operating as before.

To avoid this problem, the royal decree which created the INH suggested the existence of INH advisors in CAMPSA. These advisors, however, are appointed by the government and *not* by INH. They are nominated by the Ministry of Finance and the Ministry of Industry and Energy in conformity with the INH's administrative council. The duality-of-powers problem was thus not eliminated. In administration, power struggles between INH and CAMPSA are inevitable. Clarification of administrative powers of the petroleum monopoly and its distribution system are determined through the government and the Ministry of Finance. In other words, the Ministry of Finance has the final word in disputes between CAMPSA and INH. The outcome is likely predetermined since the Ministry of Finance directs CAMPSA. INH, as a new administrative part of the public energy sector, was thus born relatively impotent. Its creation did not alter the existing structure of power within the public apparatus for energy policy-making.

The continued exclusiveness of control of CAMPSA by the Ministry of Finance brought strong criticism from, among others, the European Commission: "This dependency constitutes in certain cases an obstacle to the implementation of the National Energy Plan in the area of hydrocarbons."[45] Prior to Spain's joining the EEC, the European Commission also asserted that the creation of INH did not ameliorate a central institutional loggerhead that characterized energy policy-making in Spain—between the Ministry of Finance on one hand and the public energy companies, either under INI or INH, on the other. Any future conflicts between CAMPSA and INH will require the arbitration of the Council of Ministers. This, in effect, means that the resolution of such a dispute will greatly depend upon the personality of the directors of the two organizations. And if past history is any indication, the Ministry of Finance generally wins out. A new institution has been created to coordinate petroleum-related energy policy-making, yet the central and more powerful national petroleum monopoly and its guiding force in the Ministry of Finance remain outside its control.

The creation of INH also left other questions unanswered. For example, how would INH affect the acquisition of crude? At that time, acquisition was controlled by the state's quota and executed by HISPANOIL, based on CAMPSA's requests as the monopoly's administrator. The result was that during the transition to democracy, policy-making continued unchanged due to administrative indecision.

Other aspects also remained unclear. In affirming that "we don't have any interest in administering the quota. That depends on the Ministry of Economics and Commerce," INH's President Boada implied that policy-making processes would remain the same as in the past.[46] Furthermore, policy inertia existed at least for awhile in that with INH controlling petroleum other areas of energy like coal, electricity, uranium, and solar energy were left within INI.

In sum, the structural organization of INH suggests that domestic policy-making in petroleum will essentially remain unchanged. The creation of INH did not significantly alter the underlying structural-power relationships. Extreme optimism prevailed when officials stated that the creation of INH was "as important as the establishment of the monopoly in 1928, as the prolongation of the life of the monopoly and of the administrator in 1948, and as the creation of INI in the sense of what INI entailed in the petroleum sector in that epic."[47]

Other, more limited, reorganization occurred as well in other areas of energy. In the coal sector, the Ministry of Industry and Energy created Carbonex in January 1980. The central objective of this public company was to provide foreign coal supplies analogous to HISPANOIL's role in petroleum. These supplies, fundamental to the success of PEN, were contracted for long-term periods and in increasing amounts. Such institutional reorganization had strong political support when no one's bureaucratic "turf" was encroached upon. Furthermore, Carbonex's coal imports are used by three consumers: electric generating plants, which burn coal when hydroelectric production is down; the cement industry, which began substituting coal for oil; and the new generating plants designed specifically for imported coal. Thus this public corporation for coal tended to serve as a conduit of fuel supplies for the well-established industrial companies. Spanish businessmen found its creation advantageous.

Spanish policymakers in energy used several policy instruments during the transition to democracy. I initially considered their economic policy response to the immediate problems caused by the 1973–74 oil crisis. The three periods analyzed—the late Franco regime, the early transitional period, and the early democracy—all ultimately relied on the day-to-day control to bank liquidity by the Bank of Spain as an instrument of economic management. For different reasons, none of these policy-making groups were able to ameliorate the country's economic problems. Emphasis on monetary policy to fight inflation ultimately led to the demise of the Moncloa Pacts. Macroeconomic instruments such as control of bank liquidity which often assist in fine-tuning an economy were simply not applied stringently enough to manage a central economic problem: energy.

With other policy instruments, governments in both Francoist and democratic Spain did not utilize more direct policy instruments such as energy pricing. Gasoline, electricity, and coal prices, all of which the Spanish government determines, consistently remained low. Gasoline remained extremely cheap by European standards. The price of electricity, in real terms, actually declined consistently over the years. And a proposal in PEN to rationalize the pricing policy of coal quickly fell into disuse. This history of pricing of these three major sources of energy strongly suggests a lack of significant change in energy management during Spain's transition to democracy.

Investment policies in energy appear to have followed a similar pattern. Projections for investment in the Francoist version of PEN and later revisions all strongly emphasized the development of nuclear energy. While PEN's later versions, particularly those under the Socialists, placed a more realistic burden on coal to generate electricity, investment projections in PEN still sought to channel enormous sums into the construction of nuclear plants. The source of the funds remained consistent with the past—generated on the open bond market, thus benefitting the financial community in Spain.

Spain also witnessed some institutional coordination in energy during the early stages of the transition to democracy. The implementation of energy policy through the creation of the National Institute of Hydrocarbons did not greatly alter the administrative style of policy-making found during the Franco regime. Despite parliamentary oversight, administratively speaking, the need for greater institutional coordination and the actual attempt by the INH suggest the protection of many interests institutionalized during the previous regime.

In sum, several central instruments of energy policy did not change in composition or usage following the end of authoritarian rule. Energy policy in general and the National Energy Policy in particular utilized policy instruments in a manner remarkably similar to the Franco regime. These instruments, and the policy directions they imply, naturally raised political questions and opinions. It is to these politics of energy policy that I turn next.

# 5

## Public Opinion and Political Opposition

Spain's orientation to energy management and the government's energy policy instruments do not appear to have significantly changed during the country's transition to democracy. One possible explanation for this is that little pressure was brought to bear on policymakers to alter energy policy. The absence of significant and effective pressure for policy change—by the general public, interest groups, and political parties—was particularly relevant given Spain's transition to a more open political system.

Some Spaniards had strong objections to the National Energy Plan. Nevertheless, the politics of energy policy transcended many of PEN's particularities. More generally, the institutional arrangements within which energy policy was made drew political fire. Many critics considered Spain's unique interface of public and private energy companies and institutions as economically inefficient. They did not perceive this structural configuration with its overlapping ministries, agencies, and other energy-related institutions to be conducive to effective policy-making. Additionally, these political antagonists questioned critical components of the implementation of energy policy in Spain. Organized labor, some interest groups, and environmentalists criticized many aspects of energy policy in the early stages of the transition. They criticized the government's choice of policy instruments, the motivation behind their use, and their timing and emphasis.

This chapter focuses on the political criticism of energy policy in Spain before and during the transition to democracy. It considers the nature of political pressure on Spain's national energy policy and assesses the opposition to both PEN and the country's overall energy program. This opposition is treated at several levels. First, several energy-oriented interest groups and associations are discussed. Next, I focus on the positions of the major political parties. The basic position of each of the four parties on energy policy is outlined. Third, I compare public opinion on Spanish energy policy. Survey research from both the late Franco period and early in the political transition suggests general opposition to many key components of PEN. Several political parties in Spain and the general public agreed that the government should have pursued conservation policies. Given these findings, the final section considers the failure of policymakers to pursue energy management on the demand side.

## Interest Groups in Energy

The earliest opposition to energy policy in Spain came from small ecological and regional groups. AEORMA—the Spanish Association for Environmental Control—was the only national environmental group to criticize PEN-75 during the Franco regime. It focused on general environmental questions. In addition, AEORMA created much of the early anti-nuclear publicity in Spain. On a regional level, the Asturian association ANAN, the Leonese Cultural Club and Friends of Nature, and Sementcira, the cultural association of Vivero (Lugo) also actively opposed the Francoist version of PEN. The ecological group Amigos de la Tierra (Friends of the Earth) also spoke out against the plan shortly after the legalization of such groups in early 1977. They produced one of the few comprehensive written responses to PEN.[1] This strongly criticized PEN's nuclear emphasis, its neglect of alternative energy sources, and the power and centralization of capital which controlled energy production in Spain. Amigos de la Tierra, like all these groups, was small, leftist-oriented, organizationally fractured, and financially hard-pressed.[2] It relied heavily on self-motivated environmentalists, anti-nuclear activists, and political authors who wrote many anti-nuclear studies.[3] These groups and individuals, while quite vocal in their opposition, had minimal effect on national energy policies.[4] Spain did not witness the creation of a formidable Green party, despite the fact during this period it was second only to France in having the most ambitious nuclear energy program in Europe. Even opposition to NATO and U.S. nuclear arms did not instigate such broad political organizations. The consolidation of a democratic system appears to have facilitated the co-optation of such groups by larger political associations closer to the center of power—particularly leftist political parties such as PCE and PSOE and the labor unions. The same aversion to existing political parties found in Green movements, as in West Germany, was not present in Spain early in the transition.

The strong push in PEN for construction of nuclear plants focused the attention of these environmentalists. The lightening rod of the anti-nuclear movement in Spain was the Lemóniz nuclear plant on the Bay of Biscay near Bilbao. The controversy over the construction of Lemóniz beginning in 1972 encapsulated many issues central to those opposed to Spain's nuclear program. First, opponents feared Lemóniz as a health hazard. Besides the normal health arguments concerning cancer and other diseases made against nuclear plants throughout the world, critics further cited the plant's proximity to the greater Bilbao metropolitan area and the heart of the Basque industrial belt (the most concentrated economic zone in Spain). Environmentalists also sided with Bay of Biscay fishermen who were concerned about the rise of water temperatures and the possible destruction of the crab industry.[5] Strong emotions were also generated by the picture emphasized by these environmentalists of a potentially dangerous mass of steel and concrete rising against the backdrop of the blue ocean and rolling green hills surrounding Lemóniz.

Most importantly, Lemóniz was a political symbol reaching beyond these environmental concerns. Opposition to Lemóniz also grew from political emotions: Lemóniz became a symbol not only of the treatment the Basque country received under the Franco regime and its authoritarian policy-making processes but also of the perpetuation through energy policy of a tradition in which all policy emanates from Madrid.[6] Lemóniz was thus perceived as a legacy of Francisco Franco and a political symbol of the powerlessness of the Basque nation. Despite movement toward limited home rule, many Basques saw Lemóniz as the product of centralized power emanating from Madrid.

Madrid-dominated power, Basque activists argued, was controlled by the industrial-financial oligarchy created under the Franco regime. Iberduero, S.A., built and owned Lemóniz. In the eyes of the activists, this company was part of the same oligarchy that turned Bilbao into one of the two centers of industry in Spain with all the negative consequences such as some of the worst pollution in the world. Iberduero, these opponents contended, did not consult the Basque people, did not operate under democratic norms, and even worse, continued to play by Francoist political rules. For example, they argued that when lawsuits contended Lemóniz was illegal because the site had been zoned a "park," the company simply went to the Francoist Vizcaya Provincial Council and had it rezoned as "industrial."[7]

Political opposition to Lemóniz had a violent side as well. The military branch of ETA, the Basque separatist organization, directed several attacks against the installation and its employees. An ETA explosion killed two construction workers in mid-March of 1978. ETA killed Lemóniz's chief engineer in 1981. ETA's bombs also destroyed Iberduero property in neighboring locations such as Bilbao and Pamplona.[8] Despite the strong condemnation of such violence by moderate Basque political leaders, this violence had some popular support. As one "man in the street" said, "I don't believe in violence, but if ETA and bombs will stop Iberduero, I am for ETA."[9]

Leftist Basque parties also opposed Lemóniz on the political front. Both Euskadiko Ezkerra and Herri Batasuna, the political wing of ETA, were strong, organized supporters of these anti-nuclear activities.[10] Euskadiko Ezkerra, for example, believed "the Lemóniz nuclear plant continues being one of the central controversies in Basque political life."[11] This party had long called for a halt to Lemóniz's construction, concerned over the social, economic, and political impact this plant would have on the Basque country.[12] Euskadiko Ezkerra heavily criticized both PSOE and the Basque National Party (PNV) for not supporting the construction stoppage and for dragging their feet on taking a firm policy stand on Lemóniz. In May 1981, Angel Pascual Mugica, the successor to José María Ryan, the chief engineer for Iberduero who was killed by ETA-m, was also murdered. All work on the plant was suspended on 13 February 1982, primarily due to ETA-m terrorism. The Basque National Party (PNV) called for a referendum on Lemóniz. Euskadiko Ezkerra viewed the proposal by the PNV as too accommodating. They also found as too compromising of Basque national interests the agreement reached in 1982 between Iberduero and the Basque government. This accord permitted Lemóniz to operate under the control of a specially created "Lemóniz management company," a public entity of technicians and experts paid by Iberduero but under contract to the Basque government.[13] Thus Iberduero surrendered operational control of the plant to the Basque government on 5 May 1982, while Iberduero retained ownership and financial control of the facility and Madrid remained responsible for the safety of the plant. By 1986, the plant was 97 percent complete but no date had been set to start operations.[14]

Euskadiko Ezkerra's opposition to the official energy policy went far beyond its opposition to Lemóniz. Even before legalization in 1977, this party adamantly opposed PEN. The party's most formal statement, an extensive work on the subject, was written under a cloak of secrecy.[15] They argued that PEN took a critical step "for the State's future politics and economics. Under a supposedly technical facade, PEN supports and justifies policy choices clearly favoring the oligarchy, and these were basically made and initiated during the Franco era."[16] They contended that the electricity industry was the key sector in the energy plan. They saw the private control of the electricity industry and the push for even larger profits as the motivation for

PEN's consideration of nuclear energy as the state's "energy solution." Euskadiko Ezkerra members were particularly worried that the financing of the nuclear program would come out of the pockets of the working class through higher electricity prices. They believed UNESA had the power to obtain these increases from the government, although Table 4-2 raises doubts about their claim. Euskadiko Ezkerra, in sum, not only opposed PEN for reasons very specific to the Basque country but also on a much more general level.

Organized labor also paid close attention to energy policy. The socialist union, UGT, and the Communist Workers Commissions (CCOO) both wanted to protect the interests of their members throughout the political transition and the development of PEN. Similar to their sister political parties, PSOE and PCE, these two major labor unions initially took tentative pro-nuclear positions only to reverse themselves later. For example, prior to early 1979, CCOO supported PEN's construction of nuclear plants. The party naturally wanted to defend the jobs of its members, particularly engineers in CCOO's case.[17] UGT's early favorable view of nuclear energy emanated from the potential creation of numerous construction and other jobs. Both unions believed in the late 1970s that the nuclear industry could provide many new opportunities for employment.

Following the Harrisburg, Pennsylvania, nuclear accident in March 1979, the unions reassessed their position and have since taken a strong anti-nuclear stand. This reversal left the unions somewhat redfaced, but they quickly attempted to minimize their self-embarrassment:

> It is true we spent two years searching for reasons to support nuclear energy . . . [I]n two years we haven't found a single reason to favor nuclear energy from a democratic socialist point of view. We have now also searched for reasons not to support it and we have found many.[18]

Justifications for UGT's anti-nuclear and pro-conventional sources position, nevertheless, still emphasized employment.

> Adherence to their earlier logic but with a totally different conclusion is often heard: the nuclear sector carries the most investment and least work produced relative to investment; we believe the correct focus should be jobs per unit of investment and in this sense the nuclear industry generates the fewest number of job openings of any other.[19]

Spain's transition to democracy, supported by both business and labor, obviously facilitated the airing of criticisms of other aspects of energy policy.

UGT, for example, produced some extremely detailed publications in opposition to PEN.[20] Coordinated by the Energy and Mining Federation of the union, one book provided an extensive account of UGT's position on nuclear energy. A second volume broadened its scope of criticism to include all aspects of the nation's official energy program.[21] For its part, UGT advocated large increases in investment in the domestic coal industry, a doubling of investment in natural gas, a total halt to the nuclear program, and a strong emphasis on energy conservation. Many union leaders and some PSOE party officials hoped these two documents would influence energy policy when PSOE came to power in late 1982.[22] They were generally disappointed on this score.

Anti-nuclear proponents did not have a monopoly in the debate. Pro-nuclear forces responded with their own association for "creation of public awareness." The best-known pro-nuclear association was the Spanish Atomic Forum (FAE). The Forum's creation in the mid-1970s was an attempt by business to counter growing anti-nuclear sentiment in Spain. FAE's approach to developing a pro-nuclear sentiment with the public was much subtler than the anti-nuclear demonstrations. Its attempt at public education included organizing conferences and producing studies favoring Spain's nuclear program.

The Spanish Atomic Forum was the organization for publicity for the electrical industry, the Nuclear Energy Council (JEN), and related pro-nuclear companies, many of which were members of CEOE, the Spanish business association. FAE's link to these energy-related companies could most clearly be seen at the top. One of the first presidents of the FAE was Alfonso Alvárez Miranda, the last Minister of Industry of the Franco regime, under whom the first PEN was written. The policy preferences and ideological orientation of FAE under Sr. Alvárez Miranda were oriented in much the same direction as policy first formulated in the Franco regime. For example, at an FAE-sponsored conference entitled "A Non-Nuclear Society?", information expert Juan Luis Calleja addressed the anti-nuclear movement on behalf of the Forum: "We are falling short in the war of communication. . . . [T]he resistance to nuclear energy is one of the strategy tactics against the Christian way of life represented, economically, by the free-enterprise system."[23]

## Major Political Parties and PEN

During the earlier period of the transition to democracy, the politics of PEN split the Spanish party system. The center-right, through the Union of the Democratic Center (UCD), the first party to form a democratic government, and the right-wing Popular Alliance (AP) staunchly defended the National

Energy Plan. UCD governments produced PEN-79 and PEN-82. As the government party, it directed the ministries that wrote these plans, the consultations that influenced them, and the parliamentary deliberations on them. Popular Alliance, later the centerpiece of the Democratic Coalition (CD), pressed for the continuation of Francoist elements in the plans. AP consistently supported UCD's energy policies, thus protecting the interests of business and the past arrangements of economic institutions. The political left, on the other hand, attacked PEN with varying degrees of intensity. Like the major labor unions, the Socialist Party (PSOE), and the Communist Party (PCE) both underwent a certain "learning experience" regarding energy policy. Early on, both parties made numerous wide-ranging calls for reforms in private energy only to back off later—particularly PSOE as it moved closer to and later acquired power. Both the PCE and the PSOE adopted stringent anti-nuclear positions, but only after the 1979 accident in Harrisburg, Pennsylvania.

Each of the four major political parties during the transition addressed energy policy on many different occasions. In doing so, each party, in many ways reflected the broader ideological views it held on economic policy and institutional reform and its proximity to power. Of course, while the PCE and PSOE were partisan critics of PEN, they were in parliamentary opposition until December 1982. They thus did not possess the numbers in parliament to produce major changes in energy policy. These two parties were ideologically and institutionally linked to Spain's major labor unions. The fact that little changed after the PSOE came to power, however, should not be forgotten. More significant change might come from EEC membership, but that is beyond the scope of the present work.

During the early stages of the transition to democracy, the Left's vocal opposition to PEN, its overall policy direction, and its implementation methods increasingly moderated. It nevertheless continued to reflect a basic ideological concern over private economic power. In the mid-1970s, the PSOE called for the nationalization of the electrical sector.[24] PSOE argued in April 1977 that the electrical industry was a public service whose management responded primarily to private interests. PSOE asserted that private initiative had lost its raison d'être in this industry. Electricity companies assumed no risk, PSOE argued, because of an increasing monopolistic market. The industry bore no risk, they claimed, since the state and consumers supplied the bulk of the capital, particularly in the unprofitable area of rural electrification. PSOE feared that once the public capitalization of rural electrification was complete, control would pass to the private sector. PSOE nevertheless moderated its call in 1979 for the nationalization of electricity by targeting only the delivery system of high-tension lines, something they did implement in the mid-1980s. PSOE modified its positions on energy policy because of the impossibility of tackling a "financial Goliath," transferability of control, and awareness of the potential protection by the military of such a fundamental economic sector. This change in position appeared to be more a modification of political tactics than policy desire.[25]

Regarding petroleum, PSOE believed in the early days of the transition that CAMPSA was an uneconomical structure, one which perpetuated investment disincentives. However, it did not provide a solid and detailed alternative plan for CAMPSA's restructuring—one of the reasons the EEC deadline of 1992 will force some changes. It also suggested that public participation in petroleum exploration and refining should be grouped in a single public company to assure the management of petroleum prices. As previously mentioned, the refining industry was controlled by seven private refining companies who bought from the public company for external exploration, HISPANOIL, and sold to CAMPSA, all at prices designated by the Ministry of Commerce. Regarding coal, initially after the end of authoritarian rule PSOE called for nationalization but then suggested reform of the coal mines, a sector they claimed obtained unjustifiable profits for marginal explorations through the public-controlled HUNOSA.

In 1977, the Communist Party called for the nationalization of all areas of energy. The PCE asserted that energy, along with the industrial advancement of a country, had a public character and that its production and use should benefit all society. The PCE considered public ownership and management not only feasible but necessary since the sector tended toward monopolization for technical reasons. Nationalization of energy, the PCE argued, would provide greater planning and coordination, assist in the efficient development of both the sector and the economy, and, through more rational use, end the serious waste and abuse of energy. They claimed that greater planning in energy use, transportation, and final consumption could produce a 15 percent savings. The PCE further argued that the state should have placed greater emphasis on domestic energy production, better coordinated existing sources, and avoided financing that had long and exorbitantly benefitted the sector's large monopolies. The PCE also consistently emphasized research and development of new energy sources, especially solar, wind, and geothermal. It believed these sources of energy had received little attention because they conflicted with the immediate interests of the large national and international monopolies. Nevertheless, like PSOE, the PCE moderated its call for strong nationalization measures in 1979. After this time, they placed emphasis on national planning and financial controls.[26]

The PCE, and the PSOE in particular, slowly altered many of the policy positions they articulated between early 1977 and 1979. Under the leadership of Felipe González, the PSOE increasingly came to adopt a philosophy, and a set of policies once in government, consistent with liberal economic thinking. Ideologically it questioned its position on nationalization. And it changed its position on nuclear energy. Initially, both the PCE and PSOE mildly favored nuclear energy. As late as the Moncloa Pacts, they and their affiliated labor unions supported the essence of the Spanish nuclear energy program. The PSOE remained concerned primarily with the private control of nuclear energy but clearly understood the potential it held for the creation of jobs. In early 1978, for example, a PSOE spokesman stated, "Given conventional energy sources, some increase in nuclear energy is going to be indispensable"[27] and "considering industrial growth rates and the population's standard of living, nuclear energy is necessary."[28] In discussions on the Moncloa Pacts, PSOE called for policy reconsideration in nuclear energy, not at the convenience of the monopolistic electric companies who had directed its development but rather for the public's interest and especially for the protection of the environment.[29] For its part, the PCE called for

> a rational and planned nuclear energy policy, with complete studies on security and residual problems, with participation of the local powers and the movements concerned with the placement of new plants, and planning at the same time a diversification and a large national presence in all concerning fuel supply sources and technical incorporation.[30]

Both the PCE and PSOE supported the nuclear program at that time. Santiago Carrillo, the PCE's General Secretary, stated, "I am convinced that no modern nation can renounce nuclear plants," words he later hoped were forgotten.[31] The PSOE and PCE's favorable position on nuclear energy, however, rapidly turned following the nuclear accident at Harrisburg, Pennsylvania, in March 1979.[32] The political left thus opposed the country's nuclear program after having agreed to it in the Moncloa Pacts but before parliamentary approval of PEN-79.

The arguments of the major parties in the parliamentary debates on PEN-79 permits comparison of their policy positions at that time.[33] The debate in parliament on PEN held on 27 June 1979 was the first time the major parties publicly announced their position on the national energy program. This was not, of course, the first political confrontation in democratic Spain over energy policy. As previously mentioned, the first political compromise in policy was the Moncloa Pacts signed in October 1977. Article 9, entitled "Energy Policy and Public Enterprise Statute," contained objectives for energy policy and a proposal to send a new PEN to parliament before the end of the year. On 4 October 1978, *The Official Bulletin of the Cortes* published the UCD government's official statement accompanying PEN's resubmission to parliament. The first plenary debate in the Congress of Deputies took place on 26 October 1978. Rodríquez Sahagún, UCD Minister of Industry, presented the plan. Stating that the first quantified projection of energy demand for 1987 had been 161 million TEC, and that the government had considered reducing it to 145 million TEC with the following objectives, he highlighted these points:

- Intensify natural gas and petroleum exploration in order to obtain between 7.5 and 8.0 percent of final demand in 1987.
- Double coal production by 1987.
- Increase by a fifth hydroelectric production.
- Pursue the nuclear program.
- Create a company to manage the Central Electrical Distribution Coordinator (RECA—Repartidor Central de Cargas), containing government representation, and make a strong push against nationalization proposals.
- Restructure public participation in the petroleum sector.
- Do not include alternative energies.

Also noteworthy was that the UCD held its first party congress in 1978. At the meeting, it approved a resolution opposing the nationalization of the electrical network of high-tension lines. PSOE had advocated this policy and later implemented it themselves.

Following the presentation of PEN by the UCD government, the other parties clarified their positions. The Socialists, as the main oppositional party in parliament, divided their time between the spokesman for the Catalan Socialists and Javier Solana of PSOE. The former stated, "The only thing that PEN does is sanction the electrical companies' projections formulated before the energy crisis."[34] Solana continued this attack: "The Energy Plan presented by the Government is the result of a confrontation of interests between the most reactionary powers of the private electrical industry and the more progressive elements of the governmental party."[35] The Socialist spokesman for energy went on to conclude that this "retrospective planning" prevented a real economic break with the past.[36] The principal points of PSOE's proposal were to emphasize employment as a policy priority, to nationalize the high-tension electrical network, to establish the petroleum holding company, and to seriously curtail nuclear energy. They similarly criticized the undervaluation of coal and natural gas as well as a neglect for alternative sources of energy. The Socialists concluded by classifying PEN-79 as unacceptable.

The Communist Party considered the plan as "too little, too late." Ramón Tamames, PCE's spokesman in 1979, emphasized his party's rejection of the Moncloa Pacts and the unclear financial planning of PEN. PCE's counterproposals included the need to control the implementation of PEN—particularly its financial plans, the nationalization of RECA, the creation of a Nuclear Security Council, and a public company for nuclear energy.

Popular Alliance, although supportive of PEN-79, felt that the plan did not go far enough. AP felt the 145 million TEC projection was low. This party adamantly defended private control of energy industries, including coal, and opposed any nationalization of RECA. Given anti-nuclear protests, UCD welcomed AP's belief that the Spanish government did not place enough emphasis on nuclear energy. AP also defended the JEN—the Nuclear Energy Council.

Regional parties in the parliament also articulated their positions on energy policy. The Basque National Party (PNV) initially criticized the UCD government's failure to include PEN within a more general economic plan. It spoke against the exaggeration of short-term energy solutions, citing the structure of Basque industry, the demand for regional participation in the Nuclear Security Council, and the need for long-term energy planning.

The Catalan CiU raised objections to the UCD government's projections of energy demand. The party argued as incorrect the assumption in PEN that nuclear energy was not imported energy. Spokesmen for this regional party additionally argued that the plan failed to accurately estimate the supply or required finances for nuclear energy. They insisted on greater self-financing, reform of price scales for electricity, expansion of natural gas, restructuring of the petroleum sector, inclusion of alternative energy sources, and an annual revision of PEN.

Parliament's Mixed Group, with its catchall membership primarily of representatives from smaller regional parties, also spoke out against PEN. Its spokesman, Sr. Letamendia, focused objections on UNESA's plans, which in 1977 called for twenty-seven nuclear plants. This group thus directly confronted the nuclear energy policy. Letamendia also stated that the independent Basque option did not prevent autarchy, referring to the closed policy-making of the electrical industry in placing nuclear plants in the Basque country.

These policy positions followed PEN to the Committee on Industry and Energy in the Congress of Deputies following the initial debate. However, the general election of March 1979 interrupted this parliamentary process. The committee resumed its work following the election. Testimony from these post-election proceedings consisted fundamentally of hearing the administration and public- and private-sector representatives. Furthermore, between the end of 1978 and spring 1979, the Energy Commission (of the Ministry of Industry) had produced a new version of PEN, reconsidering some of its basic figures. The Committee on Industry and Energy ultimately accepted most of these quantitative revisions.

The final version of PEN received its full parliamentary debate on 27 June 1979. Table 5-1 contains a summary of the different parties' counterproposals and amendments. Those modifications, primarily accepted, dealt only with details. UCD's preferential treatment of CiU and PSA proposals, no doubt,

Table 5-1  Spanish Parliamentary Parties' Proposals on PEN

| | UCD | PSOE | PCE | CD | CIU | PSA |
|---|---|---|---|---|---|---|
| Energy Demand Target | 145 Mtec 1987 | 140 Mtec 1987 | | | 145 Mtec 1987 | |
| 1. Energy balance | –Validation of government's analysis shared by Congress<br>–Apply the objectives<br>–Periodic estimations<br>–Decrease petroleum to 50% | –Investment and conservation policy that permits reaching this objective<br>–Dubious government calculations<br>–Biannual forecasts | –Creation of an evaluation commission of energy demand<br>–New distribution of supply<br>–New division of financial burden<br>–PEN review and control commission | | –Bi-annual review by Industry Energy Commission<br>–Annual revision of PEN*** | |
| 2. Prices and energy conservation | –Rates and prices reflecting real costs<br>–Apply an appropriate fiscal policy<br>–Complete and reinforce conservation measures | –Develop conservation measures in 1979–80<br>–Develop self-generation<br>–Brake high consumption industries<br>–Support individual conservation | –Price and rate proposals by Control Commission<br>–Authority for Control Commission to monitor conservation | | –Quantified conservation plan in 2 months*** | –Consider territorial disequilibrium*** |

| | | | | | | |
|---|---|---|---|---|---|---|
| 3. Energy resources research | –Encourage, stimulate, and coordinate the effort<br>–Revise current legislation<br>–Spur domestic research | –Push exploration with the public sector<br>–Coordination through a medium-term plan that revises the Mining Law, later hydrocarbons, uranium, and coal<br>–Support alternative energies*** | –Directorate General of Energy Resources<br>–Law of Energy Resources Research & Resources Plan | | | |
| 4. Electoral sector | –Principles of general interests and a market economy<br>–Strengthen control of the association of electrical companies with the intervention of the government delegation with a veto right<br>–Rural electrification | –Public corporation that acquires RECA and RAT | –Mixed company for RECA and RAT<br>–Rural electrification Plan | –Government delegation in RECA and RAT<br>–Law of Rural Electrification | –Strengthen coal and hydro-electricity*** | –Electrification of Andalusian area (one plant in Almeria, one in Algeciras)***<br>–Law of Rural Electrification and development of eastern Andulsia*** |

**Table 5-1** *continued*

| | UCD | PSOE | PCE | CD | CIU | PSA |
|---|---|---|---|---|---|---|
| Energy Demand Target | 145 Mtec 1987 | 140 Mtec 1987 | | | 145 Mtec 1987 | |
| 5. Nuclear energy | −Proposed law for a Nuclear Security Council (CSN) −Restructuring of JEN and the treatment of nuclear wastes by this new entity −Financing the strategic stock | −Limitation of 1987 installed energy to 7,500 MW −CSN accountable to Parliament −Don't authorize new plants or reprocessing plants −No to the Center of Soria | −Mixed company −Creation of CSN −Revision of current legislation −Company of nuclear systems −Management plan for radioactive fuels −Redefinition of JEN-ENUSA's objectives | −Creation of CSN −Passage of current legislation −Seven in construction, four more authorized −Participation of the public sector | Creation of an independent CSN, responsible to the president, with regional coordination | −Proposed study on the radioactive dumpsite in Hornachuelos (Córdoba) |
| 6. Coal | −General assistance system −CECA preference pricing for bituminous coal −Substitution of concentrated action, Research Plan −Inventory financing | −Increased investments −Upward revision of projections −Restructuring of the assistance system and of the public sector −Miner statute | −Public-sector-management entity −Substitution of concentrated action by capital-debt subsidies. | −Preference attention −Free port −International cooperation*** | −Propitiate production through a complete program | −Strengthen Andalusian exploration −Environmental defense*** |

| | | | | | | |
|---|---|---|---|---|---|---|
| 7. Petroleum | –Exploration promotion<br>–Purchasing policy current base<br>–Coordination of public companies and conversion of CAMPSA into a corporation participated in by the Spanish refineries | –Freeze refining capacity and reform quota system<br>–Creation of a petroleum holding company<br>–Adaptation of CAMPSA*** | –Public hydro-carbons entity<br>–Crude supply plan*** | –Policy of free business pur-chases which avoid public-private rivalry<br>–Plan to improve transport<br>–Coordination of public participation | –Maintain imports in absolute terms<br>–Clarify purchasing policy<br>–Group as an entity all public participants | –Single petro-leum entity |
| 8. Natural gas | –Develop market-ing and infrastructure<br>–Push SEGAMO | –Accelerate the networks' coverage<br>–Diversification and connection with other countries | –Accelerate the gas pipeline network<br>–International connection<br>–Reorganize ENAGAS<br>–Increase con-sumption in pol-luted areas*** | | –Connect with the European network<br>–End ENAGAS's distribution network<br>–Creation of local distribution companies<br>–Gas utilization | –Resources of the Gulf of Cádiz for Andalusian people's benefit<br>–Light steel plant in Andalusian territory*** |
| 9. Alternate energy and research | –Increase and co-ordinate public companies' efforts<br>–Experimental use<br>–Encourage research | –Research and utilization plan<br>–Annual detailed plan on resources and results | –Alternate energy service from DGRE<br>–Strengthen alternative energy<br>–Subsidize domestic use | | –Alternate energy service<br>–Program for public-private university research<br>–Promote solar energy *** | –Decentralization of Center for Energy Studies*** |

Table 5-1  *continued*

| | UCD | PSOE | PCE | CD | CIU | PSA |
|---|---|---|---|---|---|---|
| Energy Demand Target | 145 Mtec 1987 | 140 Mtec 1987 | | | 145 Mtec 1987 | |
| 10. On ecology and consumer protection | –General environmental Law<br>–Prior information on environmental impact of projects<br>–Technological investigation | –Coordinated research development with universities<br>–Increase activities to protect the environment | –Basic law on environmental impact and limitation of effects<br>–Miner Statute | | –Environmental law<br>–Pollution controls★★★ | –Dismantling of Malaga crude receiving station |

★★★: Nonbinding amendments approved.
SOURCE: UGT, *Alternativa Energética*, 59–61.

stemmed from their recent support of the investiture of President Suárez. Carlos Bustelo, UCD Minister of Industry, closed the parliamentary debate on PEN. Javier Solana of PSOE closed with comments to Bustelo that revealed much about the political nature of opposition to PEN: "This is the Government's Energy Plan, and we do not feel at all represented in it."

Such opposition to PEN highlights many areas in which policy continuity was apparent during Spain's passage from authoritarianism to democracy. As leader of the parliamentary opposition on energy policy during these July 1979 legislative debates, Javier Solana summed it up:

> The Plan presented by the Government . . . doesn't try to direct the sector's future but rather to lay out the past, or more clearly stated, to justify the future operation of decisions adopted in the past, and, most gravely, trying to legitimize them.[37]

Similarly, PEN-82 did not address this criticism and did not significantly alter the energy policy established by earlier plans. In 1982, the same partisan objections were raised against PEN-82 again during other parliamentary debates. Javier Solana pursued the same line of attack in leading PSOE in opposition.

> In general terms, one can affirm that PEN-79 as much as its '82 revised version does not deal, in the desired manner, with directing the sector's future but rather plans well the past. Stated more clearly, it justifies future implementation of decisions adopted in the past and, the worst part, tries to legitimate them, perpetuating in a large way the same policy. In conclusion, the different versions of this energy policy constitute true retrospective planning.[38]

And on future directions, Javier Solana went on to say "It is not possible to prolong longer the economic growth model of past years. The society we all must build for tomorrow cannot be a mere extrapolation of yesterday's tendency."[39] Such opposition to the country's energy policy, even though now presented openly as a consequence of the transition to democracy, remained unable to influence its direction, a direction determined during the Franco regime.

## Public Opinion on Energy Policy

The direction of energy policy under the UCD did not change, in large part, because this party legitimately controlled the government until late 1982.

Parliamentary democracies, after all, are designed to reflect the will of the majority. But was this the majority's will? Did the basic direction of the National Energy Plan reflect the policy desires of the Spanish population? Or was there significant opposition among the citizenry to parts or all of this energy program? What other policy measures or instruments did they believe should be used to combat the energy crisis? Were particular measures or instruments advocated by different political, economic, or social groups? Had the desires of the population changed over time, given the transition to democracy? If so, did the changes in the energy program, i.e., the revisions of PEN, reflect this changing public opinion?

In public opinion on policy, we cannot assume public awareness or concern for any particular policy issue, even energy, with its consequences for social and economic life. Furthermore, we should not assume that the general population actually understood that a problem existed. Even if it did, the public may have believed the issue was more properly addressed by other, nongovernmental institutions. Tables 5-2 and 5-3 reveal, however, that before and during the transition Spaniards did believe the government should take steps to address the country's energy situation.

Table 5-2 indicates that in late 1973, in the aftermath of the October Arab-Israeli war, slightly more than half the respondents believed various governmental measures were necessary to address the energy crisis.[40] Less than 10 percent held a laissez-faire attitude. These respondents possibly believed the appropriate means to address the crisis were nongovernmental. More likely, however, they were stating that no such crisis existed. Regardless, many Spaniards held the opinion that public measures were necessary *before* PEN-75 had been written and promulgated.

Table 5-3 reports attitudes in June 1979 about whether or not the govern-

**Table 5-2**    Spaniards' Belief that Government Energy Measures are Necessary (December 1973)

| | |
|---|---|
| None | 9.8% |
| | (232) |
| Various | 50.3% |
| | (1188) |
| D.K./N.R. | 39.9% |
| | (942) |
| Totals | 100.0% |
| | (2362) |

SOURCE: Complied from data made available to the author by Estudios Comerciales Y Sociológicos/Gallup, S.A., Madrid.

**Table 5-3**  Spaniard's Agreement with Possible Governmental Energy Measures During the Political Transition (June 1979)

| Governmental Measure | Percentage | Cases |
|---|---|---|
| Raise prices | 7.2 | (173) |
| Rationing | 49.9 | (1199) |
| Odd/even driving | 13.8 | (331) |
| No measures should be taken | 14.9 | (357) |
| Don't know/no response | 14.9 | (341) |
| Totals | 100.0 | (2401) |

SOURCE: Compiled from data made available to the author by Estudios Comerciales Y Sociológicos/Gallup, S.A., Madrid.

ment should take steps to address the energy crisis. Five and one-half years after the first survey, well into the democratic experience, and at the time PEN-79 was being ratified in parliament, the number of those who believed the government should take some conservation measures had grown to over 70 percent. The laissez-faire group is equally significant in these data. Only a slight increase is found among those who responded that the government should take no energy policy action. This small increase is even less significant analytically given the large decrease in the "don't know" category between 1973 and 1979. Obviously, the Spanish had increased their awareness of the energy crisis and had simultaneously grown in their belief that the government had a responsibility to address it.

Evidence that in 1973 and 1979 more Spanish were not simply calling for any type of government activity in energy policy is found in Table 5-4. Increasingly the Spanish had in mind some specific policies aimed at promoting energy conservation. More specifically, gasoline rationing had support as an instrument of energy conservation as early as 1973. Even before the transition, many Spaniards supported some sort of conservation policy in energy.

These findings that show a growing desire for certain policy measures also suggest opposition to both the general direction and many of the policy instruments emphasized in PEN. They indicate increasing favor for public measures in energy conservation. While public opinion increasingly supported conservation, PEN essentially continued to neglect savings in energy consumption.

Up to now, the data on public opinion have been products of a survey which focused on energy-conservation questions. To minimize potential bias, Table 5-5 contains survey findings totally independent from the previous one, a study commissioned by the Spanish democratic government itself and circulated as internal documents. These national results collaborate the other

**Table 5-4**    Spaniards' Agreement with Possible Governmental Energy Measures
(December 1973)

| Governmental Measures | All Respondents | Drive | Don't Drive |
|---|---|---|---|
| Rationing | 23.4% | 30.0% | 21.8% |
| | (572) | (145) | (427) |
| No Sunday driving | 15.2% | 15.5% | 15.2% |
| | (372) | (75) | (297) |
| Prohibit driving on another day | 3.8% | 3.9% | 3.7% |
| | (92) | (19) | (73) |
| Impose speed limits | 25.1% | 34.6% | 22.7% |
| | (612) | (167) | (445) |
| Odd/even driving | 2.0% | 3.5% | 1.7% |
| | (50) | (17) | (33) |
| Don't know/no response | 30.4% | 12.4% | 34.8% |
| | (742) | (60) | (682) |
| Totals | 100.0% | 100.0% | 100.0% |
| | (2440) | (483) | (1957) |

SOURCE: Compiled from data made available to the author by Estudios Comerciales Y Socioló-
gicos/Gallup, S.A., Madrid.

findings that the public supported conservation, something the different governments both before and after the transition to democracy failed to undertake. Results from official polls reflect a strong leaning toward government
measures for energy conservation, with over 75 percent agreeing that the
government should prohibit excessive consumption through the use of different policy instruments, excluding price increases.[41] Taken as a whole, these
two different surveys suggest that both early in the energy crisis and much
later, the Spanish increasingly wanted strong policies for energy conservation. This was true as much in Franco's authoritarian system as in the nascent
democratic one.

Furthermore, the public's awareness of energy issues increased over time.
In 1973, much of the population, nearly 40 percent, could or did not respond
to the question in Table 5-2 asking if government measures were necessary.
Thirty percent gave no opinion or did not respond to a more detailed question in Table 5-4 on conservation policy. Issue awareness during the early
stages of the energy crisis was quite low in Spain as well as in other countries.
A general lack of issue awareness ran throughout the 1973 survey. On the
other hand, by 1979 five years of energy as a salient issue had decreased this
"don't know" category in Table 5-3 to a little over 14 percent. This trend is
substantiated in Table 5-3. Not only did the Spanish grow in their propensity

**Table 5-5**   Spaniards Beliefs Concerning Certain Energy-related Questions (July 1979) (percent)

|  | Agree | Disagree | D.K./N.R. |
|---|---|---|---|
| The government should prohibit excessive consumption | 75.4 | 16.6 | 8.1 |
| TV should end at midnight | 71.8 | 24.2 | 4.1 |
| Gasoline should be rationed | 55.8 | 31.0 | 13.2 |
| Electric restriction should be implemented | 38.2 | 52.7 | 9.2 |
| Gasoline should be raised to 50 pesetas | 11.6 | 76.9 | 11.5 |
| Petroleum should be purchased at its actual price | 16.8 | 72.0 | 11.3 |
| Electrical rates should be increased | 7.4 | 86.9 | 5.7 |
| Only 3% of the petroleum we use is ours | 59.9 | 18.2 | 22.2 |
| The people don't realize the problem | 67.5 | 28.0 | 4.4 |
| Too much energy is wasted in public buildings | 86.0 | 6.1 | 8.1 |
| It is best for the government to be an example | 95.3 | 1.7 | 3.1 |
| One should get accustomed to living worse | 26.9 | 69.3 | 3.9 |
| Nuclear plants should be constructed | 32.1 | 51.8 | 16.0 |

N = 1223
SOURCE: Opinión Pública Y Ahorro de Energía. Centro de Estudios de la Energía, 1980.

to express an opinion about conservation, they wanted a more active role by the government.

## Specific Energy Policy Instruments

The most criticized and politicized aspect of the National Energy Plan was its heavy emphasis on nuclear energy. Several major political parties and many not-so-central environmental groups expressed opposition to this push for nuclear energy. While Lemóniz, the nuclear plant constructed in the Basque country, captured the most publicity, the anti-nuclear movement in Spain and other Western European countries had a much broader concern. Many individuals and groups called for a total reassessment and change of policy in what they perceived as Spain's misdirected nuclear-energy program.

Governments of both authoritarian and early democratic Spain consistently defended the nuclear direction of PEN. Only in the mid-1980s did the

Socialist government pull back on some of this push. Proponents of nuclear energy often argued that the anti-nuclear forces were not representative.[42] In Table 5-5, results to a question on the construction of nuclear plants suggest that this is incorrect. The government's own data reveal that in 1979, 51.8 percent opposed the construction of nuclear plants. During the transition, a majority disagreed with policy decisions that formed a critical component of PEN. Public opinion on nuclear energy, however, did not immediately alter energy policy. The different revisions of PEN adjusted the number of nuclear plants authorized for construction. The overall nuclear program in Spain was also slowed by many technical problems. But political opposition played a very small role in this. Forces other than public opinion lay behind the continuation of Spain's nuclear and entire energy program.

In terms of conservation policies by public authorities, energy pricing as an instrument appeared as a major political concern to many. The different governments outlined in PEN a desire to stop the long-held policy of maintaining below-market prices for most energy products, particularly petroleum. This policy, which essentially subsidized energy consumption, was inconsistent with the formal commitment, as seen earlier, to pursue a more realistic policy of energy pricing. Little political pressure existed in either authoritarian or democratic Spain to pursue pricing as a policy instrument.

On one hand, little incentive existed for the private sector to push for increases in the price of petroleum. The private electric companies that burned large quantities of fuel-oil preferred to operate with these low regulated prices. Because rates for electricity were also regulated, electric company profits were maximized by burning, when necessary, fuel-oil purchased from the government at low prices. The lower the price the electric companies purchased their fuel-oil, the larger their profits. A strong incentive thus existed for the private electric companies to encourage the government to keep prices low.

The unique private-public blend to the petroleum industry in Spain minimized private incentive to seek price increases. Large volumes bought and sold at regulated prices kept profits up in the refining industry. The seven private refining companies in Spain bought from the state-operated HISPANOIL, which purchased overseas. They then sold most of their refined petroleum products to CAMPSA, the distribution monopoly. This business transpired at prices regulated on both ends under a quota system determined by the Ministry of Commerce. An individual refinery had its profits for the year guaranteed on the first day of January, and any price increase at one end would have required an adjustment at the other. Lower petroleum prices at both ends maintained high levels of consumption. Any rises in the price of petroleum and a concomitant decrease in domestic consumption would have slowed business, and thus profits, for each individual refinery.

Naturally such increases in the price of energy would not have pleased the average Spaniard. (Tables 5-3 and 5-4 demonstrated this.) In 1979, only 7.2 percent of those polled in this government survey believed the government should raise prices to decrease consumption. And 87 percent disagreed that the regulated rates for electricity should be increased. About 77 percent disagreed that gasoline prices should be raised and close to the same percentage disagreed that petroleum should be purchased at its actual price. Thus policymakers for energy faced potential or actual political pressure from both energy and other companies as well as the general population not to follow through on the commitment in PEN-79 and PEN-82 to restructure energy pricing. Public opinion reinforced the desires of the financial-business interests to not alter during the transition to democracy the policies of the previous regime.

These data show surprising popularity of gasoline rationing as a policy instrument. Possibly the Spaniards' propensity for public transportation and their comparatively moderate use of the automobile as a primary means of transportation explain this. Nevertheless, Table 5-4 shows that gasoline rationing only slightly trailed speed limits as the conservation measure most often selected by respondents in the survey during the Franco regime. By 1979 and the democratic system, rationing had clearly become the favorite conservation measure the government might impose. One of every two respondents in Table 5-3 selected this measure, although speed limits had been eliminated as a possible response in this later survey. The figures in 1973 and 1979 for those favoring rationing were 30.6 percent and 58.2 percent, respectively, among all those who favored some conservation measure by the government, i.e., not including the undecided respondents. Table 5-5 once again substantiates this finding. The survey sponsored by the government itself reported in 1979 that 55.8 percent agreed with rationing.

Policies strong on conservation such as gasoline rationing are generally highly political. Governments often shun utilizing such instruments of energy management for fear of political repercussions. Evidence suggests such concern for politics was misperceived in the Spanish case. Gasoline rationing, similar to other conservation issues raised in this questionnaire, appeared to be nonpartisan. During the early transition, membership in any of the four major political parties did not significantly affect opinions about rationing or other conservation measures. This can be seen in Table 5-6. Support was there for the use of several instruments for energy management not included in PEN. Party identification did not influence views on energy conservation. Despite this extensive and nonpartisan support for gasoline rationing, neither the Franco regime nor the contemporary democratic system seriously considered including it in the National Energy Plan, often stating that such a rationing scheme would be administratively difficult to organize and manage.[43] The different versions of PEN continued to emphasize increased supply over decreased consumption.

Table 5-7 and 5-8 suggest that both before and after Spain's transition to democracy rationing was favored more in the larger cities, reinforcing the earlier statement about the use of mass transportation. Tables 5-8 and 5-9 similarly reveal that in both 1973 and 1979 those who believed the government should not pursue energy conservation were disproportionately from smaller towns.

The weak relationship between place of residence and use of instruments in energy policy and the noninfluence of party identification suggests why public opinion did not strongly alter energy policy in Spain. Public opinion had a minimal impact on policy because preferences were not tied to electoral organizations. There was, in effect, a kind of bipartisan or transpartisan consensus-by-default to much of Spain's energy policy.

## Supply-Side Energy Policy

Many critics of the National Energy Plan often emphasized that the response of Spanish policymakers to the energy crisis was not only late but limited, focusing primarily on increasing energy supply. They saw little or no attention paid to conservation.[44] Such critics argued that policymakers assumed

Table 5-6    Spaniards' Agreement with Possible Governmental Energy Measures by Party Identification (June 1979)

|  | PCE | PSOE | UCD | CD |
|---|---|---|---|---|
| Raise prices | 7.0% | 8.5% | 8.2% | 12.9% |
|  | (9) | (41) | (42) | (9) |
| Rationing | 55.5% | 57.5% | 55.3% | 47.1% |
|  | (71) | (279) | (283) | (33) |
| Odd/even driving | 19.5% | 13.2% | 13.7% | 18.6% |
|  | (25) | (64) | (70) | (13) |
| No measures should | 7.0% | 12.0% | 11.3% | 10.0% |
| be taken | (9) | (58) | (58) | (7) |
| Don't know/no | 10.9% | 8.9% | 11.5% | 11.4% |
| response | (14) | (43) | (59) | (8) |
| Totals | 99.9% | 100.1% | 100.0% | 100.0% |
|  | (128) | (485) | (512) | (70) |

SOURCE: Compiled from data made available to the author by Estudios Comerciales Y Sociológicos/Gallup, S.A., Madrid.

**Table 5-7**  Spaniards' Agreement with Possible Governmental Energy Measures by City Size (December 1973)

|  | 10,000 or less | 10,000 to 100,000 | 100,000 to 1,000,000 | Madrid and Barcelona |
|---|---|---|---|---|
| Rationing | 19.0% | 21.0% | 29.2% | 30.3% |
|  | (156) | (147) | (157) | (115) |
| No Sunday driving | 14.2% | 14.3% | 16.9% | 16.6% |
|  | (116) | (100) | (91) | (63) |
| Prohibit driving on | 2.6% | 3.9% | 3.0% | 7.4% |
| another day | (21) | (27) | (16) | (28) |
| Impose speed limits | 27.0% | 25.4% | 20.5% | 25.0% |
|  | (221) | (178) | (110) | (95) |
| Odd/even driving | 2.0% | 1.4% | 3.2% | 2.6% |
|  | (16) | (10) | (17) | (10) |
| Don't know/no | 35.3% | 34.1% | 27.2% | 18.2% |
| response | (289) | (239) | (146) | (69) |
| Totals | 100.1% | 100.1% | 100.0% | 100.1% |
|  | (819) | (701) | (537) | (380) |

SOURCE: Compiled from data provided to the author by Estudios Comerciales Y Sociológicos/ Gallup, S.A., Madrid.

**Table 5-8**  Spaniards' Belief in Whether or Not Governmental Energy Measures are Necessary by City Size (December 1973)

|  | 10,000 or less | 10,000 to 100,000 | 100,000 to 1,000,000 | Madrid and Barcelona |
|---|---|---|---|---|
| None | 6.9% | 11.2% | 12.7% | 9.4% |
|  | (55) | (77) | (66) | (34) |
| Various | 46.3% | 46.9% | 53.4% | 60.8% |
|  | (370) | (322) | (277) | (219) |
| Don't know/no response | 46.9% | 41.9% | 33.9% | 29.7% |
|  | (375) | (288) | (176) | (107) |
| Totals | 100.1% | 100.0% | 100.0% | 99.9% |
|  | (800) | (687) | (519) | (360) |

SOURCE: Compiled from data provided to the author by Estudios Comerciales Y Sociológicos/ Gallup, S.A., Madrid.

**Table 5-9**   Spaniards' Agreement with Possible Governmental Energy Measures by
City Size (June 1979)

|  | 10,000 or less | 10,000 to 100,000 | 100,000 to 1,000,000 | Madrid and Barcelona |
|---|---|---|---|---|
| Raise prices | 8.4% | 7.3% | 4.5% | 7.7% |
|  | (75) | (32) | (24) | (41) |
| Rationing | 46.7% | 50.7% | 53.3% | 51.7% |
|  | (417) | (221) | (285) | (273) |
| Odd/even driving | 10.8% | 11.0% | 14.2% | 20.6% |
|  | (96) | (48) | (76) | (110) |
| No measures should be taken | 16.5% | 16.3% | 13.3% | 12.5% |
|  | (147) | (71) | (71) | (67) |
| Don't know/no response | 17.7% | 14.7% | 14.8% | 7.5% |
|  | (158) | (64) | (79) | (40) |
| Totals | 100.1% | 100.0% | 100.1% | 100.0% |
|  | (893) | (436) | (535) | (534) |

SOURCE: Compiled from data made available to the author by Estudios Comerciales Y Socioló-
gicos/Gallup, S.A., Madrid.

that Spain's answer to the energy shortage rested with providing an ample
supply. They highlighted the fact that PEN consistently overestimated the
country's energy resources and that supply goals simply could not be met.[45]
In its different versions, PEN assumed increased consumption and stated
that this could be met with its estimates of increased supplies.

The heavy emphasis on nuclear energy in PEN followed this logic—that
greater consumption would be met with increased supply. Furthermore,
PEN-75, PEN-79, and PEN-82 saw a strong nuclear program as the most
viable means to guarantee this supply. This logic showed in many statements
by the UCD government. For example, the Minister of Industry and Energy
stated in 1980 that in spite of any "conservation campaign, energy consumption should increase in order to maintain industrial growth, and there will be
no other remedy than to give a hand to nuclear energy in order to meet
demand."[46] Such logic and PEN itself conjectured that Spain would be able
to supply this energy. Many proponents of nuclear power saw, however, that
it generally took at least ten years to get such installations on line. Spain's
record on such construction made even this figure an optimistic one.

Critics argued that PEN's emphasis on supply should have been replaced
by a focus on the demand side—that is, conservation measures. For example,
restrictions and higher prices for electricity and gasoline could reduce consumption, but the government was politically hesitant to implement such

policies. Likewise, other policy-conservation instruments were not seriously considered. Critics believed that even the Energy Conservation Law had problems and major flaws. This law, according to Minister of Industry and Energy Ignacio Bayón, contained incentives and subsidies for research and development on energy savings, the self-generation of electricity, and petroleum substitution by either other fuels or alternative energy such as solar, wind, or geothermal. From its position of parliamentary opposition, PSOE criticized the law as incomplete and not going far enough, objecting, for example, that it only considered home consumption of solar energy. The UCD government responded that the law was not meant to regulate all aspects of this matter, but was only an instrument to assist its implementation. This law was so heavily amended as it passed through the Senate, finally being approved on 10 December 1980, that it was sent back to the Congress of Deputies before ultimate passage. Critics continued to contend, nevertheless, that policy on conservation was neglected, that PEN's projections substantially overestimated the use of nuclear energy, and that it underestimated an increased reliance on imported coal.

Why did Spanish energy policy continue its emphasis on increasing energy supplies with very little attention paid to energy conservation? Why were instruments of policy implementation such as pricing not adopted? Even many opponents of PEN-75, PEN-79, and PEN-82 seem to have comprehended why their criticisms fell on deaf ears. The major political parties, smaller regional parties, environmental groups, and individual critics of PEN and its emphasis on increased energy supplies acknowledged the existence of a political-financial oligarchy which controlled energy policy.[47] Energy policy in both authoritarian and early democratic Spain emphasized supply, critics contended, because it was good for the financial-business class of the country. The power and centralization of capital that controlled energy production in Spain remained a concern to more than just environmental groups. Many political groups believed it was no coincidence that PEN, as the formal public statement on energy policy, reflected the interests of the financial community and perpetuated policy made during the Franco period. More than a few citizens of Spain and their political leaders noted that energy policy ran counter to public opinion. Why was this so? One response was often heard at that time: the financial-business oligarchy.[48]

The Franco regime originally formulated the National Energy Plan. During the transition, despite opposition by the Left and in some ways counter to public opinion, such energy planning remained essentially unaltered. Why, despite such opposition to PEN and its policies by the political parties, public opinion, interest groups, and other political pressures, did the direction and policy instruments of energy management not change despite the transition to democracy? Why, given the nature of public opinion, did the UCD government continue to pursue an energy policy that was primarily concerned with increasing supply?

The lack of fundamental change in energy policy despite the political pressures described above was likely due to the close relationship between the energy policymakers and a pivotal cadre of financial-business interests. These economic interests were found in the electrical industry, the banking industry, the refineries, CAMPSA, and various government ministries that were too deeply entrenched to be easily assigned new roles. They were extremely protective of the power they held. Many formidable economic and political interests had to be overcome to produce significant policy change, interests that constrained such policy-making. The politics of challenging the basic elements of any nation's economic structure in order to alter energy policy is difficult. Therefore, I now turn to this powerful financial-business cadre which, in serving as a "pivotal" actor during the transition, proved instrumental in maintaining the direction of Spanish energy policy.

# 6

## The Role of the
## Financial Oligarchy

Spain's transition to democracy through *reforma* rather than *ruptura* left intact the country's economic system. Fundamental economic and financial institutions, practices, and preserves were not significantly altered in the transition. Capital concentration generally remained beyond democratic political control; yet this strength of the financial community could be asserted to influence economic-related public policies. Such influence characterized energy policy-making both before and during the transition to democracy.

The lack of significant change in energy policy following the end of authoritarian rule is best explained by the central role of business. Consideration of the business-financial oligarchy in Spain and its impact on key aspects of energy helps to understand policy outcomes. The banking industry, with its financial resources, was the guiding force for the position of many elite businessmen within the inner circles of energy policy-making. More specifically, the banks influenced policy decisions in the electric companies. They accomplished this through interlocking directorates: directors of electric companies were from the boards of directors of the banks. This overlapping membership then permitted a push for numerous projects that the banks managed, financed, received the international credit for; they also saw to it that their factories provided the equipment for the projects, took charge of the construction, placed their own firms on the site, and generated huge profits.[1]

The principal reason for pushing the construction of nuclear plants in Spain is because it is still an unsurpassed opportunity for obtaining huge private profits, projecting extensive collective social costs over space and time. The astronomical financing, the generous and redundant manufacturing, the never-ending engineering work and construction—through governmental connivance and control of the means of social communication—offers unsurpassed profit opportunities to national and foreign companies, to banks and other financial institutions, and to executives and middlemen at all levels.[2]

This scenario of private financial advantage went well beyond the electricity industry. It was found in Spain with the construction of superhighways, in the purchase of heavy machinery and equipment, and in the refining industry. Construction in both the refining and the electricity industry, particularly the nuclear program, meant energy planning only for supply, producing an enormous oversupply capacity. The adeptness of the electricity companies in generating demand produced an excellent business, which the banks encouraged. This demand generation became, as seen above, formal policy in PEN, a plan in which the demand for electricity grew more rapidly than that for primary energy. The relationship of the Spanish banking industry to the government, the position of the financial sector in the electrical industry, the refining industry, CAMPSA, and the profitability of investments in many other areas of energy provided both the motivation and the means to push for a continuation of energy plans formulated earlier.

In this chapter, we analyze the relationship of the business-financial oligarchy to the energy sector. We consider here the overlapping nature of Spain's most powerful financial institutions and the various components of the energy industry. First, the centrality of the energy industry is established in Spain's overall economic structure. Second, inferences are made about the concentrated and coordinated nature of policy-making in these energy companies. Third, the role of the banking industry is then introduced and its strong nexus with the energy industry is drawn. Next, with the banks' policy influence established, the analysis then outlines the links of the financial oligarchy to the government. The representation of private financial institutions in both the energy industries and at the highest levels of government provided the necessary economic linkages and government platform to politically control energy policy in Spain.[3]

## Energy Industry Centrality and Cohesion

A large number of the largest companies in Spain during the transition were energy-related. In 1976, at the beginning of the political transition, thirteen of Spain's top thirty-one companies dealt in terms of sales in either electricity or petroleum-related products. Table 6-1 shows that by 1983 fourteen of the top twenty-seven Spanish companies focused their business on energy. While some companies such as Iberia and RENFE were state-owned and operated, most of the enterprises were privately capitalized. The mixed economy in Spain thus produced several public companies of considerable size, sales, and profitability as well as many private ones. CAMPSA, at the top of this list, characterized the classic Spanish twist to a "mixed" economy through a private company holding a state monopoly. Most of the energy companies on this list, however, were privately owned and operated.

The thirteen energy companies here were also quite profitable. Table 6-1

**Table 6-1**    Top Spanish Companies in 1983 (Sales and profits in millions of pesetas)

| Company | Sector | Sales | Employees | Profits |
|---|---|---|---|---|
| 1. CAMPSA | Petroleum | 1,256,577 | 8,821 | 9,887 |
| 2. Empetrol | Petroleum | 692,788 | 5,422 | 2632 |
| 3. CEPSA | Petroleum | 493,117 | 4,149 | 4,506 |
| 4. Telefónica | Public Services | 373,806 | 66,781 | 32,620 |
| 5. El Corte Inglés | Retail Sales | 251,356 | 22,500 | 6,174 |
| 6. Iberia | Transportation | 248,735 | 24,232 | −17,126 |
| 7. Explosivos Río Tinto | Chemicals | 225,334 | 9,100 | −10,349 |
| 8. Fasa-Renault | Vehicles | 197,111 | 21,586 | 411 |
| 9. Ensidesa | Metallurgy | 193,057 | 21,012 | −24,611 |
| 10. Petronor | Petroleum | 191,524 | 705 | 3,473 |
| 11. Ford España | Automobiles | 181,722 | 8,994 | 12,091 |
| 12. Seat | Automobiles | 180,217 | 23,610 | −36,190 |
| 13. Tabacalera | Tobacco | 174,980 | 8,614 | 795 |
| 14. Iberduero | Electricity | 171,545 | 7,049 | 13,587 |
| 15. Hidroeléctrica | Electricity | 162,024 | 6,800 | 13,165 |
| 16. Union Eléctrica-Fenosa | Electricity | 161,777 | 7,444 | 8,665 |
| 17. Hispanoil | Petroleum | 160,365 | 256 | 5,939 |
| 18. Endesa | Electricity | 155,323 | 6,076 | 25,260 |
| 19. Dragados Construcción | Construction | 148,777 | 12,925 | 1,440 |
| 20. Butano | Petroleum | 141,896 | 3,336 | 1,111 |
| 21. IBM España | Information | 139,052 | 3,923 | 13,446 |
| 22. General Motors España | Automobiles | 137,738 | 8,410 | — |
| 23. RENFE | Transportation | 131,129 | 65,612 | −107,235 |
| 24. Petroliber | Petroleum | 131,025 | 796 | −1,830 |
| 25. Petromed | Petroleum | 128,209 | 439 | 3,351 |
| 26. Sevillana | Electricity | 123,116 | 6,423 | 4,857 |
| 27. FECSA | Electricity | 117,763 | 6,034 | 6,188 |

SOURCE: Tamames (1986), 228.

shows that in 1976 seven of the ten most profitable companies were involved in energy. The electricity industry particularly stood out. All thirteen of these energy companies made a profit during the year. While this does not represent all energy companies in Spain, it does strongly suggest that energy was a lucrative business.

Part of this profitability occurred because Spain has increasingly been characterized by capital concentration. Spaniards, even high-ranking public officials, often referred to this in terms of "la patronal," or an economic oligarchy.[4] This capital concentration included energy. By 1965, 98 percent of steel production, petroleum refining, and electricity generation was controlled by 300 leading Spanish financiers.[5] And as early as 1962, eight companies held 51 percent of production capacity, generating 53 percent of the electricity.[6] The energy industry in general and the electric companies in particular were at the center of this consolidation of economic power.

This economic consolidation in the electricity industry went beyond capital concentration. Some management and policy-making overlap existed, and decisions in the electricity industry were not only coordinated in UNESA. In addition, a complex network of overlapping directorates existed in electricity. While common directors do not automatically imply that decisions were closely coordinated, this overlapping board membership served to reinforce UNESA's ability to speak on behalf of the entire electrical industry.[7] Figure 6-1 shows the extent of the overlapping directorates of the six largest companies in Spanish electricity in terms of capital. The ranking for capital size of each company is presented in the lower-right corner of the rectangle representing that enterprise. Lines connecting these companies indicate the number of joint board members, with each board averaging about six board members. Thus private electric companies appear to have possessed a strong potential for management and policy coordination.

However, Figure 6-1 considers only the top six private electric companies. Figure 6-2 presents similar data, but includes state-owned companies. This enlarged picture reveals the same: overlapping directorates linking Spain's electric companies at the management level.

These figures and Table 6-1 strongly suggest that energy was a central component of Spain's economy during the transition to democracy and that these companies, particularly in electricity, were closely linked through mutual members of management. A basis for oligarchical control of energy was thus present. Further evidence of this oligarchical control requires identification of these policymakers and establishment of their connection with the governments which formulated energy policy during Spain's transition to democracy.

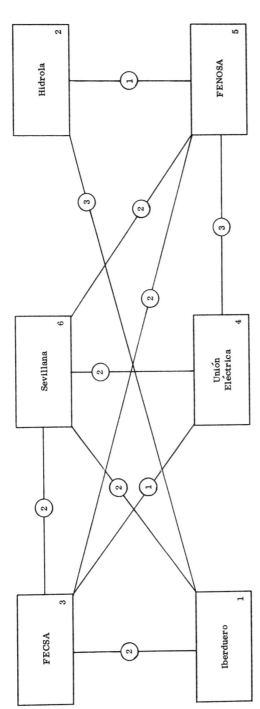

**Figure 6-1.** Overlapping Directorates in the Spanish Electrical Industry (Six Largest in Capital, 1977)
Source: Serrano and Muñoz, 1979

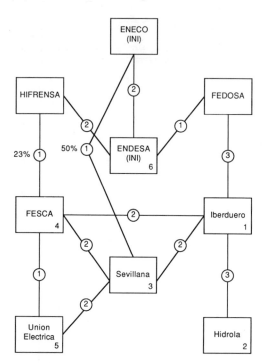

**Figure 6-2.**  Overlapping Directorates in the Spanish Electrical Industry (First Six in Production)
Source: Serrano and Muñoz, 1979

# The Banking Industry

Spaniards are generally acutely aware of and readily acknowledge the great political and economic power of the banking industry: "Financial power in Spain revolves around the banking system, so logically this system is a very important economic power in this country. The banking system is not an isolated business but determines who may participate in Spanish business life."[8] Most non-Spanish scholarly analyses of politics during the transition neglected banking's influence on public policy-making.[9] The banking system's grip on large segments of the political and economic system nevertheless largely explains the direction of much of economic policy in Spain, including energy planning.

Both before and during the transition, the Spanish banking industry was dominated by seven major banks, all with long histories and founded on old "family" money.[10] "Los Siete Grandes," as they were often called, included

Banesto, Central, Hispano Americano, Bilboa, Santander, Popular, and Vizcaya. Over the years, each of these seven banks has purchased and otherwise come to absorb other smaller banks so that eventually these "Siete Grandes" were actually seven banking groups. During the transition, these seven major banking groups were the heart of Spain's financial system. Table 6-2 lists these groups and their resources in November 1977 and June 1985.

These seven banking groups appear to have been very profitable. Table 6-3 clearly reveals that the Spanish banking industry engaged in a very healthy business during the transition to democracy. This table compares several years of profits for these major banks. These banks consistently returned double-digit profits. During the 1970s these profits were generally in the range of 11 to 12 percent, averaging 11.6 percent in 1977, 12.1 percent in 1978, and 12.4 percent in 1979. In 1986, several years later and toward the end of the transition, the banking giants had an extraordinary year, returning profits at about 22 percent. Such profitability was also reflected in the dividends paid in these same years. Although not reported in Table 6-3, these seven banks reported ratios of dividends to profits after taxes averaging 49.2 percent in 1977, 48.1 percent in 1978, 49.4 percent in 1979, and 34.4 percent in 1985. In 1986, dividends returned to the patterns of the late 1970s.

The profits of each of the "Seven Majors" were also consistent with those of the other members of the banking industry. In the years 1971 to 1979, the Siete Grandes averaged profits after capital taxes of 12 percent. During the same period, all Spanish banks turned a profit of 11.29 percent. Thus the profit figures for both the Seven Majors and the entire banking system were quite similar during this period. Most Spanish banks reaped healthy financial harvests before and during the transition period. The entire banking industry had for a long time been very profitable. After 1974, however, the Siete Grandes consistently grew more profitable than the other banks. The Seven Majors' profits were generally, yet consistently, about a percentage point higher than those of the rest of the banking industry. Spain's relatively high inflation rate and poor economic performance following the oil crisis accounted for a lessening of profits during the later 1970s. The Seven Majors' profits nevertheless remained quite solid.

The solid financial health of the banking system during the transition appeared even better when compared to the state of the general economy following the energy crisis. Comparisons can be made with any number of indicators. One such indicator is the performance of the price index for stocks. Such an indicator suggests the markets' perceived health by the banking industry. For the period 1973 to 1986, in terms of percentage change from the previous year, the price index of stocks in banking outperformed the index of general stock in ten of the fourteen years. And in two of these years, 1984 and 1985, it still grew by 12 percent and 17.4 percent, respectively.[11] These

**Table 6-2**   Spanish Banks and Assets November 1977 and June 1985 (in millions of pesetas)

|  | November 1977 | June 1985 | Percent National |
|---|---|---|---|
| Central Group | 649,720 | 1,847,500 | 11.93 |
| Central | 538,040 | | |
| Valencia | 46,653 | | |
| Fomento | 65,027 | | |
| Banesto Group (Español de Crédito) | 647,599 | 1,790,819 | 11.57 |
| Banesto | 566,677 | | |
| Bandesco | 19,341 | | |
| Guipúzcoano | 38,350 | | |
| Vitoria | 2,591 | | |
| Masaveu | 3,446 | | |
| Garriga Nogues | 12,323 | | |
| Trelles | 671 | | |
| Crédito Corporativo | 1,303 | | |
| Abel Matute | 2,891 | | |
| Hispano Group | 561,208 | 1,409,918 | 9.11 |
| Hispano | 470,861 | | |
| Urquijo | 85,945 | | |
| Mercantil Tarragona | 3,616 | | |
| Valls | 786 | | |
| Bilbao Group | 432,852 | 1,300,868 | 8.40 |
| Bilbao | 377,840 | | |
| Industrial de Bilbao | 50,520 | | |
| Comercio | 4,492 | | |
| Santander Group | 322,652 | 1,084,393 | 7.00 |
| Santander | 269,095 | | |
| Intercontinental | 50,195 | | |
| Comercial America | 3,362 | | |
| Vizcaya Group | 321,218 | 1,051,629 | 6.79 |
| Vizcaya | 276,894 | | |
| Induban | 44,324 | | |
| Popular Group | 294,617 | 753,977 | 4.87 |
| Popular | 186,716 | | |
| Eurobanco | 27,059 | | |
| Andalucia | 35,872 | | |
| Vasconia | 11,334 | | |
| Crédito Balear | 10,423 | | |
| Castilla | 13,995 | | |
| Galicia | 9,218 | | |

**Table 6-2**    *(Continued)*

|                                   | November 1977 | June 1985 | Percent National |
|-----------------------------------|--------------:|-----------|------------------|
| Rumasa Group                      | 217,217       |           |                  |
| Industrial del Sur                | 32,516        |           |                  |
| Atlántico                         | 68,613        |           |                  |
| Latino                            | 6,114         |           |                  |
| Condal                            | 18,556        |           |                  |
| Comercial de Cataluña             | 10,308        |           |                  |
| Noroeste                          | 18,674        |           |                  |
| Norte                             | 10,602        |           |                  |
| Peninsular                        | 9,323         |           |                  |
| Jerez                             | 8,360         |           |                  |
| Extremadura                       | 4,789         |           |                  |
| Sevilla                           | 6,235         |           |                  |
| Oeste                             | 3,525         |           |                  |
| Albacete                          | 2,728         |           |                  |
| Alicantino de Comercio            | 2,404         |           |                  |
| Murcia                            | 3,230         |           |                  |
| Huelva                            | 864           |           |                  |
| General Comercial e Industrial    | 10,376        |           |                  |

SOURCE: Tamames (1981) 60–61, and 1986, 588.

**Table 6-3**    Profits and Dividends of the "Siete Grandes" of Spanish Banking
(Profits after Taxes on Equity Expressed in Percentages)

|           | 1977 | 1978 | 1979 | 1986* |
|-----------|------|------|------|-------|
| Banesto   | 12.5 | 13.5 | 12.7 | —     |
| Central   | 13.1 | 11.2 | 10.6 | 18.8  |
| Hispano   | 10.2 | 11.4 | 12.5 | 13.9  |
| Bilboa    | 10.5 | 11.0 | 11.1 | 23.1  |
| Vizcaya   | 11.9 | 12.8 | 13.0 | 24.4  |
| Santander | 10.6 | 12.2 | 13.5 | 21.6  |
| Popular   | 12.5 | 12.5 | 15.0 | 30.0  |
| Average   | 11.6 | 12.1 | 12.4 | 22.0  |

*Net profits on own resources
SOURCE: 1977–79, Torrero (1982), 56. *Anuario Estádistico de la Banca Privada,* Madrid: Consejo
Superior Bancário, 1986.

figures thus reveal an important perception of the financial soundness of the banking industry. Another similar indicator is the ratio of market to quoted stock value of the different economic sectors. On 30 September 1980, a rather typical day in the period of Spain's transition to democracy, this ratio placed banking at the top of the list.[12] The market value to quoted value on this particular day was the following: commercial banks (.93); industrial banks (.72); insurance (.61); furniture investment (.57); others (.40); agriculture (.38); construction (.38); monopolies (.32); cement and construction material (.28); water, gas, and electricity (.23); automobiles (.21); chemical textiles (.21); fishing and shipping (.18); commerce and retail sales (.17); mining and metallurgy (.17); and paper (.15). These figures suggest that investors appeared to believe that the Spanish banking industry was a profitable one. Again the assumption here is that those with money to invest perceived that Spanish banks would maintain their grip on the road to solid profits.

The fact that increases in such profits corresponded with the energy crisis suggests possible energy-related profits. Research into the books of these Seven Majors to discover what percentage of these profits are energy-related is virtually impossible. Furthermore, obtainable yearly reports give only aggregate figures.[13] Banks in Spain guard their detailed account books very closely, and in a system notorious for its lack of financial transparency. Inferences can still be made, nevertheless, about the links of these banks with the energy industry.

## Common Board Members

An important indicator of the influence the banking industry had on energy policy focuses on the extent to which the banks were represented in policy-making organs and institutions. The coincidence of policymakers in both the Spanish banking and energy industries suggests one reason why energy policy remained basically unaltered during the transition.

The Spanish banking industry, with its Siete Grandes at the core of a financial oligarchy, directly controlled much of the energy policy-making. Previous discussion of UNESA and Figures 6-1 and 6-2 established that the electricity companies were woven into a coordinated management arrangement. Figure 6-3 further reveals the management links between the largest electricity companies and the major private banks. The major banks dominated many of the boards of Spain's electric companies.[14] These personnel links provided the banks the platform to influence policy decisions that affected their investments. The electric companies required large capital investments in order to grow and modernize. These funds were made available over the years by the banks, but only at a price. The price was the presence of bank representation in the decision-making organs of the electric companies.

The influence of the banking industry in electricity went beyond overlapping directorates. Spanish banks additionally sought to protect their potential for large profits in nuclear energy. Their attempt to maximize payoffs through the extension of credit to the electric companies and construction firms, which were also directly linked to the banks, meant strongly promoting research, development, and planning in nuclear energy. Nuclear energy was especially profitable to the banks. The banks loaned large sums of money to the electric companies to finance these projects. Once the loans were made and construction began, the banks reaped additional profits because they had overlapping interests in the construction firms similar to they ones they had in the electricity industry. And the banks took little risk because most of these loans were guaranteed by the state. As discussed earlier, the Nuclear Energy Council (JEN) housed all nuclear research and development in Spain. Supposedly independent, JEN was never neutral or objective; it was formed by industry representatives interested in developing nuclear energy. During the transition, JEN was open to multiple pressures from the electricity companies and the banking industry. The banking industry had direct representation on JEN's administrative board. The executive council of JEN contained representatives from the banks, the electric companies, and nuclear technology companies. These overlapping directorates almost guaranteed the impossibility of JEN to maintain independence.

An energy policy that emphasized supply maximized profits on investment in the energy industries. Capital needed for expansion and modernization was not, of course, limited to the electric companies. Other industries, both energy and other, experienced similar processes of increased management penetration by the financial community. In energy, however, the banking industry moved beyond its influence in electricity when, during the 1920s, it came to control much of another important energy industry—petroleum. In the petroleum industry, the banks had a stronghold on the private refining companies: "As is the case with the electric companies, behind each private refinery there is a bank." [15]

Table 6-4 lists the participants in the refining industry, the names and capacities of the ten refineries, and the capital structure behind them, with private capital generally referring to the domestic banking system. Figure 6-4 represents banking's nexus with the refining industry in terms of banking representatives on the refineries' boards. Some of these private refineries were directly and extensively directed by particular banks, such as Petromed and CEPSA by Banco Español de Crédito, and Central and Santander, respectively. Others such as Rio Tinto were not so strongly controlled by a single bank but contained a wide range of representatives from across the

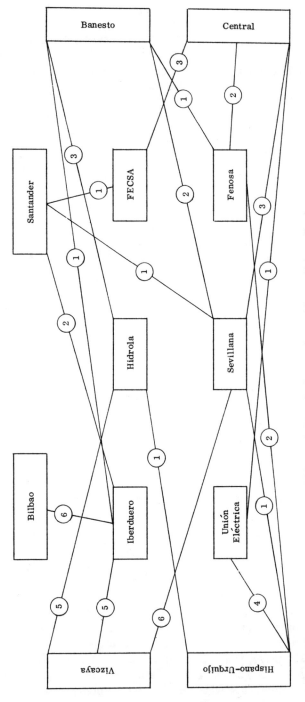

**Figure 6-3.** Overlapping Directorates of Spanish Electric Companies and Large Private Banks
Source: Costa, 1976; Serrano and Muñoz, 1979

banking industry. Even public refineries such as Enpetrol had private banking representation corresponding to ownership share on its management councils. Private credit institutions came to be tied to the petroleum refineries because most investment was financed through bank loans. This linkage existed for Banco Ibérico, absorbed by Banco Central in 1978, with respect to Petroliber, Banesto with Petromed, Urquijo with Rio Tinto, and the two Basque banks with the Petronor refinery in Bilbao. Private banks, as the source for required capital, had their interests represented in yet another critical component of the Spanish energy structure.

Petroleum's next step to the pump was transportation and distribution. CAMPSA, the holder of the monopoly for petroleum distribution, was a private company that not only generated revenue for the state but also turned a profit for its stockholders. CAMPSA's financial structure was closely monitored by the delegation of the Ministry of Finance in CAMPSA. However, the Ministry of Finance, or even individual stockholders, did not solely guide policy-making in CAMPSA. The banking industry also managed to occupy a majority of CAMPSA's management board. The banking industry's direct

**Table 6-4**   Spanish Refining Industry, 1980

| Company | Capital (percent) | Principal Private Banks | Refineries | Capacity |
|---|---|---|---|---|
| ENPETROL | 93.84 INI | Guipúzcoano | Escombreras | 10.1 |
| | 6.16 Private | | Puertollano | 6.0 |
| | | | Tarragona | 12.0 |
| PETROLIBER | 52 State | Ibérico (Central | La Coruña | 7.0 |
| | 18 Private | after 1978) | | |
| | 4 CIP | 2% of this Central | | |
| | 28 German | | | |
| CEPSA | 100 Private | Banco Central | Tenerife | 8.0 |
| | Spanish | | Algeciras | 8.0 |
| PETROMED | 100 Private | Banco Español | Castellón | 8.0 |
| | | de Crédito | | |
| Rio Tinto | 100 Private | Urquijo | Huelva | 6.0 |
| PETRONOR | 33 CAMPSA | Vizcaya 11% | Bilbao | 10.0 |
| | 33 Banks | Bilbao 11% | | |
| | 34 PEMEX | Vizcaina 5.5% | | |
| | | Monte de Piedad 5.5% | | |
| ASESA | 50 CAMPSA | Banco Central | Tarragona | 1.1 |
| | 50 CEPSA | | | |
| Total | | | | 76.1 |

Source: Self-elaboration from several sources.

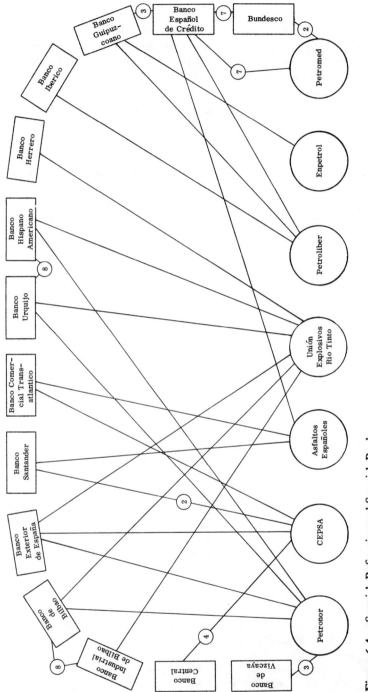

**Figure 6-4.** Spanish Refineries and Spanish Banks
Source: Adapted from Tamames, 1978, p. 209

representation on CAMPSA's policy-making body, in addition to its indirect support through refinery representation, gave banking a strong voice in the formulation of policy in CAMPSA. Figure 6-5 shows that the banks were extensively linked to CAMPSA through representatives on the company's administrative council. All major Spanish banks except Banco Central had at least one representative on CAMPSA's board. Banco Central was different because it created CEPSA's Tenerife refinery in the Canary Islands, where the Monopoly did not apply. Despite the absence of Banco Central, Spain's banking representatives undoubtedly strongly influenced decisions about the Monopoly. Thus the banks were in a position to promote their interests directly in decision-making in CAMPSA.

The overlapping directorates of the banks and the electricity companies, the refineries, CAMPSA, JEN, and other nonenergy companies reinforced the cohesion of the banking industry itself. Since many banking officials often worked together with colleagues from the other major banks through third companies such as those in electricity and refining, information and perspectives were readily shared. A set of common economic and political norms came to guide the membership of this oligarchy. These norms were continually reinforced. The nature of these norms was important because the banks owed their position in the financial community to pre-democratic regimes.

## Government Overlap in Regimes

As discussed earlier, the Franco regime placed little priority on economic policy during its early years. With the passage of time, the lifting of economic sanctions by the United States in the early 1950s, the continuation of economic hardship, and finally the domestic economic reforms of 1959, economic policy increasingly became important to the government.[16] Spain's economic miracle of the 1960s and early 1970s was both produced by and a consequence of increased need for government economic policy-making and planning. With the increased importance of economic policy and concern for industrialization and modernization, government reliance on Spain's financial elite grew. This reliance led to an increased concentration of "technicians" in the later Francoist cabinets.[17] This technician group became the largest group in the Francoist Council of Ministers in 1963 and came to dominate it by 1969, surpassing men with "military" and "political" (Falangist, or monarchist) backgrounds.[18] The twenty-eight "technicians" in the various Francoist Council of Ministers included sixteen who were related to business or banking.[19] This technical group provided a foundation for policy continuity during the transition to democracy. Not only did the Franco regime increas-

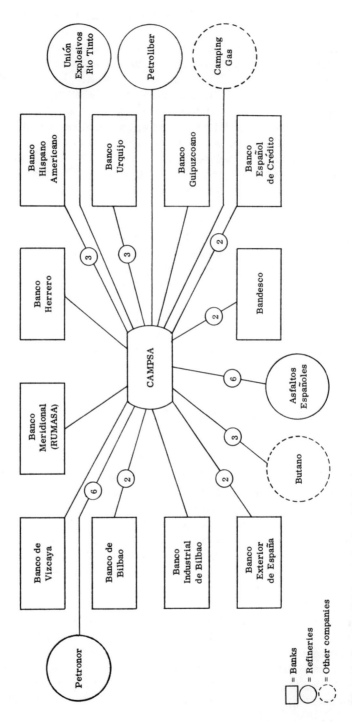

**Figure 6-5.** CAMPSA and the Spanish Banks
Source: Adapted from Tamames, 1978, p. 209

□ = Banks
○ = Refineries
○ = Other companies

ingly rely on the domestic economic community for political support, but economic policy came to be formulated with the assistance of this financial and business community.

Many of these technicians were members of Opus Dei, the secret Catholic lay organization. Through its broad investments in the economy, its influence in the universities since the Civil War, and its political connections with key officials, Opus Dei came to provide an increasing number of the technocrats in Franco's government.[20] Opus Dei proved to be a central influence in economic planning and policy management. Early on, Opus Dei placed three economic-related ministries under its influence: Finance under Navarro Rubio, Commerce under Ullastres, and the Presidency of the Government under Luis Carrero Blanco. Much of the success in Spain's economic planning during the 1960s and early 1970s grew out of shared policy norms and coordination between these and other ministries. Particularly evident was that "hostility between budgeters and planners was muted by close ties between" the Planning Commission and the Ministry of Finance. The latter was headed by Mariano Navarro Rubio, an Opus Dei technocrat.[21] A "sharing (of) similar policy values (especially a belief in the value of rapid economic growth under 'trickle-down' economic policies) and a common factional membership" mitigated potential conflict.[22] Opus Dei fell into disfavor during the latter part of the Franco regime. Nevertheless, its influence on policy remained openly present in Spain's administrative structure even after the transition to democracy.[23]

The banking industry was, however, a more direct link in policy-making continuity from authoritarianism to democracy. Table 6-5 reveals the Franco regime's growth in reliance on the financial community for policy-making assistance. The regime consolidated itself in the years immediately after the Civil War through a heavy reliance on Franco's military colleagues. Beginning in 1946, Franco's decision-making circle relied quite heavily on the families that comprised Spain's economic elite and, more specifically, on the powers behind the banking system. Overlapping directorates in government's top executive positions and the board of directors of the private banks gave banking direct representation in the immediate post-war period. Its greatest direct representation came, however, during the latter years of the Franco regime. The private banks had fifty-five representatives in high public positions at one time or another in the six years between 1969 and 1975. Seventeen of these fifty-five were directly linked to the major banks. The fact that Urquijo, with strong ties to Franco's family, was part of the Hispano banking group helps explain the high representation of Hispano in these governments. An additional forty-two officials were indirectly connected to these banks by virtue of their family's economic holdings and investments. Both these direct and indirect linkages between Franco's policymakers and the apex of the financial oligarchy not only provided a sufficient position for self-enrichment, but also created a basis for policy-making inertia during the transition.

We can draw further inferences about policy continuation during the transition to democracy by contrasting Table 6-5 with Table 6-6. The second table reveals executive overlap between the government and the private banking interests during the early years of the transition. Table 6-6 shows that the first four post-Franco cabinets included a total of twenty-six ministers directly linked to the banks and twenty-four indirectly connected through their families. While down from the 1969–75 period, we can see that despite movement toward democracy, Spain's executive leadership chose to continue to include in its inner circle numerous officials of the private banks.

The government of Carlos Arias Navarro, which took power immediately after Franco's death, reflected its basic Francoist orientation. The immediate inheritor of the Francoist standard sought to perpetuate in as many ways as possible the regime Franco had created. This overlap in executive power nevertheless occurred even after more democratic steps were taken. The first government of Adolfo Suárez, appointed by the King and confirmed by the Francoist parliament, did not make any immediate political changes.[24] This cautious political stepping included cabinet composition. Suárez's first cabinet contained as many representatives of the banking industry as the Arias government. Suárez's second government, formed after the 15 June 1977 elections, contained five ministers directly connected to the private banks: Justice and Foreign Affairs each occupied by men from Banesto, and Commerce, Culture, and Industry and Energy each with Hispano-Urquijo people. The last Suárez government, formed in 1978, contained more bank-

**Table 6-5**   Overlapping Directorates of the Governmental Executive (Ministers, Subsecretaries, and Director Generals) and Spanish Private Banks

|  | 1939–45 | 1946–59 | 1960–68 | 1969–75 |
|---|---|---|---|---|
| Banesto | 1 | 2 | 1 | 4 (11) |
| Hispano Group | — | 6 (10) | — (2) | 7 (15) |
| Central Group | — | — (4) | — (3) | — (2) |
| Bilbao Group | — | — | 3 (7) | 1 (5) |
| Vizcaya Group | — | 1 | — | 3 (3) |
| Popular Group | — | 4 | 3 | 2 (4) |
| Rumasa | — | — | — | — (2) |
| Other Banks | — | 8 | 9 | 38 |

First numbers: individual relations
Second numbers: family relations
SOURCE: Adapted from González et al., 1981.

ing representation than any of the previous post-Franco governments. In this last cabinet reshuffling, Alberto Oliart—a board member of the Bank of San Sebastian from 1974 to 1976, director general of Banco Hispano Americano between 1974 and 1977, and board member of Banco Urquijo between 1974 and 1978—was replaced by Agustin Rodríques Sahagún, allied with the Bilbao group.

Table 6-7 elaborates the banking representatives in Suarez's third government. It lists the names of the representatives, the bank they served, and the ministry they headed. It is fair to say that the positions these individuals occupied were not peripheral ones. The banking industry had strong representation at the highest levels of government even well into the transition. The government's use of the banking system as a recruitment pool provided a personal nexus with the Franco regime: "Many institutions under the UCD remained largely in the hands of the same people as before" the transition.[25] Thus, most policy-making in the public arena was not insulated from the influence of the financial oligarchy.

The personnel overlap in the government and banking industry could also be found in the legislature, creating policy continuity beyond just the executive or cabinet level. In the first parliament after the 1977 election, both Manuel Fraga's Popular Alliance and the UCD had seats held by men who sat in the Francoist Cortes. Many of these had been in the Cortes since 1968,

**Table 6-6**  Spanish Governmental Executive Power and Relations with the Private Banks

| Bank Groups | Arias Government formed 11/75 | First Suárez Government formed 6/76 | Second Suárez Government formed 6/77 | Third Suárez Government formed 8/78 |
|---|---|---|---|---|
| Banesto | 1 (1) | 2 (1) | 2 (2) | 2 |
| Hispano | 3 (1) | 2 (1) | 3 (1) | 3 (4) |
| Central | 1 (1) | — | — (2) | — |
| Bilbao | 1 | 2 | — | 1 |
| Popular | — (1) | — | — | — |
| Santander | — | — | — | — (1) |
| Rumasa | 1 | — (1) | — | — (2) |
| Madrid | — | 1 | — | — (1) |
| Others | — | — | — | 1 (4) |
| Total | 7 (4) | 7 (3) | 5 (5) | 7 (12) |

First numbers: direct ties
Second numbers: family ties
SOURCE: Adapted from González et al., 226.

**Table 6-7**    The Third Suárez Government and the Spanish Banks

| Name | Ministerial Position | Bank |
|------|---------------------|------|
| Leopoldo Calvo Sotelo | E.E.C. Relations | B. Urquijo (Board Member) |
| Manuel Clavero Arevalo | Culture | Sevilla Savings (President) |
| Julian García Anoveros | Finance | B. Urquijo (Head of Research Services) |
| António Ibañez Freire | Interior | B. Comercial Español (Board Member) |
| Marcelino Oreja Aguirre | Foreign Affairs | B. Guipuzcoano (Board Member) |
| Agustin Rodríquez Sahagún | Defense | B. Bilbao (Board Member) |
| Juan Rovira Tarazona | Health and Social Security | B. Exterior (Board Member) |
| Jesús Sancho Rof | Public Works and Urbanism | B. Rural y Mediterráneo (Spokesman) |

SOURCE: González et al., (1981), 224.

when family representatives were first elected. Most were of a younger generation who participated in the less authoritarian years of the regime. Most started their political careers in the youth organization, the Sindicatos, or public bureaucracy, and often closely associated with Opus Dei. With the initial steps toward democracy, these individuals quickly donned democratic coats, generally with either AP or UCD party labels. While many UCD members, unlike AP, did not defend the past, the political biographies of some in the leadership of UCD reflect an orientation of continuity.[26] Many of these men, whose political lives began under the rules of the Franco regime, still considered this a useful experience and wanted to see the previous regime and their role in it respected. They nevertheless accepted democratic principles.[27]

The parliament formed after the March 1979 elections provides a good opportunity to verify at the legislative level the continuation from Spain's nondemocratic past of the representation of financial interests. The second democratic parliament had strong banking representation through the UCD, the party in government, and AP, later part of Democratic Coalition, as well as the ultra-right National Union, the Basque National Party, and the Catalunya Democratic Pact. The elections of 1977 did reduce private bank representation in parliament from its higher level in the Francoist Cortes. Bank representation nevertheless remained quite strong. Of the 350 deputies in the Congress, forty-seven had direct private banking connections, twenty-five personally and twenty-two through their families. Eleven of the deputies were with the UCD, three of which had served in the last Francoist legislature, and AP had four, who all served in the last Francoist Cortes. This decrease was partially compensated for by some of the forty royal senators named directly by the King. Thus it is safe to say that even with democratic reform, a constant and significant voice of the domestic banking industry continued to be heard in the circles of government that made energy policy. Such overlap in personnel provided an additional basis for continuity in energy policy.

The banking industry often directly translated its economic position into political influence. Domestic banking strongly influenced UCD, the party in government until late 1982. Table 6-7 demonstrates that many UCD ministers were directly tied to the banking industry. Its influence also took a more overt political form. For example, at one point during a particularly rough period, representatives of Los Siete Grandes met with then-president of UCD Rodríquez Sahagún to guarantee protection of their interests and promotion of their concerns. They told the president of UCD that his party would be defeated in the next election through support by the banks of forces that would defend business interests if the government did not change its policies.[28] And such pressure was also applied through specific energy-related concerns. For example, the construction of nuclear plants was a particularly lucrative business in Spain, so much so that the election of UCD in 1979 was financed in large part by the principal beneficiaries of this business. In addition, sizable contributions to UCD's campaign came from electric-company funds.[29]

## Power Base Continuation

The domestic banking industry was a major power behind energy policy in Spain during the transition to democracy. The influence of banking on energy policy and planning was felt by many others involved in the politics of the transition. Specialists in the politics of domestic energy in the Socialist labor union, UGT, for example, spoke often of the oligarchy's influence on energy policy. As an example, they highlighted the close working relationship between UNESA and the banks.[30] These energy specialists expressed opinions that the power of the banks was total.

During the transition, attempts to alter "business as usual" in energy politics were often thwarted. For example, while in opposition to the UCD, the Socialists and Communists proposed a public company statute that sought to fix the criteria for the operations of public companies, whose existence the Constitution recognizes equally with private enterprise, to avoid their subjection to the criteria of the different ministries. The Communists argued that no controls existed over the public companies or over INI. The Left suggested that UCD gained benefits from this lack of control over public companies.[31] A conflict over coal importation between Carbónex (public) and Aprocar (private) exemplified this shortcoming. Simply stated, these two companies were locked in a competition over business "turf." The more recently created Carbonex sought a greater hand in coal importation. The UCD Minister of Industry and Energy nevertheless considered any public company statute unnecessary.[32] The UCD government resolved this conflict in its own way with a "gentleman's agreement" with Pérez Iturrioz, an employee of Banco Central and the firm behind Aprocar, being named to the administrative board of Carbónex. Later, on 16 December 1980, the Committee on Industry and Energy in parliament rejected the broader bill on public companies given its lack of backing by the government.[33] Energy management, with strong direction given by private business and banking interests, continued as in the past.

The Socialist victory in the election of October 1982 and its ascension to power in December of that year in many regards meant the completion of Spain's transition to democracy. The peaceful transition of power stemmed from Spain's moderate party system.[34] This moderation signaled little change in the structural arrangement of economically oriented public policy-making.[35] Such moderation dashed many analysts' beliefs that a real change of economic policy-making would come with a change in government. Because the development of interest groups effectively faltered during the transition, Spain's political parties were given the onus of responsibility for the management of conflicts.[36] But since 1979 and following its 1982 electoral victory, PSOE advocated one of the mildest programs of any major European socialist party. As discussed later in greater detail, between PSOE's victory in 1982 and the 1 January 1986 entry of Spain into the European Economic Community (EEC), very little changed in terms of economic policy-making. The PSOE did little to alter the basic relationships within the country's economic system. Virtually no radical reforms or nationalizations followed the Socialists' victory, unlike, for example, Mitterrand in France in 1981. The one promise PSOE made along these lines in energy, the nationalization of the high-tension delivery system for electricity, was quite mild in comparison to its rhetoric of the 1970s. The only public takeover suggested that the financial oligarchy remained quite strong.

In early spring of 1983, the government "appropriated" the financial conglomerate Rumasa.[37] The reasons behind the appropriation were numerous. During the 1960s, Rumasa established an extremely secretive business style, one that raised many questions among its competitors concerning the legality of some activities. This company had grown extremely fast and quickly became very powerful. More interesting than why Rumasa was appropriated is the question of why the Socialists were able to accomplish this without opposition from the banking community. One possible explanation is that the other banks resented this newcomer to the industry. Given the eccentric behavior surrounding Rumasa's operations, it had not fully established itself within the political-business community sufficiently enough to protect its position.[38] The Siete Grandes possibly did not come to Rumasa's aid since they saw it as an unfair competitor and they did not perceive themselves as threatened by nationalizations. Important to this is that PSOE made it very clear that this appropriation would go no further. The established banks perceived this action as an opportunity to fortify their positions. In terms of the Socialists' careful handling of the financial oligarchy, PSOE made clear it had no intention of maintaining public control of Rumasa. Instead, it reprivatized Rumasa by selling off its individual components. The government simply served as an instrument of anti-trust activities in a country that had no anti-trust laws.

On another front, the Socialist's victory in the 1982 election brought an interesting, although not surprising, development in the area of energy administration. When Felipe González organized his first government, a logical choice for Minister of Industry and Energy was Javier Solana, the PSOE deputy who had led the parliamentary attacks on PEN between 1977 and 1982. Solana had long been the spokesman for PSOE on energy. His outspokenness drew praise from his partisan colleagues and bitterness from those supporting PEN. Nevertheless, Felipe González passed over Solana in his choice of Minister of Industry and Energy. Once PSOE was in power and had to work with the vested economic interests, Solana's presence would probably have proved detrimental. Instead, González selected Carlos Solchaga and named Solana as minister of Culture. (Several years later he also became government spokesman.) Solana had clearly seen the overlap between public and private energy structures and the personnel linkages discussed above. He was thus quite forthright about the powers he had confronted: "The private energy sector in Spain constitutes an enormous interest group, whose power and imbrications with the State are continually demonstrated. It suffices to recall the confrontations that took place during PEN-79's writing which consumed more than eleven months, dragging with it a few officials."[39] Even Solana, to some people's surprise, was ultimately one of these officials dragged out of energy policy-making.

A policy-making nexus existed in Spain during the transition between the government, the energy industry, and the domestic banking community.

Banking was the core of the country's financial oligarchy. The existence of this financial oligarchy was established in this chapter as well as its connections to central components of the energy industry. This suggested the importance of the energy industry to the overall economy, the importance to the economy of the banking industry, and the linkages between the two. The analysis then considered the government. Evidence revealed the central position the banking industry occupied in early democratic cabinets and at the upper echelons of many ministries. On the whole, this chapter sought to present evidence, albeit indirect, that energy policy during the early transition in Spain was based on a hand-in-glove relationship between the government, the financial oligarchy, and the various industries that supplied Spain its energy.

The continued existence of the financial oligarchy and its presence in energy policy-making circles during the transition to democracy helps explain policy continuity in Spain. The banking industry's link to the government itself, which formulated policy, including energy; banking's role in many key energy companies such as in electricity, refining, and CAMPSA as holder of the monopoly for gasoline distribution; and the profitability for banks in investments in numerous areas of energy provided both the motivation and the means to push for a continuation of national energy policy. This energy policy focused almost entirely on supply at the neglect of demand management and conservation. This emphasis maximized profits for those who had invested in the Spanish energy industries. The direction of Spain's National Energy Plan thus greatly benefitted the domestic financial community. And protection of profitability on capital investment meant continued support for PEN. This economic reality was not significantly altered by political reform, such as the transition to democracy.

# 7

# International Support for Energy Policy: The International Energy Agency

The politics of energy policy-making in Spain during the transition to democracy inevitably involved more than just domestic actors. An international context to policy-making should be considered, particularly given the role of energy in world politics. This chapter looks at international influences on energy planning in Spain.

Many individuals and groups opposed the National Energy Plan for reasons other than the influence on it by the domestic financial oligarchy. Opponents of Spain's energy policy, particularly those of the Left, perceived these financial-business decision-makers as part of a broader, international economic elite. They saw energy policy, and its roots in the Franco regime, as a product of domestic collaboration with international capital. These critics argued that energy policy in Spain and the nuclear program in particular resulted from economic penetration by the United States and other Western countries into Spain.[1] Some extremists talked about a conspiracy by international capital.[2]

Factual or not, questions raised by these intellectuals and political activists about the international influences on domestic policy are relevant here. Energy policy-making during Spain's transition did not occur in national isolation; it was formulated within the domain of international politics. The previous argument about a domestic financial-business oligarchy is logically linked to questions about international support of energy policy. As mentioned earlier, Spain's nuclear program included such companies as Westinghouse and General Electric. Influences such as international capital, the flow of technological information, the ethical and legal behavior of large corporations, and anachronistic events like regional armed conflicts, e.g., the war between Iran and Iraq, had an impact on Spanish energy policy. International organizations such as OPEC, the United Nations, the World Bank, the International Monetary Fund, the Organization for Economic Co-Operation and Development, its International Energy Agency, the International Atomic Energy Agency, and the European Economic Community also influenced the direction of energy policy in Spain.

The impact on Spanish energy policy of all these international organizations, multinational companies, and unpredictable world events merits greater analysis than is possible here. Nevertheless, the crux of the arguments about international influences on Spanish energy policy requires some consideration. What type of support did policymakers in Spain receive from outside its borders? What was the relationship between Spanish domestic and international energy policymakers? And, central to this analysis, did any international organizations reinforce the policy-making role of the domestic financial oligarchy?

This chapter addresses these questions by focusing on one such organization—the International Energy Agency. The IEA is taken as an example of the broader concerns of organized international influences on Spain's domestic energy policy. The IEA is an especially good example because it was created as the West's response to the 1973 oil crisis. The IEA sought to coordinate policy responses to the changing situation of energy. Since the U.S. in large part determined the overall direction of the IEA, it serves as an example of the types of international constraints imposed on energy policy-making in Spain. Much research has been conducted on the IEA itself, but few if any studies analyze the impact of the IEA on an individual country's energy policies.[3] This chapter addresses this lacuna. It examines the link between the IEA and Spain's energy program. It assesses the specific manner in which the IEA aided in energy planning in Spain. In an indirect manner, then, this chapter analyzes the manner in which the IEA reinforced the financial oligarchy's position in energy policy-making.

I begin with a brief description of the International Energy Agency. Next the political and ideological conflicts that surrounded the IEA's influence on energy planning during the transition are analyzed. Then more specific accounts of the influence of IEA on Spanish energy planning are presented, along with Spanish participation in various programs of the Agency. Finally, IEA support of Spain's nuclear energy program is discussed.

## The IEA and Spanish Politics

The International Energy Agency (IEA) was born on 15 November 1974 as the response of the Western industrialized nations to OPEC. The 1973–74 petroleum crisis produced the initial confrontational character of the IEA. Its raison d'être was to coordinate diplomatic pressure and present a united front to OPEC. The IEA later developed a more conciliatory, cooperative-oriented posture. Its essential goals were to prevent further price increases, to reduce the dependency of member countries on petroleum, and to secure oil supplies. The IEA assisted in the coordination of national energy programs and planning. It encouraged closer cooperation in developing alternative energy supplies and helped finance research and development. The IEA's core programs were its Emergency Allocation Scheme, reflecting its earlier confrontational nature, the encouragement of more long-term energy programs, and the coordination of R & D projects between member countries. The IEA was an autonomous body of the Organization for Economic Co-Operation and Development (OECD). During Spain's transition to democracy, twenty-one of OECD's twenty-four countries were IEA members.[4] Spain was a charter member.

Spain's dependence on foreign oil and its economic susceptibility to rises in petroleum prices motivated Spanish governments to participate in IEA activities.[5] National energy planning in Spain preceded the IEA by fifteen years. Nevertheless, once organized, the IEA assisted in Spain's energy planning.[6] During the transition, the IEA figured in the politics of Spain's energy program by encouraging its general direction. Because of this encouragement, the IEA's role in energy planning in Spain revolved around the larger political conflicts of the country's energy program. Simply stated, the politics of the IEA within Spanish energy planning was part of the larger Left-Right division that characterized the early history of the National Energy Plan.

Governments during the transition, the UCD governments of 1977 through late 1982, and to a lesser degree the Socialist government of Felipe González, often used the IEA as a means to justify PEN's basic orientation. Government officials highlighted points of compatibility between PEN and the IEA in order to give credibility to domestic energy planning. For instance, the IEA figured in the parliamentary debates during the ratification of PEN-79. The two right-of-center parties, the Union of the Democratic Center (UCD) and Popular Alliance (AP), mentioned the IEA in the parliamentary debates. The minister of Industry, Carlos Bustelo, stated in his introductory remarks that

> the energy policy established by the Plan responds to the international recommendations on this question, especially those given by the International Energy Agency and the advice of the OECD and are in line with the solutions adopted by countries with socioeconomic conditions similar to ours.[7]

UCD energy spokesman Goméz Angulo made the same point:

> And these principles and measures each in their turn correspond to the twelve fundamental points suggested for the different countries facing the energy problem, outlined by the International Energy Agency created by the World Conference convened in Washington in 1974.[8]

He then proceeded to list all twelve points adopted by the IEA at its October 1977 ministerial level meeting. The spokesman for AP also mentioned the IEA in the context of conservation, emphasizing PEN's savings in industry and highway transportation.[9] The fact that IEA figured in these debates suggests that in formulating national energy plans, Spanish policy officials were cognizant of IEA recommendations.

The propensity of Spain's right-of-center parties to cast energy planning in line with IEA desires did not stop with the parliamentary debates. Officials were quick to refer to the IEA in other situations in order to justify energy policies. IEA recommendations were often used as a standard, benchmark, or goal. Responsible for much of the writing of PEN-79, Florentino Escobar of the Ministry of Industry and Energy and the Center for Energy Studies also cast consumption projections in the context of IEA recommendations.[10] The UCD minister of Industry and Energy, Ignacio Bayón, even proudly pointed out that parts of Spanish energy planning went beyond the Agency's recommendations.[11] Thus PEN was generally consistent with IEA recommendations.

During the early stages of the transition, Spanish officials projected a great deal of harmony between the IEA and domestic energy planning. The IEA reinforced the general orientation of energy planning formulated by the political Right. While some disagreement occasionally occurred, in general the Spanish Right was committed to maintaining a close working relationship with the IEA.

The Left, on the other hand, generally placed energy planning in a much broader context: political and economic power stemming from capital concentration that permitted control of the capitalistic structure in Spain. Its arguments included international economic penetration into Spain. The relationship of the IEA to Spain's energy program, they argued, was manifested in the government's failure to address national needs. The influence of the multinational petroleum- and nuclear-energy industries, e.g., Westinghouse and General Electric, in both the IEA and Spain's energy program were a major cause of this.

This perception could be seen in the Socialist labor union, the UGT:

> The nuclearization of the capitalist world is being driven principally by the large multinational companies, increasingly rich and strong. . . . These companies increasingly find within their reach the means to determine many countries' energy policies and to control their plans, power further facilitated by the actions of international organizations of integration and cooperation, in which the presence of the multinationals' interests is hegemonic.[12]

Footnoted at the end of this statement as examples of such international organizations were the OECD, implying the IEA, the International Atomic Energy Agency, the Trilateral Commission, the World Bank, and the International Monetary Fund.

At least in its rhetoric, the Left viewed the IEA as dominated by the U.S. and thus another arm of international capitalism.[13] The IEA was, it emphasized, a product of the diplomacy of Henry Kissinger following the 1973–74 OPEC oil embargo. The U.S. took the lead in proposing and organizing this attempt at energy cooperation. During Spain's transition, the Left considered the IEA as an instrument of the U.S. in the international oil market. This belief was reinforced by France's refusal to join the IEA and by others who argued that the IEA was not only a united response by the OECD to energy problems but also an attempt by the United States to mold the OECD countries into an institutional framework which it could control.[14] A prominent Socialist party member involved with energy policy expressed this understanding that the IEA was controlled by the large industrial countries: "We have almost no influence there because the influence is held by the United States, West Germany, Japan, the United Kingdom . . . no more. . . . As in OECD, the others are no more than accompaniment, the supporting cast."[15] The Left feared that collaboration with international organizations under American domination permitted only further penetration into the Spanish economy and economic planning by the U.S. and multinational companies. The Spanish Left's concern about membership in U.S. dominated organizations like the IEA strongly paralleled its early opposition to membership in NATO.[16]

The Left, however, did not perceive the IEA as the most critical issue in energy policy-making. Given its view that the IEA was only a small part of a much larger problem, the Spanish Left generally did not go out of its way to criticize this international organization. For example, the center-to-left political parties—the Socialists (PSOE) and the Communists (PCE)—did not emphasize the IEA in the parliamentary debates on PEN-79. In addition, when interviewed, PSOE members of the Congress of Deputies did not suggest that the IEA was of fundamental concern to them in their criticisms of energy policy-making.[17] Nor did ecological groups or labor unions take the offensive against the IEA.[18] When they did speak of the IEA, they indicated it was just another leg upon which PEN's heavy emphasis on nuclear energy and its controlling financial oligarchy could rest. And following the 1979 accident at Harrisburg, both the PSOE and PCE took anti-nuclear positions: they reasoned that the nuclear program incorporated in PEN benefitted the private electricity industry and the Spanish banking system. The Socialists and Communists found the IEA's encouragement of Spain's nuclear program consistent with the interests of international capital, and saw the IEA as an instrument of these interests.

Despite the political criticism and the ideological split, it is still a fact that PEN was formulated by a Francoist government and later revised by the UCD and PSOE governments. Energy policy-making in Spain was first guided by parties to the right of center, initially during the Franco period, then under UCD's democratic control of policy-making, and later by the PSOE. As discussed later, Felipe González's Socialist government did not pursue much reform in energy policy. The early views the Spanish Left held about the IEA remained largely outside the formation of energy plans. Governments willing to permit the influence of IEA and its assistance in energy policy-making characterized both authoritarian Spain and democracy during the transition. We thus turn to some particulars of how these governments worked with the IEA.

## Planning Assistance

The IEA coordinated among its member countries projects, investments, and technology relating to energy development and planning. These activities were coordinated by the Secretariat of the IEA, which served as the Combined Energy Staff of the OECD. The Secretariat acted on the policy decisions taken by the Board of Governors. The effect the IEA had on domestic energy planning in Spain during the transition can be seen in its main programs. Planning assistance came from the IEA in three ways: an emergency allocation system, a cooperative effort on energy research and development, and energy forecasting and planning. Their relation to Spain's energy program during the transition to democracy will each be dealt with in turn.

## Emergency Allocation Program

The IEA's central program was its collective contingency plan for a major disruption of oil supplies. The International Energy Emergency Allocation Program was a coordinated plan to share available oil supplies among the members in another embargo situation. The decision process to activate this plan began with the Secretariat, which monitored supplies. This process would have begun when a 7 percent shortage was anticipated in any member's total oil supplies. This figure left some room for squeezing consumption before international allocations and redistributions were to be implemented. If a shortage was found, it was to be immediately reported to the Management Committee and the Governing Board. These two bodies had to act within two and four days respectively. The decision of the governing board to activate the Emergency Allocation Program was to be implemented within fifteen days by all member countries. The decision-making procedure to activate this program was potentially highly political, especially given the nature of a complicated weighted voting scheme. Once implemented, the plan called for a mixture of restraints on consumption, withdrawal from stocks or "drawdown," and reallocation.[19] The Emergency Allocation Program also called for a stockpiling of oil supplies. Drawdown by a member during such an emergency period assumed compliance with the IEA's compulsory stockpile regulation. The level of required stockpiles was raised in 1980 from seventy to ninety days of total oil imports.[20]

Petroleum storage by IEA members was of considerable psychological importance to Spain, given its unfavorable energy situation. The stockpiling program was perceived by some Spanish officials as being the most important function of the IEA.[21] The backup supply was an important component of energy planning since Spanish authorities could apply to the compensation fund. Furthermore, Spain actively participated in it, according to one official, because it was institutionally easy to do so. CAMPSA, the petroleum monopoly, facilitated control of all petroleum-related information. Public control of this information had no equal in the world, according to this official. Known at all times were the quantity of crude in shipment, how much was stored, where it was stored, and who was consuming what.[22] This centralization, the official added, made the Spanish petroleum structure very compatible with such programs as IEA's petroleum stockpiling.

In Spain, views on the IEA's Energy Allocation Program appeared consensual. Both the Left and Right saw this program as beneficial. However, pessimism prevailed. For example, one PSOE energy official stated: "I believe this system wouldn't function if it had to be implemented but at least it is prepared."[23] Regardless of party affiliation, officials also acknowledged that the major Western powers dominated the IEA. The UCD saw Spain's vulnerability in this IEA program. Officials spoke with displeasure about the Governing Board's weighted voting system, which facilitated major power domination.[24] Ignácio Bayón, the UCD Industry and Energy minister, reflected this in his statement that to activate the Energy Allocation Program it would be necessary for "the more powerful countries less burdened by energy deficiencies carry out their promises."[25] This statement highlights Spain's susceptibility to the more powerful forces within the IEA.

## R & D and Joint Projects

An important objective of the IEA was to promote international collaboration in the development of new technology that fully utilized the national resources of member countries. The Long Term Cooperative Program, agreed to in January 1976, provided a framework for joint investment projects by two or more countries in domestic resource development.[26] Here members moved beyond mere information exchanges to a coordinated joint project. Some argued, however, that relatively little cooperative R & D development took place.[27] Hence, the coordination and specialization of effort which might have made energy R & D expenditures more effective were largely unrealized. As seen in the Spanish case during the transition, national energy R & D efforts remained independently determined. Many of the projects remained single-nation undertakings but with cooperation in investment.

For example, the IEA promoted high-temperature solar-energy production in an area of Spain that annually receives almost 3,000 hours of sun with very little rainfall. This project led to the construction of two 500KW solar plants that began operations in September 1981.[28] Situated in Tabernas, near Almeria in the south, they cost about 3,200 million pesetas. West Germany provided 37 percent of the capital investment, the United States 18 percent, Spain 15 percent, Italy 7 percent, Belgium 6 percent, Switzerland 5.5 percent, Austria 4.5 percent, and Greece 2 percent. The two plants met the needs of 1,500 area residents.[29] These two solar plants were later complemented by the CESA1 solar project in Almeria. Approved by the Spanish government in 1977, it used only domestic technology. Thus IEA-coordinated projects appeared to be a catalyst for further development.

Spain was a reluctant participant in energy R & D despite these occasional successes. Of the forty-six IEA programs and projects in 1980–81, Spain participated in only thirteen.[30] Of these, Spain joined in on five of the seven IEA-sponsored projects in solar energy, but none of the other alternative energy projects, and four of ten of the projects in coal technology. Notably absent was Spanish participation in energy conservation: only two of fifteen IEA projects, up from none of seven in the 1977–78 period.[31]

This lack of R & D in conservation reinforced the generally held belief, discussed earlier, that PEN was not concerned with the demand side of energy. Some Spanish officials justified the lack of participation in these projects by making references to a lack of resources.[32] Table 7-1 suggests that national energy R & D was a problem in Spain. Per-capita government R & D was one of the lowest in the IEA. The fact that Spanish R & D remained constant over the years indicates that Spain never committed large financial resources to energy R & D. This lack of participation occurred in part because funding and participation in IEA projects was voluntary. The IEA itself did not provide finances for these projects. It served as a coordinator, an intermediary.[33] There was no central IEA fund. Financial support was the sole responsibility of the participants. Projects were either task-sharing, with participant financing, or jointly funded, particularly with larger projects, with all participating members contributing to a common fund.[34] Constrained by domestic economic considerations, Spanish governments were reluctant to undertake many international ventures that did not have immediate economic or political benefits. Energy planning in R & D during the transition to democracy thus continued as it had since the Franco regime: constrained by the very economic conditions a lack of such long-term developments helped promote.

The absolute level of R & D funding in Spain during the transition was not very high compared to other countries. Nor did Spain heavily participate in IEA-coordinated R & D projects. Nevertheless, the IEA did figure in Spanish energy policy in the area of R & D. The IEA and its member countries played a role in the determination of the direction of Spanish R & D policy, limited as it was. Allocations of R & D funds in Spain closely paralleled other IEA members, suggesting indirect IEA influence. Table 7-2 shows that of total research and development expenditures of IEA members in 1978, 30.8 percent went to conventional nuclear fission and 29.2 percent to the Breeder and Fusion programs. This combined total of 60 percent for nuclear research and development in the IEA compared favorably to Spain's 69.9 percent. Policymakers in Spain felt that the heavy emphasis on nuclear energy in PEN was supported by the IEA and its members.[35] The same applied to the weak emphasis on conservation R & D. The expenditures of IEA members included only 6.2 percent for energy conservation, and only 14.8 percent of R & D expenditure came under renewable energy and conservation grouped together.[36] In addition, the IEA devoted 12.6 percent to conservation in industrial R & D expenditures for 1978.[37] Spain was below all IEA countries in both conservation and new energy sources. Spanish industrial R & D expenditures in the same year attributed only 10.6 percent to conservation. The IEA served as a point of reference, then, for Spanish offi-

**Table 7-1**   Government Energy R & D, Ranking of IEA Countires, 1978

| Country | Government R & D per capita (US $) | GDP per capita (US $) |
| --- | --- | --- |
| Greece | 0.1 | 2.9 |
| Ireland | 0.8 | 3.8 |
| New Zealand | 1.1 | 4.9 |
| Spain | 1.3 | 3.8 |
| Austria | 2.9 | 7.9 |
| Italy | 3.1 | 4.2 |
| Denmark | 4.8 | 10.8 |
| U.K. | 5.6 | 5.6 |
| Switzerland | 6.1 | 14.1 |
| Japan | 6.9 | 8.4 |
| Canada | 6.9 | 8.6 |
| Netherlands | 7.7 | 9.3 |
| Norway | 7.8 | 9.9 |
| Sweden | 9.9 | 10.4 |
| Belgium | 13.9 | 10.0 |
| United States | 14.8 | 9.6 |
| Germany | 15.1 | 10.4 |

SOURCE: IEA, *Annual Report on Energy Research, Development and Demonstration* (Paris: OECD, 1979), 158.

cials to compare their own policy direction. These comparisons helped justify and encourage, albeit indirectly, the continuation of domestic energy policy.

During the transition, energy R & D in Spain followed the IEA's lead in most areas, particularly in nuclear energy. In 1978, policy in energy channeled 65.2 percent of R & D resources to conventional nuclear energy and an additional 4.7 percent on more advanced research in this area. Table 7-3 suggests that this nuclear emphasis was not just limited to R & D. Much of Spain's financial investment in energy followed this same pattern. The electricity industry strongly pushed investment in nuclear energy. Since a central feature of PEN was its investment schedule, these figures suggest that the IEA's R & D emphasis influenced, or at least helped justify, the direction of Spain's nuclear program. This international support for policy did not help rectify the persistent overestimation by Spanish officials of the potential contribution of nuclear energy.

## Technology and Energy Models

A third and more direct manner in which the IEA influenced domestic energy policy-making during Spain's transition was in the area of quantitative

**Table 7-2**   Government R & D Budgets, 1978

|  | Spain | Italy | Greece | EEC | Total IEA |
|---|---|---|---|---|---|
| Conservation | 4.7% | 6.4% | — | 2.2% | 6.2% |
| Oil, gas, and coal | 9.6% | 0.2% | 11.3% | 20.0% | 6.2% |
| New energy sources | 7.3% | 3.8% | 48.9% | 8.9% | 8.6% |
| Conventional nuclear | 65.2% | 43.3% | 37.5% | 36.1% | 30.8% |
| Fast breeder and nuclear fusion | 4.7% | 44.6% | — | 24.0% | 29.2% |
| Other source and supporting technology | 8.4% | 1.6% | 2.2% | 8.1% | 12.2% |

SOURCE: Adapted from IEA, *Annual Report on Energy Research, Development and Demonstration* (Paris: OECD, 1979), 186–87.


**Table 7-3**   Investment in the Spanish Electrical Industry, 1977–80

|  | 1977 | 1978 | 1979 | 1980 |
|---|---|---|---|---|
| Hydroelectric plants | 4.5% | 9.3% | 8.0% | 5.1% |
| Conventional plants | 15.2% | 20.8% | 16.4% | 17.7% |
| Nuclear plants | 57.1% | 38.7% | 52.7% | 54.3% |
| Transportation and distribution | 23.2% | 31.2% | 22.9% | 22.9% |
| Totals (in millions of current Pesetas) | 148,250 | 162,150 | 197,378 | 260,404 |

SOURCE: Adapted from *La industria española en 1978; La industria española en 1980.*


modeling and energy forecasting. The general information system of the IEA sought to collect objective information about the international oil market. One offshoot of this was the creation of a comprehensive reporting system. Analysis and evaluation in this system included forecast modeling. In 1976, the IEA created a work group in the systems analysis staff to study the energy systems of its member countries. Organized under the IEA's Research and Development committee, this group represented fifteen IEA countries and the Commission of the European Economic Community. There were actually two parallel groups, one centered in the Brookhaven National Laboratory in the U.S. and the other in Julich, Germany. In early 1977, they published a preliminary report on the development of the energy systems of the member countries, projecting the impact that new technologies would have for them. These groups focused on a fundamental analysis of final energy demand and, above all, the transformation of the structure of industry necessary to satisfy it.

In March 1977, the IEA decided to extend this project to include the analysis of energy demand. The result was the model MARKAL, which permitted the quantification of the impact of most factors in energy systems. MARKAL was a dynamic optimization model which could be used as a planning instrument to help reduce arbitrary judgments. It calculated, among other things, the percentage of the participation of each energy source and the capacity of installed equipment at five-year intervals, minimizing the total actual costs of the energy system until the year 2020.[38]

This optimization model developed by the IEA aided Spanish policymakers in assessing their energy situation. More specifically, the MARKAL model became an important instrument for energy planning in the Ministry of Industry and Energy. The energy-planning division in the Ministry used MARKAL during the transition to assess the country's energy situation, and its projections were incorporated into energy policy-making. The nexus between the IEA models and energy planning in Spain was emphasized by the person who drafted PEN-79: "We form part of the IEA, with full participation in the agency . . . where an optimization model has been created called MARKAL in which almost all the members have participated."[39] This official also spoke of demand analysis: "We use complicated energy models, considering consumption by industries, utility consumption, etc., that we have in a model called EL PROCER with which we proceed to estimate national energy demand and then we optimize according to the existing technologies through the model MARKAL."[40]

Tables 7-4 and 7-5 present some quantitative projections of the MARKAL model for Spain and those of PEN-79. Its projections clearly incorporated MARKAL's estimates. The slight differences between the two were attributable to the developmental hypothesis of certain variables that did not exactly coincide in the case of PEN-79 and the IEA; the MARKAL model had to be robust enough to include definitions for eighteen countries.[41] In sum, the use of energy policymakers of these models suggests that the IEA significantly contributed to Spanish energy planning in some key technical areas.

## Published Recommendations

Despite direct, technical assistance to Spanish energy planners, the IEA had its own perception of its influence. The IEA viewed its own fundamental role in each country's domestic energy planning as limited to advice and recommendations. In interviews, IEA officials went out of their way to emphasize that the agency was not an executive body but a consultative organization, a

**Table 7-4**   Projected Spanish Primary Energy Utilization (in percent)

|  | (PEN-79) | (MARKAL Model) | | | |
|---|---|---|---|---|---|
|  | 1987 | 1985 | 1990 | 1995 | 2000 |
| Coal | 16.2 | 18 | 21 | 25 | 27 |
| Natural gas | 5.3 | 5 | 5 | 4 | 2 |
| Nuclear | 14.8 | 12 | 16 | 18 | 25 |
| Petroleum | 54.3 | 55 | 49 | 44 | 38 |
| Renewable | 9.4 | 10 | 9 | 9 | 8 |
| (Hydraulic and others) | | | | | |

SOURCES: Ministerio de Industria y Energía, Plan energético nacional: 1978/1987 (Madrid: Servicio de Publicaciones, 1978, 44. Juan Alegre Marcet "Previsión sobre la demanda de energía en España hasta en año 2000," Boletín Informativo 99: 22. (Madrid: Fundación Juan March.)

**Table 7-5**   Projected Spanish Electrical Generation (in percent)

|  | (PEN-79) | (MARKAL Model) | | | |
|---|---|---|---|---|---|
|  | 1987 | 1985 | 1990 | 1995 | 2000 |
| Coal | 26.8 | 27 | 29 | 26 | 19 |
| Nuclear | 37.7 | 32 | 39 | 45 | 48 |
| Petroleum | 10.7 | 14 | 9 | 8 | 3 |
| Renewable | 24.8 | 27 | 23 | 21 | 20 |
| (Hydraulic and alternative energy) | | | | | |

SOURCES: Ministerio de Industria y Energía, Plan energético nacional: 1978/1987 (Madrid: Servicio de Publicaciones, 1978) 35. Juan Alegre Marcet, "Previsión sobre la demanda de energía en España hasta el año 2000," Boletín Informativo 99 (1980): 22, (Madrid: Fundación Juan March; and Primo González Ortiz, "Problemas de la energía," Cuadernos de Política Económica 4 (1981): 24.

coordinator, and a facilitator of information. They viewed the IEA primarily as an agency to prepare reports and recommendations to be considered by the government once it is sent, say, to Madrid.[42] An annual review of the national energy policies of member countries was the IEA's principle public means to influence domestic energy policy. Energy policy reviews became the most important aspect of ongoing IEA activity in long-term cooperation.

These regular reviews monitored the policy achievements of IEA members. The Spanish government, like others, submitted a detailed report to the IEA on an annual basis. The IEA responded directly to the Spanish government. This response was later reported in the annual review. Besides summarizing Spain's and other countries' plans and steps taken in the previous year, the IEA generally commented on these policies. These comments were often quite critical, and the reviews sometimes contained finger-pointing criticisms and the pledges of members to do better. Despite criticisms, these reports were perceived by Spanish officials as being more or less neutral and objective.[43] This may be attributable to the fact that IEA national reviews improved over the years in their quality of analysis. They nevertheless remained rather general in nature.

The major influence of the IEA's annual reports on energy policy during Spain's transition to democracy was on the nuclear program. The IEA consistently encouraged the general direction of energy-planning in Spain and PEN and nuclear energy in particular. A sampling from several of these policy reviews illustrates this. In 1978, IEA comments on Spanish policy were quite favorable:

> The energy policy outlined in PEN is generally consistent with the IEA objective of reducing dependence on imported oil.[44]

In 1979, the IEA continued this support:

> The concept of the National Energy Plan appears to be very sound. Rapid acceptance by Parliament is an essential step to reduce the country's dependence on imported oil. It . . . also envisages significant increases in the production of solid nuclear fuels.[45]

By 1980, the IEA seemed pleased to report that

> According to Spanish authorities, the seven nuclear plants under construction are nearing completion, making the achievement of the ambitious nuclear programme almost a certainty. It is hoped that the Spanish Government will be able to ensure, in the future, that the construction of the three additional nuclear plants will proceed on schedule.[46]

The following year, however, the tone of the report changed when Spanish officials admitted that the nuclear construction program was facing a difficult challenge. The IEA became concerned:

> A great area of concern is the slippage in the nuclear programme for both 1985 and 1990 compared with last year's submission. This slippage is caused by difficulties with local authorities. . . . To avoid further slippage in the nuclear programme, rapid approval and im-

plementation of the Law for Interprovincial Compensation is necessary. Otherwise, local authorities would not be eager to approve the site of a nuclear power plant without adequate compensation for developing the economy of their region.[47]

These reports clearly demonstrated the IEA's desire for energy policy in Spain. IEA encouragement of future domestic energy planning followed similar lines:

> The IEA's greatest concern lies with Spain's nuclear programme. The authorities should make every effort to adhere to the target production identified during the 1979 review and consider the possibility of developing an accelerated programme.[48]

In sum, the published recommendations of the IEA strongly encouraged Spain's emphasis on nuclear energy. Energy policymakers were cognizant of the IEA's desires to steer PEN in this direction, even if they would not straightforwardly state the degree of influence.[49] The recommendations of international organizations such as these IEA published reports were particularly important to all Spanish governmental officials who at the time of the transition were eagerly attempting to be "accepted" as full political members of Western Europe.

## International Support

Most Spanish officials for energy policy asserted that the IEA, like the United Nations, was not a very powerful international organization.[50] They realistically understood IEA's prime role as a forum for discussions about energy, since it was without legislative powers like some other international organizations. They were aware that the cooperation was very limited in the IEA between Spain and the other importing countries on such subjects as conservation, import levels, development of supply alternatives, and contingency planning for emergency shortages. They had seen such efforts frequently undercut by the attempts of individual members to make bilateral deals with cartel members to secure supplies and compensate for high prices.[51] These Spanish officials were also aware that many of the IEA's problems were due to the varying capabilities of its members. Spanish officials knew the IEA remained a politically and economically weak organization, that its potential had not been fully realized.[52] They remained cautious of the IEA's more powerful members and those less burdened by energy deficiencies.

Spanish officials also maintained that, limited as it is, the IEA did serve a purpose. They were pleased that the IEA had become an organization promoting cooperation for consumer nations on data collection, policy coordination, and facilitating R & D efforts. The IEA, they contended, provided a ready setting to communicate Spain's energy concerns. For example, the ministerial-level meeting of 21 November 1980 in Paris at the outbreak of the conflict between Iran and Iraq was quite important to Spain. At that time, Spain received about 22 percent of petroleum imports from these two countries and was quite concerned about a cutoff of petroleum supplies.[53] Although eventually not seriously affected by this war, Spanish officials appeared pleased to have had this institutionalized means for a quick airing of concerns during this crisis period.

The IEA influence on domestic energy policies during Spain's transition to democracy, however, went beyond this limited institutional availability. The IEA subtly influenced the scope of Spanish energy planning both directly and indirectly. The emergency allocation system was a potential source for an emergency allocation of petroleum. Although of questionable efficiency, this emergency allocation program provided authorities in Spain with a short-term backup system. Such a system was a policy necessity for a country that so heavily utilized petroleum yet pushed a long-term nuclear solution. The existence of this emergency allocation system gave Spanish officials some short-term psychological support—policy breathing room until more nuclear plants were to come on line.

More directly, the IEA encouraged Spain's ambitious nuclear program. The cooperative high-technology programs in R & D, the agency's regular monitoring of members' energy planning and implementation, and most importantly, policy forecasting based on formal models made available to member countries all promoted PEN's emphasis on increasing energy supplies through greater utilization of nuclear power. These programs and other IEA recommendations all became part of Spanish energy policy. These IEA recommendations and programs were incorporated into Spain's National Energy Plan. This international organization supported the general direction of Spain's National Energy Plan and its ambitious nuclear component at the end of the Franco regime as well as during the transition to democracy.

The International Energy Agency supported Spain's National Energy Plan while giving special encouragement to the development of a strong nuclear program. The IEA communicated this encouragement to policymakers through domestic policy reviews, coordination of joint R & D projects, and particular planning instruments such as formal models. This support gave policy-making officials yet another base, this time an international one, upon which to defend logically the direction of energy policy. The IEA's support for PEN-75, PEN-79, and PEN-82 encouraged the perpetuation of the direction for Spain's energy policy. By promoting the status quo of Spain's energy planning, the IEA supported, intentionally or not and as much indirectly as directly, the control of energy policy-making by the financial oligarchy. By promoting the emphasis of energy policy during the transition to democracy, the IEA simultaneously reinforced the role played by Spain's financial oligarchy.

The relationship between the IEA and energy policy in Spain fundamentally underscored some domestic politics. During the transition, Spanish political parties and officials ideologically to the right-of-center were quite concerned about policy performance. Policy consistency and policymaker solidarity was a major reason the Spanish right-of-center favorably viewed these relations with the IEA while it was in power in Spain, i.e., prior to late 1982. They contended that Spain's relationship with the IEA had generally been a positive one and that at worst it did nothing to hinder the national energy program. More positively from their perspective, this relationship encouraged the UCD governments to continue PEN's nuclear emphasis. The UCD did not hide this fact, welcoming international support for its policies.

On the other hand, the Left's perception of this relationship was quite different, at least prior to PSOE's victory in October 1982. Reflecting its early anti-nuclear position, the Left believed the IEA added weight to Spain's emphasis on nuclear policy. It highlighted the commonly known fact that the U.S. was a leading power in the IEA. This served to strengthen the Left's perception that the IEA was an instrument of multinational business, those who greatly benefitted from the use of nuclear energy. On the domestic front, the Left contended that PEN's emphasis on nuclear energy, particularly high technology, permitted greater penetration into the domestic economy by the multinationals. IEA assistance was often perceived as stemming from and in the interests of those who benefitted from nuclear energy. To the Left, the IEA was simply one of many international organizations which supported the central position of the financial-business oligarchy in energy policy-making. After late 1982, however, the PSOE government of Felipe González did little to change this situation.

Before winning the October 1982 election and coming to power, the Socialist party obviously overstated its case, particularly with regard to any conspiracy among international corporations. Until that victory, the Left nevertheless continued to push its argument in many different political arenas. Regardless of why PSOE changed its tune, this chapter has suggested that international organizations such as the IEA did defend certain national energy programs, which knowingly or not were advantageous to entrenched financial interests. International organizations such as the International Energy Agency did play a role, albeit a limited one, in perpetuating the scope and direction of Spanish energy policy during the country's transition from an authoritarian political system to a democratic one.

# 8

# Energy Policy Under the Socialists: Steps Toward Change?

Following the Spanish Socialist Workers Party's (PSOE) victory in the election of October 1982, energy continued to be an important component of the country's overall economic policy. The government of Felipe González undertook several visible steps in energy policy in the years prior to 1 January 1986, when Spain became a member of the European Economic Community. In this chapter, we consider several topics of energy policy. First, the National Energy Plan of 1983 (PEN-83) is discussed with reference to its predecessors. Second, the reorganization of Spain's petroleum distribution monopoly, CAMPSA, is analyzed in light of Spain's entry into the European Community. Third, PSOE's nationalization of the high-tension system of electricity is discussed as an example of an energy-related policy that the PSOE had pushed for many years. And fourth, an agreement reached between the government and the electric companies suggests that the post-Franco pattern of elite accommodation continued despite the Socialists' control of the government. These four areas of energy policy under PSOE leadership reflect the degree to which such policy changed during Spain's transition from an authoritarian system to a western liberal democracy.

# The National Energy Plan of 1983

As outlined earlier, Spain's policy response to the 1973–74 energy crisis came in the form of the National Energy Plan of 1975 (PEN-75), a second plan during the transition to democracy (PEN-79), and a revision of this plan (PEN-82). Following the assumption of power, the Socialists produced their own version of the National Energy Plan in 1983 (PEN-83). All of these versions of PEN, taken together, reflect the degree of continuity of public policy in this area from authoritarian to democratic Spain. PEN-83 also suggests the degree to which the Socialists broke with the past in energy policy-making.

Spain's PEN-83 was similar to its predecessors in many respects. First, the PSOE's plan followed a pattern of previous governments in terms of its lateness. PEN-83 was actually not approved by Parliament until 28 June 1984. Despite the fact that PEN-79 called for a reassessment and revision of Spain's energy situation every two years, the Ministry of Industry and Energy was not fully prepared to present a final version to the government until a year after the time mandated by law. Second, PEN-83 systematically focused on the different energy sectors—electricity, petroleum, coal, natural gas, etc. It determined supply and the anticipated demand for the period 1983–92, a period similar in length to the previous PENs. PEN-83 also focused on such concerns as investment, prices, and production in the different energy sectors and fields. Third, prior to its formal approval, the plan itself came under much debate and criticism in the press and in parliament at both the committee and plenary stages.[1] Finally, PEN-83 outlined future undertakings in energy policy in the area of institutional restructuring. Some of the more important of these reforms, such as the vertical integration of CAMPSA and the nationalization of the system of high-tension electricity, merit further discussion here given the significance of these changes.

As outlined in its first chapter, PEN-83's basic objectives included (1) the reduction of the vulnerability of Spain's energy supplies; (2) the improvement of efficiency in the consumption and transformation of energy, with a push for savings and conservation; and (3) optimally utilizing resources to satisfy demand. This third objective included correcting the excessive supply capacity of the energy sector and improving the financial health of domestic energy companies. The Ministry of Industry and Energy acknowledged that a total achievement of these goals in the plan's ten-year framework was not possible.[2] Like its predecessors, nevertheless, PEN-83 was to serve as a guideline for the pursuit of these goals.

In general terms, PEN-83 fixed a probable rate of growth for energy consumption over the 1983–92 period. Supply figures and other projections were then matched to these consumption estimates. Table 8-1 outlines PEN-83's basic objectives for energy consumption. Three features stand out here. First, the Socialist government anticipated an absolute increase in primary energy consumption of about 30 percent from 1982 to 1992—104.69 to 135.65—in TEC. Such realistic projection figures added credibility to the plan, particularly following the openly acknowledged lack of realism contained in the goals of the Francoist PEN-75. Second, the government anticipated little change over the next decade in the percentage of coal and natural-gas consumption, with about a 2.5 percent increase in hydroelectric consumption. Third, PEN-83 predicted a large—9.7 percent decrease in petroleum consumption by 1986, an amount it projects to be replaced by nuclear energy.

How different are the projections of energy consumption contained in PSOE's National Energy Plan and the previous PENs? Table 8-2 compares PEN-83's projections of the areas of energy consumption with those of PEN-75, PEN-79, and PEN-82. While comparisons with the first two PENs are a little misleading given that each PEN dealt with a slightly different time period, it is clear that the Socialists placed a strong emphasis on more traditional sources of energy. PEN-83 projected a larger percentage increase in consumption of coal- and petroleum-generated energy in 1990 as compared to PEN-79's projections. In terms of Spain's energy consumption of nuclear-produced energy, PSOE anticipated a lower percentage of consumption than

**Table 8-1**   PEN-83 Projections for Primary Energy Consumption (thousands of TEC-tons equivalent of coal)

| Source | 1982 | 1986 | 1990 | 1992 |
|---|---|---|---|---|
| Coal | 25.9% | 25.4% | 24.3% | 25.2% |
| | (27.05) | (29.54) | (31.52) | (34.16) |
| Petroleum | 59.6% | 49.9% | 47.6% | 47.1% |
| | (62.43) | (57.98) | (61.56) | (63.89) |
| Natural gas | 3.1% | 3.6% | 4.9% | 4.6% |
| | (3.38) | (4.10) | (6.33) | (6.33) |
| Hydroelectric | 8.6% | 11.1% | 11.4% | 11.3% |
| | (8.89) | (12.96) | (14.79) | (15.31) |
| Nuclear | 2.8% | 10.0% | 11.8% | 11.8% |
| | (2.94) | (11.55) | (15.22) | (15.96) |
| Totals | 100% | 100% | 100% | 100% |
| | (104.69) | (116.13) | (129.42) | (135.65) |

SOURCE: Plan Energético Nacional, 1983–92, vol. 1 (Ministerio de Industria y Energía, 1984) 14.

did the UCD in either PEN-79 or PEN-82, and certainly much less than the unrealistically pro-nuclear PEN-75 of the Franco regime. PEN-83's upward estimate of petroleum consumption and its lowered projections for nuclear consumption appeared to reflect a policy adjustment. Important to note, however, was that being in power did not lead the PSOE to take Spain totally away from nuclear energy as its earlier rhetoric suggested it might. Policy inertia proved difficult to overcome. Constraints on policy continued to exist.

PEN-83 outlined several major policy goals, such as the reorganization of CAMPSA, the nationalization of the electrical delivery system, and assistance for improving the electric companies' financial health. PEN-83 nevertheless also covered additional energy-policy concerns. For example, in the area of pricing policy, increases in electricity prices after 1983 were consistent with the call in PEN-83 for a more realistic pricing program. While Spain continued to lag considerably behind its Western European neighbors in a strong reliance on the pricing instrument, energy prices in Spain increasingly reflected real costs of production and thus provided a strong incentive to conserve. Spain still had a great distance to go, however, in reducing the differences between domestic and industrial prices, reducing special prices, and establishing a new system of compensations.

**Table 8-2**  Comparison of Projections for Spanish Primary Energy Consumption (thousands of TEC)

| Source | PEN-75 (1985) | PEN-79 (1987) | PEN-82 (1990) | PEN-83 (1990) |
|---|---|---|---|---|
| Coal | 14.7% | 16.2% | 22.8% | 24.3% |
| | (25.5) | (23.5) | (34.7) | (31.5) |
| Petroleum | 43.0% | 54.3% | 45.2% | 47.6% |
| | (74.4) | (78.7) | (68.7) | (61.56) |
| Natural gas | 11.1% | 5.3% | 6.1% | 4.9% |
| | (19.1) | (7.7) | (9.3) | (6.3) |
| Hydroelectric | 9.2% | 9.4% | 9.2% | 11.4% |
| | (15.9) | (13.6) | (14.0) | (14.8) |
| Nuclear | 22.0% | 14.8% | 15.1% | 11.8% |
| | (38.1) | (21.5) | (23.0) | (15.2) |
| Other | | | 1.6% | |
| | | | (2.4) | |
| Totals | 100% | 100% | 100% | 100% |
| | (173) | (145) | (152.1) | (135.7) |

SOURCES: PEN-75: Ministerio de Industria (1975), 3. PEN-79: Ministerio de Industria (1978), 44. PEN-82: *El País*, 6 December 1981, 53. PEN-83: Ministerio de Industria y Energía (1984), 14.

In the area of energy savings beyond price incentives, the PSOE government created the Institution for the Diversification and Savings of Energy (IDAE). This institution, in collaboration with the autonomous communities, sought to increase contact between public authorities and domestic industries, companies, large energy consumers and, in general, with all the country's energy users that possess a strong savings potential.[3] According to its director, the IDAE's chief role was different than its predecessor, the Center for Energy Studies.[4] IDAE primarily sought to stimulate investment by financing selected public and private projects. By 1985, however, IDAE remained too small to significantly influence Spain's overall energy picture.

## CAMPSA's Reorganization

The entry of Spain into the EEC on 1 January 1986 motivated officials to consider the impact this entry would have on the petroleum industry in general and CAMPSA in particular. EEC membership, of course, means that in energy as well as most other commercial products, Spain must open its domestic markets to other member countries. Spanish officials grew concerned about the effect this opening to the multinationals would have on CAMPSA. Government and business officials feared that CAMPSA would not be competitive enough to survive the opening, according to the Treaty of Accession, of the borders after 1992.[5] While the full impact of EEC membership on Spanish energy is beyond the scope of the present study, it is important to note that some changes were undertaken in anticipation of entry on 1 January 1986.

In order to face future competition, the PSOE government began a preaccession process of vertical integration of the domestic petroleum sector. This structural reorganization was initiated in late 1984 when the National Institute of Hydrocarbons (INH)—the state's energy holding company—coordinated an attempt to purchase CAMPSA's privately owned stocks at 250 percent their nominal value. INH successfully purchased 97 percent of these stocks. In December 1984, this "public" CAMPSA acquired ownership of the primary distribution network of petroleum products from the state patrimony at a price the Ministry of Finance estimated at 109,000 million pesetas (approximately $623 million). The next phase in CAMPSA's transition occurred in January 1985 with the entry of the capital of the six public and private Spanish refineries—EMP, Petroliber, Petromed, CEPSA, Petronor, and ERT—according to preestablished percentages. The private participation in CAMPSA nevertheless preserved majority public ownership.

Following the completion of CAMPSA's vertical integration, only the six Spanish refineries that owned a share of CAMPSA distributed their products through the distribution network. In other words, the "new" CAMPSA continued to be the sole distributor of the six refining companies. Each refinery is to sell its refined petroleum products only to CAMPSA at a determined price. CAMPSA, in turn, will be the sole domestic distributor of these products. Thus, while the goal of this vertical integration in the Spanish petroleum industry is to make the entry of the petroleum multinationals into Spain more difficult, the reality of this "change" is that while the integration rationalizes the petroleum industry to some extent and unquestionably increases its competitive potential before the multinationals, it does not change the monopoly status CAMPSA has had since its creation in 1927 as the sole domestic distributor. It will remain unlawful for other Spanish companies to enter this market.[6]

# Nationalization of the High-Tension System

Similar to petroleum, the government of Felipe González sought to rationalize the electric industry, increase the efficiency of its management, and improve the product delivery of this vital energy source. In May 1983, the Ministry of Industry and Energy and the major companies of the electric industry reached an agreement to nationalize the country's electrical high-tension network. These companies, Iberoduero, Endesea, Hidroeléctrica Española, FECSA, Sevillana de Electricidad, and Unión Eléctrica-Fenosa, agreed to the nationalization given the government's commitment to a pricing policy with a sufficient profit for the electric companies.

Why nationalization? What made it possible? This nationalization of the high-tension system through majority public participation in a new mixed company was the latest attempt to achieve what Franco pursued in the National Electrical Plan of 1969: to assist in coordinating, and therefore increase, the management efficiency of the national electric system. The two participants in the agreement—the PSOE government and the electric companies—were both to benefit. The PSOE, for its part, fulfilled its 1982 election promise of nationalizing the high-tension system and creating a mixed company to manage this system that would have as its object "the optimization of the operation of all the installations of production and transportation."[7] In the negotiations on this agreement, the Ministry of Industry and Energy also explained its desire to facilitate the sector's management on behalf of the present companies and to place the nuclear plants Almáraz (I and II) and Asco I on line as well as the others included in PEN-83. By creating a central control for electricity, PSOE assured, through corresponding technical regulation, the necessary coordination and subordination of the different technical offices of the companies with their central offices. The electric companies accepted this as coordinating operations of the production system. For their part, the electric companies obtained recognition for the quality of their management, the guarantee that the high-tension system would be the only part of the system nationalized, and the promise that the prices would be adjusted to the real costs of energy production. This statement by PSOE assuring the electric companies there would be no further nationalizations was extremely important to the business community in general and the electric companies in particular.[8]

To carry out the principles of the pact, the Ministry and the electric companies agreed to three points: (1) to audit the data on costs and expenses on operations of the electric companies to determine an adequate profit; (2) to analyze the process and the means most appropriate to implement the projected revision of PEN-83, with special reference to the coming on line of new nuclear plants and their operations with the rest of the installed potential; and (3) to study immediately the creation of the mixed company and its effect on the stock value of the companies.

How did the companies react to this nationalization? UNESA, the sector's patron, complained following the drafting of the law that the project "greatly exceeded the words contained in the protocol signed between the companies and the Ministry of Industry and Energy."[9] Nevertheless, despite this statement that the text of the project-law as it was presented to parliament had not been agreed to by UNESA, PSOE's nationalization of the high-tension system was without political costs since most parts were not opposed by the electric sector. UNESA did not obtain everything it wanted in these negotiations but ultimately saw a law it could live with. UNESA stated on several occasions that it would cooperate with the new arrangement, and has few fundamental objections to public ownership of the delivery system since it will still carry UNESA's programs. The ten months of hard negotiations before the project-law reached parliament were necessary for UNESA to assure its position. These protracted negotiations were also part of the reason why PEN-83 experienced a year delay.

The nationalization itself actually occurred with the Unified Operation of the National Electric System on 26 December 1984.[10] Red Eléctrica Española (REDE), the Spanish Electric Network, was created a month later on 29 January 1985.[11] REDE's principal concern was the unified management of the national electric system through the high-tension network. As a public company, REDE determines and controls the domestic system of electricity and defines the general lines of operations for hydroelectric reserves. REDE thus controls the operations of the national electric network and establishes the program for electrical generation. REDE also directs the international exchanges of electrical energy that Spain maintains especially with France, Portugal, and Andorra. In sum, REDE seeks the efficient operation of all production and transport installations and guarantees quality of service.

REDE's administrative council contains representatives of state capital as well as of private companies integrated into UNESA. Leadership in this area of energy, part of the heart of the Socialists' desire for change, has not changed much. Consistent with other areas of energy, the head of Aseléctrica, the company that previously carried out many of these responsibilities, directs the company along with the government delegate of REDE.[12]

Who paid for this nationalization? The value of the total assets of the nationalized system was approximately 100 million pesetas at the time of its creation.[13] The capital of REDE was mixed, with majority public participation. The capital structure was the following: public companies carried 23 million pesetas of the assets and the 459.7 million by INI constituted 51% of the capital, giving the State a majority. The private sector, for its part, held the remaining 49 percent, through 23 million pesetas from ENDESA-Empresa Nacional de Eléctricidad and ENHER (Empresa Nacional Hidro-eléctrica del Ribagorzana). The difference of 82 million in the system's value of private ownership, that is, 59 million pesetas, became a medium-term debt. This 60 percent debt will be amortized around the year 2004.[14] Thus the balance of the new company consisted of 23.5 million in public capital, 22.5 million in private capital, and 55.3 million in debt.

## Spain's Nuclear Program

Prior to its victory in 1982, the PSOE expressed strong opposition to what it perceived as a heavy supply-oriented program in energy.[15] The PSOE, and the UGT labor union argued that a "proper" energy program should not focus predominantly on increasing the potential for the generation of energy, particularly electricity.[16] Nevertheless, Carlos Solchaga, the first minister of Industry and Energy for PSOE, affirmed in an initial appearance before parliament that the production of electricity would continue growing at the level outlined in PEN-82.[17] Solchaga emphasized increased supply by stating that in 1984 and 1985, in effect, eight coal and two nuclear-generating plants would increase Spain's electrical supply by 5300 megawatts, a figure equal to 15 percent of the installed potential at the end of 1983. He also said that given increments in electrical consumption of 4.25 percent in 1983 and 4.48 percent in 1984, the possibility existed in the near future for full use of generating potential. Furthermore, PEN-83 anticipated increments in consumption of more than 3.3 percent. This increased consumption was to be due primarily to the special rates to promote growth in certain industries such as metallurgy, the production of aluminum and chemicals and other electricity-intensive industries, the placing of other energy sources in the domestic petroleum market, and the failure of the application of conservation measures. Such anticipated increases gave the impression that the Socialists were not seriously raising objections to the push by the electric industry for growth in energy consumption. Thus earlier criticism by PSOE of supply-oriented policies did not seem to be of central concern following its assumption of power. This included the continued use of nuclear energy.

The commitment of the government of Felipe González to supply Spain with the energy it needed did not mean that PSOE totally abandoned its previous opposition to nuclear power. While it did not stop the use of nuclear energy, the PSOE government did take the controversial step of suspending construction on five nuclear plants: Trillo II, Lemóniz I and II, and Valdecaballeros I and II. This decision was significant in many respects. In terms of investment, these five plants accounted for 18.5 percent of 1982's fixed-capital formation in the nuclear sector. The construction stoppage significantly altered investment in energy. Nevertheless, PEN-83 foresaw the reactivating of construction if growth in energy consumption surpassed estimates in PEN's annual revision. Despite its early rhetoric, while in power the PSOE appeared willing to live with nuclear power in Spain.

However, the construction moratorium was motivated by economics as much as by politics. For example, progress in the construction of Valdecaballeros between the first demonstration for a nuclear moratorium after PSOE came to power and the actual work stoppage suggested nonideological motivations. In fact, the nuclear industry was simultaneously reaching a similar conclusion about the economic feasibility of nuclear energy. Given soaring costs, the nuclear industry had already decided to limit Spain's nuclear-generating potential to 7,500 megawatts. The construction costs of nuclear plants had surpassed prices by 3.9 percent, according to industry estimates. Thus, except for the political problems surrounding Lemóniz, the question of the moratorium on nuclear construction was motivated by economics. The Ministry of Industry and Energy remained sympathetic during the mid-1980s to a significant role for nuclear power. The Socialists remained sensitive to the relationship between industrial expansion and the need for increased supplies of energy. Their concern for the economic effects of EEC membership and the economic modernization of the Spanish economy implied that practical economics took priority over political or ideological orientation.[18]

Nonetheless, the construction moratorium and the Socialists' overall energy program predictably came under attack. Consistent with its strong support of earlier PENs, the International Energy Agency (IEA) was one source of criticism. In a February 1985 report, the IEA expressed grave doubts that the Socialists could implement the objectives of their energy program.[19] Beginning on a positive note, the IEA stated that PEN-83's objectives seemed appropriate for the current situation of energy in Spain and reflected a solid analysis of the current problems. The means PSOE chose to achieve these goals were also deemed appropriate. The IEA, however, doubted that the government could reach its energy policy goals in the 1983–92 period. For example, the IEA opposed the moratorium on the construction of nuclear plants. If the demand for electricity continued surpassing the estimates of PEN, Spain would require additional production capacity. IEA argued that the continuation of at least part of the construction should be considered, given the capital already invested. Stated directly, the IEA believed that Spain should have continued its investment in nuclear plants already under construction instead of building new coal or fuel-oil generating plants.

The IEA also criticized the policy that passed the cost of the construction of nuclear plants on to the consumer after the plant was placed in service. "This system," IEA argued, "drives up the financing costs for the companies that will ultimately be paid for by the consumers."[20] The IEA maintained that such construction costs should be included in the consumers' bills from the beginning of construction. The IEA also believed the electricity companies were going too far into debt. These companies spent enormous sums of money in constructing nuclear plants within the specific guidelines of the previous PENs. They felt that it was more rational to pay for the plants as they were being built, giving the companies a strong source of additional revenues, indebting them less, and—since they had to pay the interest on the debt—making it cheaper in the long run for the consumer. Despite such arguments, Spanish utilities still proved quite profitable. In 1986, they had profits of 87 billion pesetas ($674 million). This permitted a 1.1 billion peseta ($8.5 million) reduction of debt, down to 4.1 billion ($32 million).[21]

The IEA also strongly criticized PEN 83 on several other points. First, the IEA argued that the petroleum quota system—the previously discussed practice established during the Franco regime in which a quantity is fixed for the refineries' purchases and a price determined for CAMPSA's purchases from these refineries—continues to drive an inadequate refinery structure. The IEA believed the quota system produced an underutilization of the refining system. Second, the Spanish refining system's long-term level of competitive efficiency, in terms of comparisons with foreign refineries, will ultimately depend on the restructuring of CAMPSA induced by the Common Market. A complete restructuring will probably not occur prior to the market's opening in 1992. Third, and consistent with most of its reports on Spain, the IEA criticized the poor quality of data on Spain's energy program and operations, arguing that improvements in statistical collection procedures are vital to maintain the necessary flexibility for policy adjustment to changing market conditions.

## The Electrical Pact

The 1986 profits for the electricity companies were, in part, a consequence of another energy-related policy of the Socialist government in the mid-1980s. The electricity companies and the nuclear industry argued in the late 1970s and early 1980s that they increasingly faced serious economic problems. The distortion between supply and demand in the generation of electricity, in part a consequence of overproduction, the optimism behind the building of nuclear plants, and the divergence between energy reality and energy projections contained in both PEN-75 and PEN-79 had negative economic implications. The electric companies argued that they were in an economically indefensible position. The industry's investment of two trillion pesetas in generating plants, many of which were nuclear, looked bad in the early 1980s given projections that these nuclear plants would not be heavily utilized once, and if, they were placed in service. Several electric companies were thus concerned that these plants would not generate enough resources to pay off the debts.

Following the 1982 election, the government of Felipe González initiated discussions with the electric companies about these economic problems. They reached an agreement in May 1983. First, this accord permitted the nationalization of the high-tension system. Second, the pact sought to help the electric industry get its economic house in order through a financial "interchange." Third, and most important to the electric companies, the agreement assured a "sufficient profit" for all the companies through an adequate pricing policy.[22] Fourth, and related to the other points, as reparation for the moratorium on the construction of nuclear plants, the pact established a compensation for the affected companies consistent with a 3.9 percent surcharge above the existing prices. Outside the question of nationalization, the heart of this agreement focused on the financial condition of the electric companies.

Reaching this agreement was not an easy task. Several issues proved difficult. Iberduero had not resolved the problem of Lemóniz. The stoppage of the construction for political reasons had created additional expenses which exceeded compensation from the financial "interchange." The nature of the compensation was uncertain. The presidents of the private electric companies were also worried about functions to be carried out by the company that would manage the network of high-tension lines. And if this wasn't enough, Hidrola paid no attention to the collective search for solutions, surprisingly acquiring Hidroeléctrica de Cataluña in the middle of these negotiations. Nevertheless, the tensions were overcome and a pact eventually signed.

With the "interchange," Iberduero, Endesa, and Hidroeléctrica Española obtained assets of the most financially troubled companies. These three large companies were themselves in a strong financial situation. In exchange for a reasonable increase in their indebtedness, these healthy companies were to improve their productive capacity and their participation in the market. Debts and previous overinvestment kept FECSA, Union-Fenosa, Hidro-Cataluña, and ENHER from participating.

The pact also outlined that through Endesa the public sector would grow 413 megawatts, or 9 percent, in installed potential. Endesa simultaneously enlarged its market with the purchase of Eléctricas Reunidas de Zaragoza (ERZ), also ending part of ERZ's final distribution through FECSA. This purchase meant a national increase of 4.5 percent in the number of kilowatts sold by public firms. The private sector, on the other hand, also gained through the pact. For example, Iberduero increased its disposable potential by 700 megawatts through what it obtained from Union-Fenosa. Iberduero also sold its 20 percent participation in ERZ to Endesa. Hidroeléctrica de Cataluña, with a distribution market similar to ERZ, enlarged by a third the potential of its group of companies through the assumption of debt.

In many respects, this financial interchange removed the appearance of "holes" in the companies most indebted. The PSOE government hoped that this interchange would maintain the financial equilibrium of the electricity sector and help it optimally use its resources to satisfy demand and improve efficiency. Nevertheless, some foreign banks who had loaned the electric industry more than one trillion pesetas deemed these measures insufficient for obtaining a healthy financial situation. In order to placate them, the PSOE Secretary General of Energy explained the new pricing policies to them in London in the summer of 1984.

After the pact, Spanish electricity was financially fortified, although with a lessening of its solvency. The PSOE government accomplished an operation that permitted it to strengthen its management of energy policy through the employment of instruments such as pricing policy, the use of a nationalized network of high-tension lines, the power for the authorization of generating plants, and expanded activities of public companies. Politically, the costs of this strengthened policy hand await future assessment. Political reactions to a financing process which may ultimately place the burden on the consumer have not yet fully manifested themselves. It is the consumer after all who, through increased prices, will determine the profitability of the electric companies and their healthy operations. This same consumer also casts a vote in general elections. However, as discussed earlier, the democratic expression of public opinion tends to be a nonbinding constraint on energy policy-making.

## Steps Toward Change?

Parliamentary passage of PEN-83, CAMPSA's reorganization, the decisions about a moratorium on the construction of nuclear plants, the nationalization of the system of high-tension lines, and the electrical pact have all occurred between the time PSOE came to power followings its victory in October 1982 and 1 January 1986 when Spain joined the European Economic Community. How much, however, really changed in policy direction under the Socialists during this time? Has energy policy under PSOE constituted a significant break with the past?

No doubt the PSOE government made some policy decisions that were very different from those of previous governments. The moratorium on construction of nuclear plants did slow the push for this method of generating electricity that had begun in authoritarian Spain and continued during the transition to democracy. However, PSOE's call for a total halt to nuclear energy prior to its success in the 1982 election suggests that the moratorium on construction was motivated more by economic and business concerns than by ideology. Worldwide, the nuclear industry cut back considerably during this time, given enormous cost overruns and the increasing unprofitability of nuclear generation. Spain was not that different from other countries. The Socialists broke with the recent past in terms of modifying the future use of nuclear energy. However, the plans of the previous governments were not totally abandoned. The Socialists only slowed them down—possibly temporarily. Pressures from different groups and organizations such as the IEA, Spain's business community, and the electricity industry will insure that energy policy does not radically deviate from the past.

On another front, the reorganization of CAMPSA—through its vertical integration and rationalization—was an example of how the Spanish left-of-center was very concerned about economic efficiency and business' competitive advantage in the marketplace. In many ways, the PSOE was oriented more toward liberal economics than the Right in terms of economic and management efficiency, increased reliance on pricing as a policy instrument, and concern for profitability in the energy field. The PSOE challenged some more "traditional" business relationships through the nationalization of the high tension system and the "new" CAMPSA. It should be emphasized, however, that this was motivated by a desire for improved efficiency and rationality in business, not by an ideological drive for public ownership. The limited nature of these nationalizations and the promises to the business community that the government would go no farther with such "buyouts" clearly indicated this nonideological, pro-efficiency motivation by PSOE. In energy and other economically related policies, the PSOE has been a reformist party seeking to modernize the Spanish economy. In terms of policy, the PSOE is one of the mildest, most centerist, socialist parties in Western Europe. Policy moderation is the norm.

The PSOE's moderation energy and other economically related programs, ipso facto, suggest the lack of a significant break with past policy. PEN-83 continued the series of energy plans that began under the Franco regime. PEN-83 did not alter the basic structure of Spain's energy program; it only modified it. While it did decrease projections for the consumption of nuclear energy, it did so primarily by calling for the return to coal-burning plants. In this respect, given the economic constraints imposed by high energy costs, Spain had returned full circle to the earlier days of the Francoist period and prior to the energy crisis when decisions were made to convert to fuel-oil given its cheapness over coal. More importantly, the Socialist government continued the established practice in Spain of formal, negotiated pacts between the government, business, and, often, labor leadership. This neocorporatist style of policy-making, as seen in the electric pact, continued to leave a great deal of power for energy policy in the hands of the private companies. Thus the private electric companies continued to be solidly entrenched as the base upon which much of Spain's energy policy ultimately rested. Some of the changes that have occurred may, however, be the beginnings of decline in the influence of the financial oligarchy and the business community. If change occurs, it will probably come not as a direct consequence of democracy itself but as an indirect one: through reforms and changes prompted through membership in the European Economic Community.[23]

# 9

---

# Conclusion

## Political Change in Spain

The transition to democracy in Spain was unique. Authoritarian regimes rarely legally abolish themselves and almost never replace themselves with a viable pluralistic parliamentary democracy. This transition to democracy in Spain was marked by several historical roadmarks: the death of Franco in November 1975, the ratification of the constitution in December 1978, the peaceful alternation of power in late 1982 following the electoral victory of the Socialists, and Spain's membership in the European Economic Community on 1 January 1986. Many of these and other critical steps—the political reform law of November 1976, its popular referendum a month later, the June 1977 election, the ratification of the constitution in 1978, and the 1982 alternation of power—all *politically* resolved issues about the *political* system. This transition was a remarkable feat in political behavior, the development of democracy in the West, and world political history.

Nevertheless, this transition through *reforma* rather than *ruptura* left intact many of the economic structures of Spanish policy-making. The reforms following Franco's death in late 1975, with the broad changes in government structure and the apparently successful construction of a viable parliamentary democracy, did not change the basic relationships between economic structures and the state. Large private interests in the Spanish economy remained central to the apparatus of public policy-making. The Spanish business community and its important component of economic elites, which prospered under the Franco regime, along with the structures within which they grew, were not profoundly altered during the transition to democracy. The opportunity for labor unions, the newly reestablished political parties, and other organized interests to resurface and freely articulate opposing views following Franco and authoritarianism came, in part, from the general lack of opposition to the reform from the business community. The need to include, or at least solicit, the support of most important members of the business community in the post-Franco political coalition, particularly given the early threat of military intervention, placed these individuals in a strong position to protect their financial interests.

The transition to democracy in Spain began just as the world economic crisis of the 1970s reached this Iberian country. The political steps toward democracy were taken in the middle of a depression from which Spain has yet to emerge. And the success of the contemporary Spanish democracy may ultimately depend on the country's economic conditions, the government's ability to address the economic crisis, and the degree to which the electorate holds the government accountable for economic conditions. Yet why, despite the economic crisis, did the business community play such an important role in the transition to democracy? Why were participants with economic interests to protect so readily accepted into the circles of policy-making in the new democracy?

Elsewhere I have argued that the tribulations and uncertainties of democratic reforms forced poor economic conditions and issues to take a political backseat to the consolidation of democracy.[1] The need for a politics of consensus meant that serious economic reform had to be postponed. Given that a peaceful transition to democracy was far from assured, the need for political moderation dominated. The major participants who directed the transition focused their initial attention on political reform and not economic change. Other problems were simply deemed more important. For example, Spanish leaders were more concerned about a young and unstable party system, the emotions of regional politics, and the desire not to alienate those of the old regime to such an extent that memories of the Civil War would be relived. The difficulties in pursuing political reform and stringent economic measures simultaneously were too enormous. Spanish political leaders thus undertook a strategy that first called for the strengthening of the norms, rules, and procedures of democratic decision-making. Then, if they desired, they believed they could address economic problems. Furthermore, many believed that successful political reform would naturally lead to the resolution of the country's other problems, such as the need for economic reform.

Thus the transition to democracy in Spain occurred in a situation in which, despite very serious economic problems, politics took precedence over economics. The strategy of a politics of consensus rather than one of radical change was the manifestation of this ordering of priorities. In hindsight, such tactics proved extremely useful for the ultimate success of the consolidation of democracy. Nevertheless, such a strategy did have important consequences. Public policy in economics was undoubtedly affected by it. This politics of consensus meant leaving essentially unaltered the position of the domestic economic community. Central to our concern, this position in Spain's transition to democracy had a significant effect on the continuity of economic and economically related policy.

## Effect on Energy Policy

At a general level, the analysis reported here is intended to increase understanding of the consequences of a peaceful transition to democracy on an important issue in public policy. It reassesses the problems inherent in policymaking in energy during Spain's transition from its democratic beginnings prior to the death of Francisco Franco in November 1975 to the country's membership in the EEC on 1 January 1986. More specifically, this research seeks to answer why Spain's transition to democracy did not produce a significant alteration in energy policy. The basic argument presented here is that when political or governmental structures change but economic structures remain essentially unaltered, basic orientations of policy also remain unaltered. Change in political or governmental structure is generally not a sufficient condition to change economically related policy. The argument is made that a transition to democracy that does not alter the influence of important economic forces on economically related policy-making will not produce significantly different policy outcomes.

The development of this argument essentially takes a two-pronged approach. One line of reasoning is that continuity in energy policy during the transition to democracy in Spain existed because certain individuals and well-established economic and financial institutions held central positions in both Franco's authoritarian regime and the constitutional democracy that followed. Spain's political transition left fundamental economic structures unaltered. The economic elites in these structures had become institutionalized during the Franco period. These financial entities included the major Spanish banks, other financial institutions, and many large companies, which became well-situated during the Franco regime. This growth included a large financial interest in the domestic energy industry. Spanish energy policy in general, as formulated in the PEN, and its means of implementation reflected the interests of these financial members and their representatives in government and other policy-making positions. In other chapters, this analysis discussed PEN and the choice of instruments to implement this energy program. The transition to democracy produced little significant change in energy policy because private financial forces had an economic interest in producing continuity in energy policy. These financial elites were central to energy policy-making because of the capital-intensive nature of energy production, the nation's need for investment in energy development, and the general requirement during industrial and economic development for increased supplies of energy. Furthermore, the financial elites had penetrated the ranks of government policy-making in both the Franco regime and the liberal democracy. Such penetration encouraged the support of the business community for each regime while simultaneously permitting the financial elite to protect its own economic interests in economically-related policy, including energy. Many groups and individuals pushed for democratic reform in Spain before and during the transition. While treatment of all these is beyond the scope of this book, it is clear the business/financial community generally did not oppose such reforms, nor did it oppose change in economic policy when such change served its own economic interests. Structural reforms in government were supported as long as they were not accompanied by reform in the economic structures they opposed. This limitation to the extent of the reform was also made possible because organized labor wanted democratic reforms in order to legalize its participation. Labor understood the need for the support of the business community. Business and finance representatives were thus "pivotal" members of the Spanish governing coalition. The financial oligarchy undoubtedly lost some of its governmental power during the transition to democracy. And Spain's entry into the EEC will probably also lessen some of its influence in domestic politics because of increased international competition. Nevertheless, as suggested in the analysis of the number of banking representatives in various cabinets during the early stages of the transition and in the discussion of policy change under PSOE, such losses do not lessen its desire to defend policies that are economically advantageous to the business community.

A parallel or analytical prong of the argument addressing the question of why the regime change in Spain did not produce significant changes in energy policy centered on the nature of constraints on policy-making. This argument proposed that the transition to democracy did not produce significant change in energy policy because alternative sources of policy were impossible for political, economic, or other reasons. I argued, for example, that while political parties, labor unions, public opinion, and alternative sources of policy advocated different positions, these policy preferences could not affect decision-making.

There were numerous reasons for the nonbinding nature of these constraints. For example, many alternative energy proposals were advanced by political parties declared illegal during the Franco regime or in the parliamentary opposition until December 1982, when the PSOE came to power. Such alternative policy was not politically possible given that those proposing them did so from political and governmental opposition. I propose, however, that once the PSOE did gain control of the government, energy policy remained characterized by an absence of significant change in policy. The parties and individuals who had previously suggested change in policy were unwilling to bear the costs of such change. For example, despite its rhetoric prior to late 1982, the PSOE later found itself constrained by the reigns of power and other factors. Changes that were implemented, such as the reorganization of CAMPSA, appeared to be more in response to future membership in the EEC than to the transition to democracy itself. In addition, the analysis of public opinion on questions of energy shows that while a strong desire existed for energy conservation measures, the Spanish population was equally strong in its unwillingness to bear the costs for conservation through higher prices for energy. Since individual citizens wished to avoid such costs, there was little reason to expect that a political party, once in power, would be any more willing to bear the political costs for this or other measures such as rationing. Any attempt by a political party to force the public to bear the costs of conservation through rationing would likely have received as equally hostile a reaction as a proposal to raise the prices of energy—despite the general support for energy rationing. Such alternative proposals for policy were not politically possible.

Beyond conservation, however, most alternative proposals for energy policy by major political parties, labor unions, and public opinion could not get on the political agenda either. Strong opposition to the emphasis of energy policy on nuclear generation did not constrain policy-making. In part, this was the case because energy policy generally continued to be determined by other constraints of a more binding characteristic. The discussion of policy instruments, the analysis of the interests and investments of the private financial sector in the energy industry, the description of energy policy support and encouragement by the IEA, allusions to the more recent economic pressures on nuclear energy, and the potential for change created by membership in the EEC all provided examples of more binding constraints on policymakers. The financial advantages to private interests involved in the direction of the Spanish national energy program, with its emphasis on maintaining a high level of supply, were particularly important. These private interests, e.g., the private domestic banks, had a strong incentive to maintain the direction of Spain's energy policy because they were financially linked to this supply-oriented program. Despite some fluctuations, the Spanish energy industry has been very profitable for a long time, particularly for the private electric companies, and the Spanish financial community was strongly connected to this industry. The desire of these financial interests to maximize profits in the area of energy dictated continuity in Spanish energy policy. The domestic business community was able to prevent significant reform in energy policy in order to protect its economic stake. It accomplished this through penetration of the mechanisms of public energy planning and policy-making.

## Other Policy Areas?

These conclusions about energy policy-making during Spain's transition to democracy raise a series of additional descriptive, comparative, and theoretical questions about the effect of political transitions on public policy. The finding that energy policy changed little despite the transition to democracy leads one to question whether or not the same conclusions would have been reached in analyses of other macroeconomic policies. Does the centrality of a political-business elite in the energy industry also occur in other Spanish economic sectors? Has this elite's motivations for profit-seeking similarly affected policy in other areas during the regime transition? Were policymakers in other macroeconomic areas held accountable to the same forces as energy policymakers were? Were government policymakers equally insulated from popular sentiment in other areas of policy as they appeared on such issues as the nuclear generation of energy?

Taken as a group, these questions essentially ask whether additional insight would be gained from comparing policy outputs and decision-making processes. Are the conclusions reached here with regard to energy policy generalizable, or are they specific to Spanish energy policy? The role of the Spanish financial oligarchy and the nature of the constraints on policymakers may be quite different in such economically-related areas as budgetary policy, other fiscal policy concerns, taxation policy, monetary policy, governmental banking practices, other aspects of economic regulation in things like securities and the financial markets, and such policy issues as social security. Did changes only appear to be paid as membership with the EEC approached? Would other conclusions have been drawn if different economically-oriented policy issues had been studied?

While a detailed analysis of another such policy area was beyond the scope of this book, a few general comments may be made. Some research has begun on other policies in Spain entailing economically related issues. For example, monetary policy in Spain did not appear to be specifically affected by the transition to democracy. In both Francoist Spain and during the transition to democracy, Spanish monetary-policy authorities appear to have utilized the bank rate of interest as their central economic instrument.[2] Other research substantiates this finding.[3] Future investigations into monetary policy should verify this and question why. Such research could focus directly on the links of the banking industry and the financial community to monetary policy-making in the Bank of Spain. Research on government popularity, electoral politics, and their influence on monetary policy, borrowing from the large literature on political-business cycles, could offer insight into whether or not monetary policy was altered by the transition to democracy in Spain and the other southern European countries.[4] Such research on the relationship between regime type and use of different monetary instruments would provide insight, particularly in southern Europe.

Greater change might be expected in fiscal and taxation policy than in monetary or energy policy following the political transition. Budgetary planning and policy outputs are often quite susceptible to partisan and electoral politics.[5] Liberal democracy is often viewed as having different budgetary priorities than authoritarian or military regimes. Such work in the Spanish case would build on a strong foundation. Richard Gunther's excellent analysis of the budgetary process in Francoist Spain should be replicated in democratic Spain.[6] Many of the processes of budgetary decision-making processes have probably changed, e.g., greater legislative participation and ultimate cabinet and parliamentary accountability. Nevertheless, budgetary outputs may not have changed following the transition to democracy. A two-fold reasoning makes this possible. First, the central issue for budgetary policy in Spain since the late 1960s has not focused solely on priorities for spending. Instead, it has been the size of the budget relative to the GNP and overall state spending. Growth in the budget deficit has been a central problem since the days of Franco. Attempts to come to grips with many of the budgetary problems characteristic of modern welfare politics appears to have more to do with welfare politics than with authoritarian structures per se.

A second reason why we might expect an absence of significant change in fiscal policy stems from the fact that the PSOE's brand of socialism has proven to be extremely mild—one of the least reformist in Western and southern Europe. Many journalistic accounts of budgetary politics under the Socialists suggests that they were more concerned with managing the inherited deficits than with promoting immediate changes in policy directions. Many of the fiscal policy changes that are being undertaken, such as taxation reform, are again being pursued given requirements imposed from without by Spain's entry into the EEC. We must leave it to future research to untangle the independent effects of the transition to democracy and membership in the EEC on economically-related public policy.[7]

Additional research into social security in Spain would also shed greater light on the effects of transitions to democracy on public policy with economic orientations. The Spanish social-security program grew during the later years of the Franco regime into a system as extensive and large as any in other Western European countries.[8] During the Franco regime, the system incorporated most working citizens and their families into a complete plan for medical care. Most doctors worked in the social-security system, which included a full range of services from neighborhood clinics throughout Spain to large regional hospitals to university research facilities.[9] Besides medical care, the system also provided psychiatric services, pension programs, disability allowance, child assistance, and unemployment benefits.[10] The important point about the social-security system is that it was quite extensive during the Franco regime. Democratic politics did not appear to alter significantly the nature of the program itself or the services it provided. The financing of the system and consideration of reforms to create greater efficiency are where significant change appears to have occurred. In terms of percentage of state expenditures, the Spanish social-security system was the largest of all the twenty-one OECD member countries.[11] The high percentage not only pertained to the democratic system but was also characteristic of the Franco regime. In 1973, for example, 42 percent of all state expenditures went to the social security program. By 1980, this figure had grown to 47.1 percent. In both years, Spain ranked the highest of all OECD countries. The demands for financing such a large system were increasingly met through deficit financing. Democratic Spain has struggled to reach a policy decision on how to manage the growth of these deficits. The important point to be understood through future research is the effect of the transition on this public policy question, not that it is a democratic government that must address this problem. Most observers of and participants in the Spanish social security system acknowledged that it was a problem the Franco system created. Any successor regime, authoritarian or democratic, would have had to tackle it.

## Any Capitalist Country?

The strong influence of the financial community on energy policy before and during Spain's transition from authoritarianism to parliamentary democracy raises another important theoretical question. Is the fact that Spain was a capitalist country the best explanation for the absence of significant change in energy policy-making during the transition to democracy and not the pivotal role of the financial community? Do both the Franco regime and the capitalistic characteristics of the parliamentary democracy provide all that is necessary to explain the decisions on energy policy? After all, wasn't Spain's energy program similar in many respects to other Western democratic and capitalist countries that have not recently experienced such a major political reform?

Answers to these questions should begin by acknowledging that a more radical regime change, one which eliminated or highly altered the private nature of many of Spain's established economic structures, would have probably produced significant change in energy policy. For example, the total nationalization of the banking industry by violent revolutionary means would have undoubtedly had enormous repercussions for policy in the energy sector. Even less radical reforms such as deprivatization would have produced different energy policy outcomes. Such radical reforms would have fundamentally changed the central position of the financial oligarchy. They would also have altered the very core of capitalism—a strong public-private division. With such radical reform, Spain's capitalistic economic system would have been changed, and energy policy along with it.

Other, less radical, reforms could have been undertaken during the transition to democracy which would have produced significant differences in energy policy while not altering capitalism as Spain's economic system. The elimination of the cozy public/private relationship in the Spanish refining industry, for example, would have significantly affected energy policy (one would probably have seen a closing of many of the private Spanish refineries) but not challenge capitalism per se. Such reform would have challenged only certain entrenched economic interests within a capitalist system. As a matter of fact, some reform in Spain's structures dealing with energy would have made the system even more market-oriented. It is this type of reform that the EEC will increasingly impose on Spain. For example, the elimination of the petroleum monopoly and CAMPSA's administering of it, and not simply its restructuring, would have permitted freer supply-and-demand to dictate patterns of petroleum distribution. Such decontrol might have resulted in higher prices for petroleum given that this would have amounted to the removal of the state subsidy on petroleum—since CAMPSA's regulated purchase price was often below market price. Vested economic interests in a capitalistic system, and not capitalism per se, thus best explain the absence of changes in energy policy outputs during Spain's transition to democracy. Revolutionary change of the capitalist system would definitely have produced the conditions necessary for the production of new energy policy outputs. Radical changes to capitalism as a system would have concomitantly affected the very existence of the private financial oligarchy. Reform of the grip of the financial oligarchy on energy policy-making would have been a necessary and a sufficient condition to produce significantly different outcomes in energy policy. Any weakening of this grip did not appear to come through the transition to democracy itself. Only the future will tell if the EEC and its emphasis on transnational liberal economies produces this effect.

Spain's energy policy during the transition to democracy was quite similar to energy policies in many other Western capitalistic countries. Many of these similarities can easily be explained by the technical and resource constraints imposed upon all countries in this era of high energy demand. Was Spanish energy policy different, however, in other aspects? The discussion of policy instruments in Spain revealed that gasoline prices were relatively low in comparison to other Western European countries. Other European capitalistic and mixed economies did not generate the same energy policy outputs as Spain, despite similarity in general economic structure. Why? I have argued that a financial oligarchy existed and that it penetrated the core of both public and private energy policy-making in Spain. Spain was different in energy policy, despite economic similarities with other Western systems, because the decisions of the financial community were binding in nature. While this may also have been true in other European systems, the continued lack of influence of other social, economic, and political interests did not permit the pluralistic policy-making characteristic of many other systems. Pluralism existed in Spain during the transition to democracy but, in many areas, the long shadow of a previous authoritarian regime did not permit it to flourish.

# Notes

## Preface

1. This work shares many central questions with the theoretical literature on political development. It should be considered in the context of discussions on the causal and sequential relationships of societal change, political action, economic advancement, and institutional differentiation and specialization. In this regard, it is a study of comparative history and politics. For useful bibliographies on the extensive literature on political development, see Ronald H. Chilcote, *Theories of Comparative Politics* (Boulder: Westview Press, 1981), 330–46; James A. Bill and Robert L. Hardgrave, Jr., *Comparative Politics: The Quest for Theory* (Lanham, MD: University Press of America, 1973, 1981), 239–54; and Howard J. Wiarda, ed., *New Directions in Comparative Politics* (Boulder: Westview Press, 1985), 213–24.

Most of the early literature on political development left virtually untouched serious theoretical thinking about the consequences of political development and change. This literature failed to analyze the effects of such change. The developmental theorists saw the most typical results of political development as being increased capabilities of the system: its regulative, extractive, distributive, responsive, and symbolic potentiality. Does this, however, assist us in making predictions about the effects on policy-making and its application of a relatively rapid yet peaceful change of the basic structural components of the governmental system? Transitions to democracy should be considered as part of political development.

Most of the developmental literature has thus been concerned more with explaining social change and with investigating its influence on political and institutional development than with studying the effects of this development. Research on political change has generally used a variant of general modernization theory. It has assumed that there is essentially only one successful development strategy: defining "success" as a change that makes a peripheral nation more like one of the European liberal democracies. Developmental theory has been characteristically concerned with maximizing economic development on one hand and political stability on the other. This literature has thus tended to center its questions on "What are the effects of social change?" or "How can the needs be politically or economically met given that this social change exists?" These questions, while important, are neglecting the effect of institutional change on policy options and outcomes.

2. Barrington Moore, Jr., *Social Origins of Dictatorship and Democracy: Lord and Peasant in the Making of the Modern World* (Boston: Beacon Press, 1966), chapter 1; Robert T. Holt and John E. Turner, *The Political Basis of Economic Development: An Exploration in Comparative Political Analysis* (Princeton: D. Van Nostrand Company, 1966); and Douglas C. North, *Structure and Change in Economic History* (New York: W. W. Norton, 1981).

3. Other comparative policy analysis has considered the issue of type of regime, regime change, and policy-making. For example, see Howard J. Wiarda, "The Aftermath of the Trujillo Dictatorship: The Emergence of a Pluralist Political System in the Dominican Republic," Ph.D. dissertation, The University of Florida, on the political transition from totalitarianism to democracy in the Dominican Republic; Frederic L. Pryor's *Public Expenditures in Communist and Capitalist Nations* (London: Allen and Unwin, 1968) on public spending in liberal and communist

states; Harold L. Wilensky, *The Welfare State and Equality* (Berkeley: University of California Press, 1975), for a cross-national study of social-security benefits and equality; Barbara Gitlin Salmore, "Political Structure, Economic Development and Social Security Policies: A Cross-National Study," Ph.D. dissertation, Rutgers University; and Howard M. Leichter's, "Political Regime and Public Policy: A Study of Two Philippine Cities," Ph.D. dissertation, The University of Wisconsin, for an analysis on the different socioeconomic histories of two provincial Philippine cities. For cross-national analysis, see Bruce E. Moon and William J. Dixon, "Politics, the State, and Basic Human Needs: A Cross-national Study," *American Journal of Political Science* 29 (1985): 661–94; and Dixon and Moon, "The Military Burden and Basic Human Needs," *Journal of Conflict Resolution* 30 (1986): 660–84.

4. For example, see David E. Apter, *The Politics of Modernization* (Chicago: University of Chicago Press, 1965); C. E. Black, *The Dynamics of Modernization* (New York: Harper and Row, 1966); Joel S. Migdal, *Peasants, Politics, and Revolution: Pressures toward Political and Social Change in the Third World* (Princeton: Princeton University Press, 1974); and A. F. K. Organski, *The Stages of Political Development* (New York: Alfred A. Knopf, 1965).

# Chapter 1

1. See, for example, Victor Alba, *Transition in Spain: Franco to Democracy* (New Brunswick, N.J.: Transaction Books, 1978); E. Ramón Arango, *The Spanish Political System: Franco's Political Legacy* (Boulder: Westview, 1978); Raymond Carr and Juan P. Fusi, *Spain: Dictatorship to Democracy* (London: George Allen & Unwin, 1979); John F. Coverdale, *The Political Transformation of Spain after Franco* (New York: Praeger, 1979); Robert Graham, *Spain: Change of a Nation* (London: Michael Joseph, 1984); Paul Preston, *Spain in Crisis: The Evolution and Decline of the Franco Regime* (London: Harvester Press, 1976); Thomas D. Lancaster and Gary Prevost, *Politics and Change in Spain* (New York: Praeger, 1985); José Maravall, *Transition to Democracy in Spain* (New York: St. Martin's Press, 1982); Paul Preston, *The Triumph of Democracy in Spain* (London: Methuen, 1986); Donald Share, *The Making of Spanish Democracy* (New York: Praeger, 1986); and Juan J. Linz, Manuel Gómez-Reino, Francisco A. Orizo, and Dario Vila, *Informe sociológico sobre el cambio político en España, 1975–1981* (Madrid: Fundación Foessa, 1981).

2. Examples of the literature on Spanish political parties include: Juan J. Linz and José R. Montero, eds., *Crisis y cambio: electores y partidos en la España de los años ochenta* (Madrid: Centro de Estudios Constitucionales, 1986); Richard Gunther, Giacomo Sani, and Goldie Shabad, *Spain After Franco: The Making of a Competitive Party System* (Berkeley: University of California Press, 1986); Mario Caciagli, "Spain: Parties and the Party System in the Transition," *West European Politics* 7:84–98, and reprinted in the Geoffrey Pridham, ed., *The New Mediterranean Democracies: Regime Transition in Spain, Greece and Portugal* (London: Frank Cass, 1984); Jorge de Estaban and Luis López Guerra, *Los partidos políticos en la España actual* (Barcelona: 1982); and Juan J. Linz, "The New Spanish Party System" in *Electoral Participation: A Comparative Analysis*, ed. Richard Rose (Beverly Hills: Sage, 1980).

3. For examples of the literature on elections and voting in Spain, see Howard R. Penniman & Eusebio M. Mujal-León, eds., *Spain at the Polls, 1977, 1979, and 1982* (Durham: Duke University Press, 1985); Peter McDonough and Antonio López Pina, "Continuity and Change in Spanish Politics." In *Electoral Change in Advanced Industrial Democracies*, ed. Russell J. Dalton, Scott C. Flanagan, and Paul Allen Beck, (Princeton: Princeton University Press, 1984); Samuel H. Barnes, Peter McDonough, and Antonio López Pina, "The Development of Partisanship in New Democracies: The Case of Spain," *American Journal of Political Science* 29 (1985): 695–720; Peter McDonough, Samuel H. Barnes, and Antonio López Pina, "The Legitimacy of Democracy in Spain," *American Political Science Review* 80 (1986): 735–60; and Thomas D. Lancaster and Michael S. Lewis-Beck, "The Spanish Voter: Tradition, Economics, Ideology," *Journal of Politics* 48 (1986): 648–74.

4. As an excellent discussion on part of the political left, see Eusebio Mujal-León, *Communism and Political Change in Spain* (Bloomington: Indiana University Press, 1983). See also Gary Prevost, "Change and Continuity in the Spanish Labor Movement," *West European Politics* (Win-

ter 1984), and J. A. Bengoechea, J. A. Sagardoy, and David León Blanco, *El poder sindical en España* (Barcelona: 1982).

5. For examples of the literature on economic policy in Spain, see Ramón Tamames, *Estructura económica de España*, 17th edición (Madrid: Alianza Editorial, 1986); Charles W. Anderson, *The Political Economy of Modern Spain* (Madison: University of Wisconsin Press, 1970); Richard Gunther, *Public Policy in a No-Party State: Spanish Planning and Budgeting in the Twilight of the Franquist Era* (Berkeley: University of California Press, 1980); Joseph Harrison, *An Economic History of Modern Spain* (New York: Holmes & Meier, 1978); Eric N. Baklanoff, *The Economic Transformation of Spain and Portugal* (New York: Praeger, 1978); Sima Lieberman, *The Contemporary Spanish Economy: A Historical Perspective* (London: George Allen & Unwin, 1982); Victor Pérez Díaz, "Políticas económicas y pautas sociales en la España de la transición: La doble cara del neocorporatismo" in *España: un presente para el futuro*, ed. E. Garcia de Enterria (Madrid: Instituto de Estudios Económicas, 1984); Luis Gámir, *Política económica de España* (Madrid: Alianza Universidad, 1980); Alison Wright, *The Spanish Economy, 1959–1976* (New York: Holmes & Meier, 1977); Joan Esteban, "The Economic Policy of Francoism: An Interpretation" in *Spain in Crisis: The Evolution and Decline of the Franco Regime*, ed. Paul Preston (London: The Harvester Press); Peter McDonough, Samuel H. Barnes, and Antonio López Pina, "Economic Policy and Public Opinion in Spain," *American Journal of Political Science* 30 (1986): 446–79; and J. V. Sevilla Segura, *Economia política de la crisis española* (Barcelona: Editorial Critica, 1985).

6. See my "Economics, Democracy, and Spanish Elections," *Political Behavior* 6 (Dec. 1984): 353–67. Reprinted in Heinz Eulau and Michael S. Lewis-Beck, *Economic Conditions and Electoral Outcomes: The United States and Western Europe* (Agathon Press, 1985).

7. Salustiano del Campo, José Felix Texanos, and Walter Santin, "The Spanish Political Elite: Permanency and Change" in *Does Who Governs Matter? Elite Circulation in Contemporary Societies*, ed. Moshe M. Czudnowski (DeKalb: Northern Illinois University Press, 1982), 147.

8. Paul Preston, *The Triumph of Democracy in Spain* (Methuen, 1986), 76.

9. Richard Gunther, et al. *Spain After Franco: The Making of a Competitive Party System* (Berkeley: University of California, 1986).

10. Ibid., 144.

11. Ibid., 74.

12. Most political regimes are controlled by an elite group of policymakers. This cadre generally claims to represent the whole of society as the embodiment of the "general interest." The individuals or representatives of groups or organizations struggle over control of the regime's patterns, processes, and structures of political recruitment, representation, and mediation. Competition for this control creates a situation in which logrolling and trade-offs characterize the maneuvering among the political participants. This political jockeying takes many forms: institutional reorganization, rule changes, role redefinition, etc. Underlying each of these is an attempt by all political participants to gain on the other competitors. In most situations, a single political participant is unable to monopolize control. Instead, a coalition of decision-makers eventually emerges from a process of proposed or actual tradeoffs among the competing political participants. Each coalition member rationally agrees to a particular set of government policy-making rules and procedures because of perceived advantages. This policy coalition formation comes at the exclusion of other participants, unless of course it is a coalition of the whole. New participants are permitted entry only when that entry benefits another participant or group of actors who have sufficient strength in the coalition to force this decision, i.e., when they can buy their way in or the payoff vector is exogenously altered.

Once a coalition gains control of policy-making, it naturally seeks to protect its interests. All members guard against encroachments on their powers by formalizing the exercise of them. In other words, the institutionalization of policy-making processes occurs because the members of the policy-making coalition believe their regularization will guarantee ample benefits. One means of achieving this is through the institutionalization of the patterns of recruitment, representation, and mediation. This and the regularization of the processes of policy-making thus create a regular flow of benefits for the members of the ruling elite. The implementation of this institutionalization is often most intense immediately following the elite's gaining control of governmental decision-making.

The composition of a political system's policy-making elite is thus at the center of a political regime. The nature of the trade-offs and payments, either positive in the sense of payoffs or negative in the form of threats of violence, and the institutional structures which reflect the governing coalition's protection of its policy-making control differentiate regime types. A political regime stabilizes as the decision-making elite institutionalizes particular patterns, processes, and structures of political recruitment, representation, and mediation. Any significant shift in the membership of the policy-making elite that alters payoffs, even if due to an exogenous shock, brings a reorganization of these patterns, processes, and structures. Such a large-scale reorganization comes as a change in regimes.

13. On the role of the military in the Spanish political system, see, for example, Vicenç Fisas, *El poder militar en España* (Barcelona, 1979); Julio Busquets Bragulat, *Pronunciamientos y golpes de Estado en España* (Barcelona: 1982); Jesus Ynfante, *El ejército de Franco y de Juan Carlos* (Paris, 1976); Julio Busquets Bragulat, *El militar de carrera en España*, 2d ed. (Barcelona: 1971); José Luis Morales and Juan Celada, *La Alternativa militar: El golpismo después de Franco* (Madrid, 1981); and Carolyn P. Boyd and James M. Boyden, "The Armed Forces and the Transition to Democracy in Spain" in *Politics and Change in Spain*, ed. Thomas D. Lancaster and Gary Prevost (New York: Praeger, 1985).

14. See Ramón Tamames, *La oligarquia finánciera en España* (Barcelona: Editorial Planeta, 1977).

15. See Eusebio Mujal-León, *Communism and Political Change in Spain* (Bloomington: Indiana University Press, 1983). For a history of the PCE during the Franco era, see Guy Hermet, *The Communists in Spain* (Lexington, Mass.: Lexington Books, 1974).

16. Major works on the labor movement during the Franco period include Jon Amsden, *Collective Bargaining and Class Conflict in Spain* (London: Weidenfeld and Nicolson, 1972), and José Maravall, *Dictatorship and Political Dissent: Workers and Students in Franco's Spain* (New York: St. Martin's Press, 1979). An excellent, and specific, discussion of the PCE in the labor movement is found in Eusebio Mujal-León, *Communism and Political Change in Spain* (Bloomington, Ind.: Indiana University Press, 1983). For a thorough history of Spanish anarchism, see Murray Bookchin, *The Spanish Anarchists: The Heroic Years, 1868–1936* (New York: Harper Colophon Books, 1977) and Robert W. Kern, *Red Years/Black Years: A Political History of Spanish Anarchism 1911–1937* (Philadelphia: Institute for the Study of Human Issues, 1978). For a review of post-Franco Spanish anarchism, see Gary Prevost, "Contemporary Spanish Anarchism," *Social Anarchism* (Winter 1982): 22–32.

17. Charles Anderson, *The Political Economy of Modern Spain: Policy-Making in an Authoritarian System* (Madison: The University of Wisconsin Press, 1970).

18. Carlos Moya Valganon, 188.

19. It is interesting to note that Santiago Carrillo, the then-leader of the Spanish Communist Party, was one of the most frenzied supporters of the monarchy. This political anomaly exemplifies the nature of the newly emerged dominant coalition. The king is the ultimate protector of the PCE's legal right to exist.

20. In this sense, this work has a great deal in common with much of the corporatist literature. For discussions of corporatism in southern Europe, see Howard J. Wiarda, *Corporatism and Development: the Portuguese Experience* (Amherst: University of Massachusetts Press, 1977); Philippe Schmitter, *Corporatism and Public Policy in Authoritarian Portugal* (Beverly Hills: Sage, 1975); Sima Lieberman, *The Contemporary Spanish Economy: A Historical Perspective* (London: George Allen & Unwin, 1982); Juan J. Linz, "Legislatures in Organic Statist Authoritarian Regimes: The Case of Spain," in *Legislatures in Development: Dynamic of Change in New and Old States*, ed. Joel Smith and Lloyd D. Musolf (Durham, N.C.: Duke University Press, 1979); Charles W. Anderson, *The Political Economy of Modern Spain: Policy-Making in an Authoritarian System* (Madison: The University of Wisconsin Press, 1970); and Richard Gunther, *Public Policy in a No-Party State* (Berkeley: University of California Press, 1980).

21. Preston (1976), ii.

22. Preston, ii; see also viii.

23. Preston, viii.

24. Preston, iv.

25. It is interesting to note, now that negotiations for Spain's entry into the EEC are com-

pleted, that the elimination of protective tariffs will hurt many small- and medium-size Spanish businesses unable to withstand unrestrained competition.

26. Preston, vi.

27. Esteban, 84. Also, William T. Salisbury, "Western Europe," in Cortada (1980), 103 and 116. This argument runs counter to Linz (1981), 394 when he states that "contrary to some interpretations, I see little evidence that business groups played an active role in favor of or against the political transformation in this period and even less evidence of structural alignments for or against change."

28. For example, see David E. Apter, *The Politics of Modernization* (Chicago: University of Chicago Press, 1965); C. E. Black, *The Dynamics of Modernization* (New York: Harper & Row, 1966); Joel S. Migdal, *Peasants, Politics, and Revolution: Pressures Toward Political and Social Change in the Third World* (Princeton: Princeton University Press, 1974); and A. F. K. Organski, *The Stages of Political Development* (New York: Alfred A. Knopf, 1965).

29. Besides a logical cutoff point for this analysis, Spain's joining of the EEC will affect energy policy in several ways. While Spain would not have been permitted to join the EEC without the transition to democracy, these changes in energy policy will come as a consequence of this membership, not as a result of the transition to democracy itself.

## Chapter 2

1. The literature on the Spanish Civil War is quite extensive. There are more than three thousand books on the subject. On the different social problems and political movements of the half-century preceding the war, see Gerald Brenan, *The Spanish Labyrinth* (New York: Cambridge University Press, 1943). The most celebrated treatment of the war's military and political activities is Hugh Thomas's *The Spanish Civil War* (New York: Harper, 1961). Richard A. H. Robinson's *The Origin of Franco's Spain: the Right, the Republic, and Revolution, 1931–1936* (Newton Abbot: David & Charles, 1970), gives an account of the period's right-wing politics. The Spanish Left during the Second Republic and the Civil War is analyzed by Gabriel Jackson, *The Spanish Republic and the Civil War: 1931–1939* (Princeton, N.J.: Princeton University Press, 1965) and by Stanley G. Payne, *The Spanish Revolution* (New York: Norton Press, 1970). The war's international dimension is related by Gabriel Jackson, ed., *The Spanish Civil War: Domestic Crisis or International Conspiracy?* (Chicago: Quadrangle Books, 1972), and William E. Watters, *International Affair: Non-Intervention in the Spanish Civil War, 1936–1939* (New York: Exposition Press, 1971).

2. Joan Esteban, "The Economic Policy of Francoism: An Interpretation," in *Spain in Crisis*, ed. Paul Preston (London: The Harvester Press, 1976), 83, in which he refers to Charles Anderson, *The Political Economy of Modern Spain: Policy-Making in an Authoritarian System* (Madison: The University of Wisconsin Press, 1970). Esteban argues that Anderson's formal analytical structure is misleading. On the basis of his analysis, Anderson fails "to understand that the same economic tools do not serve the same purpose in a dictatorship as they do, for instance, in a liberal democracy (ibid.)." Anderson's argument, Esteban believes, "fails to grasp the very nature of the regime" (83). Esteban is, in essence, more concerned with who supported the economic policy changes, while Anderson addresses how they were formulated.

3. Juan J. Linz, "A Century of Politics and Interests in Spain," in *Organizing Interests in Western Europe: Pluralism, Corporatism, and the Transformation of Politics*, ed. Suzanne Berger (Cambridge: Cambridge University Press, 1981).

4. Discussed in Esteban, 80. See Juan J. Linz, "An Authoritarian Regime: Spain," in *Mass Politics: Studies in Political Sociology*, ed. E. Allardt and S. Rokkan (New York: The Free Press, 1970), for the distinctive characteristics of the regime. See also Richard Gunther, *Public Policy in a No-Party State* (Berkeley: University of California Press, 1980). The more authoritarian tendencies of the regime's early stage are discussed in Juan J. Linz, "From Falange to Movimiento-organización: The Spanish Party and the Franco Regime, 1936–1968," in *Authoritarian Politics in Modern Societies: The Dynamics of Established One Party Systems*, ed. Samuel P. Huntington and Clement H. Moore (New York: Basic Books, 1970).

5. See Gunther, 35–41, and Kenneth N. Medhurst, *Government in Spain: The Executive at*

*Work* (Oxford: Pergamon Press, 1973). Much of the following section relied extensively on Gunther, 35–36.

6. Franco relinquished daily governmental duties to his friend Admiral Luis Carrero Blanco, who had headed the staff of the Presidencia del Gobierno since 1940, and to Carlos Arias Navarro after the admiral's assassination in December 1973.

7. This was slightly liberalized in 1974, a year before Franco's death, when a limited program of elections provided mayors and senior local officials. Preston, iii.

8. See Juan Linz, "Legislatures in Organic Statist-Authoritarian Regimes—The Case of Spain," in *Legislatures in Development: Dynamics of Change in New and Old States,* ed. Joel Smith and Lloyd D. Musolf (Durham, N.C.: Duke University Press, 1979). See also E. Ramón Arango, *The Spanish Political System: Franco's Political Legacy* (Boulder: Westview Press, 1978), 159–63, and José Amodia, *Franco's Political Legacy: From Fascism to Facade Democracy* (London: Penguin Books, 1977), 57–61.

9. Gunther, 31–32.

10. See Anderson, 1970; Gunther, 1980; Arthur P. Whitaker, *Spain and Defense of the West: Ally and Liability* (New York: Praeger, 1961); and J. W. D. Trythall, *Franco: A Biography* (London: Rupert Hart-Davis, 1970).

11. Amando de Miguel, *Sociología del franquismo* (Barcelona: 1975). See also Paul Preston, ed., *Spain in Crisis: The Evolution and Decline of the Franco Regime* (London: The Harvester Press, 1976). Besides early ideological affinity, the church also became quite economically dependent on the state. Reliance formed a political partnership because the church needed the state for financial support (Linz, 370).

12. Joseph Harrison, *An Economic History of Modern Spain* (Manchester: Manchester University Press, 1978), 158. See also Preston, 1976, and pages 160–61 of Harrison. The Franco regime's coalitional alignment began to shift during the latter part of the regime. The regime's pursuit of a distinctive industrial policy shrunk its own agrarian support. The agricultural sector was deliberately run down after the Stabilization Plan of 1959, with labor being permitted to emigrate. The Franco regime ignored the traditional agricultural society, which cost it support toward the end of the regime.

13. The ACN de P is an elitist Catholic lay organization whose prominence in Spanish politics goes back to the Second Republic. Throughout its history it has recruited high civil servants, professionals, and academics. The Franco regime recruited personnel from the ACN de P, with it reaching its greatest influence during the 1950s, when Alberto Martín Artajo and Joaquin Ruíz-Giménez held key cabinet posts. The ACN de P declined in importance following the 1957 shift in economic policy when Opus Dei began its dominance. See A. Sáez Alba, *La Asociación Católica Nacional de Propagandistas y el caso de Correo de Andalucia* (Paris: Ruedo Ibérico, 1974).

14. Opus Dei is also a religious organization whose predominantly lay membership expresses the pursuit of spiritual values and identification with Christ in their professional as well as personal lives. Its philosophy is best stated by the Aragonese priest José María Escriba de Balaguer, who founded this lay religious order in 1928 when he wrote that "idleness is sinful, that man can best sanctify himself through labor, and that he can most readily find God not by withdrawing from the world but by remaining in it and attaining the greatest possible degree of skill and perfection in the practice of his profession." Members are morally expected to shun consumerism. Instead, they are to commit themselves to the creation of new wealth, for the national good as much as for personal accumulation.

Opus Dei remained a relatively small organization until 1939. It flourished under the Catholic zeal that characterized the early Franco regime. A key in its development occurred in 1947, when the Vatican recognized the order as the Catholic Church's first secular institute. Since then, Opus Dei has prospered as a worldwide organization. It has remained the strongest in Spain, although an official membership count is impossible given the secrecy that surrounds the organization. Its membership has permeated influential positions in the Spanish academic, financial, industrial, and, particularly until 1974, high governmental-administrative worlds. See David Artigues, *El Opus Dei en España, 1928–1962* (Paris: Ruedo Ibérico, 1971). J. Ynfante's *La prodigiosa aventura del Opus Dei: génesis y desarrollo de la Santa Mafia* (Paris: Ruedo Ibérico, 1970) heavily condemns the organization, as does ex-member A. Moncada in his *El Opus Dei: una interpretación* (Madrid: Indice, 1974).

15. Charles Halsted in James W. Cortada, ed., *Spain in the Twentieth-Century World: Essay on Spanish Diplomacy 1898–1978* (Westport, Conn.: Greenwood Press, 1980), 76.

16. Linz (1981), 374. See also Edward Malefakis, *Agrarian Reform and Peasant Revolution in Spain: Origins of the Civil War* (New Haven: Yale University Press, 1970).

17. Manuel Roman, *The Limits of Economic Growth in Spain* (New York: Praeger, 1971), 93.

18. Halsted in Cortada, 44.

19. Roman, 112.

20. Roman, 113; see also 160–61 of Harrison.

21. See "The Working Class under the Franco Regime," in Preston by Sheelagh Ellwood. See also Amsden (1972) and Witney (1965).

22. See Anderson, especially 66–73.

23. Gunther, 28–29.

24. Gunther, 271.

25. Medhurst, 34.

26. Medhurst, 172.

27. Linz (1981), 291.

28. Pike, 201.

29. Witney, 17.

30. For a description and analysis of earlier Spanish economic history, see Harrison (1978); Eric N. Baklanoff, *The Economic Transformation of Spain and Portugal* (New York: Praeger, 1978); and Sima Lieberman, *The Contemporary Spanish Economy: A Historical Perspective* (London: George Allen & Unwin, 1982).

31. Esteban, 89.

32. Harrison (1978), 153.

33. Esteban, 85; see also the Southworth article in Payne (1976).

34. Linz (1981), 381.

35. See Harrison; Lieberman; and Ramón Tamames, *Introducción a la economia española*, 12th edition (Madrid: Alianza Editorial, 1978), and *Estructura Económica de España* (Madrid: Alianza Universidad, 1980).

36. Lieberman, 169–70.

37. Esteban, 91.

38. Pedro Schwartz, "Politics First: The Economy After Franco," *Government and Opposition* 11 (1976): 84–103.

39. Harrison, 162.

40. Witney (1965), 23–39.

41. Payne (1967), 60.

42. Esteban, 92.

43. Pike, 189. Esteban argues (92) that it was financed partly by tax revenue and partly by servicing the public debt. The taxation system was and remains highly regressive. See also Payne (1967), 60.

44. This statement is supported by Lieberman's analysis in which he states: "The slow growth of Spanish exports is largely explained by the persistent internal inflation, the Spanish rate of inflation being one of the highest in Europe" (180).

45. Harrison, 1978, 153.

46. Harrison, 153–54.

47. Harrison, 154.

48. Esteban, 94.

49. Lieberman, 181.

50. Harrison (1978), 154.

51. Payne (1967), 63.

52. See Anderson, 118, and Gallo (1971), 257–99.

53. See Anderson; Lieberman, chapter 4; Esteban, 96–100; and Harrison, 155–56.

54. Harrison, 151.

55. Esteban, 295.

56. Pike, 179.

57. Harrison, 155–56.

58. What was the source of the economic boom? Why was the Spanish Stabilization Plan so successful? Although some attribute the plan's success to the economic policy introduced by these technocrats, skilled domestic economic management was not as central as the windfalls of tourism, foreign investment, and the remittances of Spanish workers abroad. (See Baklanoff (1968) and Roman (1971) for a treatment of tourism and foreign investments. See also Esteban, 99, and Harrison, 156.) Others suggest that $420 million of foreign support guaranteed the plan's success. (Anderson, pages 30–31, points out that this sum included $100 million in credits from the OEEC, $75 million in IMF drawing rights, $70 million in commercial credits from the Chase Manhattan and First National City banks, and $30 million in loans to foreign companies from the U.S. Import-Export Bank.) There is little argument that the economic development could not have occurred without heavy foreign investment because Spanish savings alone were insufficient. (See Harrison, 165). In terms of the relationship of the political institutions to this strong economic performance, Esteban questions whether or not Spain's political system of the Franco regime contributed to the Spanish economic success. His conclusion that the economic growth occurred despite the political system appears sound because tourism became such a central part of the Spanish economy. The huge influx into Spain of large volumes of foreign exchange from tourism occurred without a great deal of effort on the part of the Franco regime. Tourist revenues in Spain also doubled between 1959 and 1960 by simply lifting restrictions. The relationship between the values of capital-goods imports and tourist revenues between 1961 and 1968 supports the argument that the Spanish economy's expansion was highly "related to the rapid introduction of new capital goods into the industrial sector made possible by the flow of foreign exchange provided by tourism" (See Roman, 45). Tourist revenues are undoubtedly linked to the domestic price level. As Table 3–3 indicates, between 1959 and 1973 the number of tourists increased eight times and their receipts twenty-four times, which equalized the otherwise large balance-of-trade deficit. "In reviewing overall effects of the devaluation and the Stabilization Plan, it appears that the achievement of domestic controls over prices and wages was not as crucial for the future of economic development as were the waves of tourism and foreign exchange that followed" (Roman, 40).

59. Esteban, 97. See the International Bank for Reconstruction and Development's 1963 report.

60. Harrison 1978, 157, explains that "the social element was added only as an afterthought when earlier drafts were in circulation" and was added for political reasons.

61. Esteban, 97–98.

62. Roman, 131.

63. Roman, 51.

64. Roman, 50.

65. Roman, 55 and 51. To add to this, the state's stimulation and enormous expansion of the service sector impeded significant industrial growth. And, on another note on longer range planning, the Development Plan seriously neglected the importance of professional training for economic development. Technical and scientific research and training accounted for only .01 percent of the plan's final year's spending while only 6.0 percent of total investments were allocated for labor training and education.

66. Esteban, 98.

67. For a discussion of "growth pole" planning see Lieberman, 220–23. Of particular interest is the idea (221) that "pork barrel"-type politics in an authoritarian regime may have come into play here in the sense that the establishment of a particular "pole" was personally ordered by Laureano López Rodo to please General Franco.

68. See Dionisio Martín Sanz, *En las Cortes españolas: crítica del segundo plan de desarrollo* (Madrid: A. Aguado, 1969).

69. Gunther (1980).

70. See Comisaría del Plan de Desarrollo Económico y Social, *III Plan de Desarrollo, 1972–1975* (Madrid: Imprenta Nacional del Boletín Oficial del Estado, 1971). For criticism, Martín Sanz, Dionisio, *La planificación española en la olimpiada de las ideologias: Critica del III Plan de Desarrollo* (Madrid: Afrodisio Aguado, 1972).

71. Gunther, 261.

72. Gunther, 313–14 n. 146.

73. Harrison (1978), 152.

74. Gunther, 6 and 31. Linz (1964 and 1973) also argued the notion of a "limited pluralism." Linz (1981) 391 clarified this notion of "limited pluralism" which he says was coined to compare the situation with the totalitarian ideal type. Linz suggests one might also use the term "unitary pluralism." All interest politics were subordinated to Franco's ultimate power as evidenced by the fact that the system excluded all working-class autonomous organizations. Gunther, in his solid analysis of the budgetary process in Francoist Spain, asserted that "the heterogeneous nature of the Nationalist coalition ruled out certain courses of action which might otherwise have been possible: no single group was in a sufficiently powerful position to become dominant within the new Spanish state" (Gunther, 6). A limited pluralism did not prevent a political business elite from becoming dominant. The pluralism Gunther is addressing existed, I argue, within the political business elite.

75. Gunther, 32.

76. Anderson argues that, despite their institutional differences, policy-making in an authoritarian system is not unlike that in Western liberal democracies. He suggests that economic decision-making in Spain was similar to that in other Western countries in that the political processes did not involve widespread participation. He argues that similarities between the policy processes in Spain and those in Western democracies existed not because Spain was less authoritarian than conventionally believed but because the Western democracies were more so. Anderson suggests, in effect, a convergence of the political processes of economic decision-making in "democratic" and "authoritarian" political systems.

Anderson gives special attention to how policy-making procedures were defined and functioned under Spanish authoritarianism as compared to the procedures of western representative countries. Anderson generalizes about the political process of Spanish economic decision-making from his analysis of the 1959 Spanish Economic Stabilization Plan.

Anderson's conclusions about economic decision-making in authoritarian Spain are challenged by Richard Gunther (1980) and Joan Esteban (1976). Gunther asserts in his study of the Spanish budgetary process that there were characteristics of economic decision-making within the Spanish state under Franco that clearly differentiated that regime from democratic regimes at similar levels of economic development. He argues that the source of Anderson's erroneous conclusions stem primarily from his reliance on the public record for information. All too often governmental officials regard these published accounts, which they themselves have frequently written, as little more than public-relations exercises. The reports upon which Anderson based his study, Gunther contends, often bear little resemblance to political reality.

Esteban considerably disagrees with Anderson. Although he does not dispute Anderson's claim that the Spanish economic system under Franco resembled Western European economies in most respects, he does disagree with Anderson's conclusion that the range of policy objectives and available economic instruments in Spain was at least as wide as those of other European nations.

77. See Muñóz (1969) 60–65.

78. Anderson, 76.

79. Roman, 96.

80. Payne (1967), 56.

81. Pike, 188.

82. Harrison, 161.

83. Pike, 189. See also Linz (1981), 367. This monopolization is probably facilitated by the geographical over-concentration of the Spanish economy in Madrid, Barcelona, the Bilbao-San Sebanstian area, Valencia, and Sevilla.

84. Lieberman, 219.

85. Wright, 59.

86. Lieberman (1982), 216.

87. Harrison, 156.

88. I strongly disagree with Gunther's assertion (269) that this coercive resource was relatively unimportant. Gunther's statement is based on his study of the Francoist budgetary process. I believe other political economic issues would have revealed the centrality of the leverage the private sector held in economic planning.

89. Linz (1981), 391.
90. Linz (1981), 392. Also, Carlos Moya Valganón, "Las elites económicas y el desarrollo español," Campos Urbano, *La España*, 1.
91. It was disclosed in the March 1968 budget discussions that Opus Dei's University of Navarra, legally a private university, was receiving huge governmental subsidies (Amodia 211). See also Pike, 199, and Amodia, 211. The publications include *Actualidad Económica* and *Actualidad Española*.
92. The social, economic, and political climate that Opus Dei advocated during the Franco regime was interestingly stated by Laureano López Rodo, an Opus Dei technocrat and a central figure in Spain's development plans: "One of the urgent necessities of our time is political stability, without which the government cannot comply with its commitment, each day more complex, of directing state action, above all in what bears on socio-economic development. For this it is convenient that the government not be at the mercy of parliamentary debates" (Laureano López Rodo, 85, (Madrid, 1970), cited in Pike, 197). Cited in Pike, 196, from Escriba de Balaguer's book *Camino (The Way)* first published in 1939, which contains 999 aphorisms or maxims promoting individual success in one's professional life.
93. Linz, 392.
94. Amodia, 210.
95. Discussed by Amodia, 211.
96. Juan J. Linz and Amando de Miquel, *Los empresarios ante el poder público* (Madrid: Instituto de Estudios Políticos, 1966), 121.
97. Medhurst, 172.
98. Gunther, 260.
99. Linz and de Miquel, 121.
100. Gunther, 282.
101. Gunther (1980), 282. We must note that in a regime change parts of the state bureaucracy lose, or are threatened to lose, some of their policy-initiating powers. As its power decreases, the existing branches or administrative bodies within the bureaucratic structure will fight to protect their previously delegated power. Intensity of interministerial power struggles and protection from encroachment of powers might become fiercer in the structural reorganization of the regime change.
102. Gunther, 262. For a description of the contemporary bureaucratic elite, see Beltrán (1977). For the historical background, see Linz (1981).
103. With respect to the nature of the ministerial hierarchy during the Franco regime, the Minister of Finance coordinated policy in economic areas such as energy. See Gunther, 163.

## Chapter 3

1. OECD, *Energy Balances of OECD Countries, 1960–1974* (Paris: OECD, 1976), and IEA, *Energy Balances of OECD Countries, 1975–1979* (Paris: OECD, 1981).
2. Ibid.
3. See R. Magaña Vázquez, "El carbón español en el futuro energético," *Información Comercial Española* 501 (May 1975): 57–67; and Raimundo Lasso de la Vega, "La economía del carbón," *Economía Industrial* 149 (May 1976): 48–588.
4. Ramón Tamames, *Estructura Económica de España* (Madrid: Alianza Universidad, 1980), 396.
5. See Antonio Téllez de Peralta, "El gas natural en España, *Boletín Informativo* 96 (September 1980): 3–16. Fundación Juan March.
6. Paul Preston, ed., *Spain in Crisis* (London: The Harvester Press, 1976), iv.
7. Several very good works on the contemporary Spanish constitution have been written, generally from a legalistic point of view. For example, José Belmonte, *La Constitución: texto y contexto* (Madrid: Prensa Española, 1979); Andrés de Blas, *Introducción al Sistema Político Español* (Barcelona: Teide, 1983); Luis Sánchez Agesta, *El sistema político de la Constitución Española de 1978*, 3d ed. (Madrid: Editora Nacional, 1984); E. Sánchez Goyanes, *Constitución Española Comentada*, 12th ed. (Madrid: Paranfino, 1984); and E. Sánchez Goyanes, *El sistema*

*constitucional Español* (Madrid: Paranfino, 1981). See also Thomas D. Lancaster and Micheal W. Giles, "Spain" in *Legal Traditions and Systems: An International Handbook*, ed. Alan N. Katz (Westport, Conn: Greenwood Press, 1986).

8. Mark N. Hagopian, *Regimes, Movements, and Ideologies* (New York: Longman, 1978), 163.

9. See Richard Gunther's *Public Policy in a No-Party State* (Berkeley: University of California Press, 1980), and Juan J. Linz, "From Falange to Movimiento-organización: The Spanish Single Party and the Franco Regime, 1936–1968," in ed. Samuel P. Huntington and Clement H. Moore, *Authoritarian Politics in Modern Societies: The Dynamics of Established One Party Systems*, (New York: Basic Books, 1970).

10. The name change—to the Ministry of Industry and Energy—did not occur until 1979.

11. As reported in a personal interview conducted on 10 September 1981.

12. Emphasized in a personal interview held on 16 July 1981.

13. Pedro Schwartz and M. J. González, *Una historia del Instituto Nacional de Industria* (Madrid: Editorial Tecnos, 1978).

14. Sima Lieberman, *The Contemporary Spanish Economy: A Historical Perspective* (London: George Allen and Unwin, 1982).

15. Lieberman, 172–73.

16. All service stations in Spain only sell CAMPSA gasoline. The use of other, private, oil-company names on many service stations does not mean they are selling other than CAMPSA gasoline. Private companies operate such stations at CAMPSA's discretion in order to sell their own nongasoline products. CAMPSA's monopoly applies only on the peninsula—the Canary and Balearic Islands are nonregulated zones.

17. It was also during this time that Iberia, RENFE, the creation of the chain of official hotels or paradores, and other state penetration into the economy occurred.

18. For an excellent analysis and description of CAMPSA, see José Mariá Marín Quemada, *Política Petrolífera Española* (Madrid: Confederación Española de Cajas de Ahorros, 1978).

19. A good comparison of the French, Italian, German, British, and Norwegian national oil companies (but unfortunately not CAMPSA) may be seen in L. E. Grayson, *National Oil Companies* (New York: John Wiley & Sons, 1981).

20. Tamames (1980), 408.

21. These figures include updated data not appearing in the charts.

22. Much of this information concerning the Ministry of Commerce's quota was provided in interviews with officials in the Ministry of Commerce and CEPSA in July, August, and September 1981.

23. "Centro de Estudios de La Energía," (1979) 3, a public-relations brochure published by the CEE itself.

24. The CEE's governing body, the Administrative Council, had the following composition:

| | |
|---|---|
| President: | Commissioner of Energy and Mineral Resources |
| Vice Presidents: | General Director of Energy |
| | General Director of Industrial and Technology Promotion |
| Member: | General Director of Hydraulic Works |
| | General Director of the Nuclear Energy Committee |
| | General Director of the Center for Energy Studies |
| | General Subdirector for Energy Planning |
| | General Subdirector for Liquid Fuels |
| | Director of the National Coal Institute |
| | A representative of the Ministry of Transportation and Communication |
| | A representative of the Ministry of Finance |
| Secretary: | A state employee from the General Energy Council. |

The fact that the general director of the CEE was only one of several members of the Administrative Council while the top three positions remain occupied by high officials from the Ministry of Industry and Energy strongly suggests that the CEE remains subordinate to this ministry.

25. The CEE, with the help of the Ministry of Industry's Energy and Mineral Resources

Commission, monitors Spain's energy situation. These data are published monthly, with an eye on OECD methodology, in *Coyuntura Energética*.

26. A personal interview with a senior official of JEN held on 17 July 1981.

27. José Borrell Fontelles, "Notas sobre la estructura de la industria del refino en España," *Información Comercial Española* 542 (October 1978): 31–40.

28. Spanish law grants strong preferences to Spanish refineries through, for example, a taxation scheme that forces the national petroleum companies to use ships sailing under the Spanish flag. Each company that owns a refinery generally owns its own shipping fleet.

29. UNESA is the acronym for Unidad Electrica, Sociedad Anonima.

30. Ramón Tamames, *Introducción a la economía española* (Madrid: Alianza Editorial, 1978), 214.

31. These twenty-four companies are the following: Iberduero, Fuerzas Navarras, Hidroeléctrica Española, Cia. Riego de Levante, FECSA, Sevillana, Union Eléctrica, ENHER, FENOSA, ENDESA, CESA, Unión Eléctrica de Canarias, Energía Eléctrica de Córdoba, Cia. de Langreo, Salto del Nansa, Minero-Siderurgica Ponferrada, Salto del Guadiana, Fuerzas Hidroeléctricas Segre, Energía e Industrias Aragonesas, Eléctrica Reunidas Zaragoza, Hidro. de Cataluña, Eléctra Cantabrico, Electra Viesgo, and Terminidor.

32. IESA, *The Spanish Energy Sector* (Barcelona: Instituto de Estudios Superiores de la Empresa, 1981), 22.

33. Angel Serrano and Juan Muñoz, "La configuración del sector eléctrico y el negocio de la construcción de las centrales nucleares," *Ruedo Ibérico* 63–66: 153.

34. See Kenneth N. Medhurst, *Government in Spain: The Executive at Work* (Oxford: Pergamon Press, 1973).

35. For a discussion of UNESA and the technical, nonpolitical, side of its investment policies, see Elio Núñez García, "Pricing Spanish Electricity," Ph.D. diss., University of Minnesota, 1972. Núñez García states that UNESA set up an indicative investment program that results from the optimal solution of a linear program similar to those popularized in this field by Electricite de France. He goes on to add that UNESA's 15 percent discount rate, which was used to reach this optima solution, was too high (30–31). He concluded that this rate discriminates against long-term investments (91).

36. See editor's note, "Producción, distribución y consumo de combustibles gaseosos en España," *Información Comercial Española* 542 (October 1978): 119–23.

37. For a concise discussion of this broader economic planning in Spain, see Eric N. Baklanoff, *The Economic Transformation of Spain and Portugal* (New York: Praeger, 1978), 27–32.

38. See, among other articles, "La planificación energética en España," *Situación* (August 1979): 34–48.

39. An earlier plan covering the period 1955–63 was produced by the electrical industry with little governmental participation.

40. J. M. Marín Quemada, "Política de Energía," in *Política Económica* 2: *Autonomias, sectores, objectivos* ed. Luis Gámir (Madrid: Alianza Editorial, 1980), 699–702.

41. Ibid., 701–2.

42. For a discussion of this postponement of economics for politics during Spain's transition, see Thomas D. Lancaster, "Economics, Democracy, and Spanish Elections," *Political Behavior* 6 (1984): 353–67, and reprinted in *Economic Conditions and Electoral Outcomes*, ed. Heinz Eulau and Michael S. Lewis-Beck (New York: Agathon Press).

43. Ministerio de Industría y Energia, *Plan Energético Nacional: Balance de actuaciones* (Madrid: Comisaría de la Energía y Recursos Minerales, July 1981).

44. This belief was expressed during the course of several personal interviews with a senior official of INH, a PSOE parliamentary deputy, and a former deputy of PSOE. These interviews were conducted in Madrid during the summer of 1981.

45. *El País*, 25 October 1980, 41.

46. *El País*, 18 October 1980, and *El País*, 25 October 1980, 41.

47. The Ministry of Industry and Energy prepared a plan of restriction for consumption in December 1980 as a result of the shortage of rain. This plan called for cutting down service by 2,000 megawatts. Fuel- and coal-burning generating plants were working to capacity to cover energy demand, and the nuclear energy plan suffered considerable setbacks that made it unable

to cover projected demand. Energy demand was almost surpassing supply. (*El País*, 16 December 1980).

48. In 1980, the energy industry, both public and private, invested 330,000 million pesetas. In 1981, these investments were to be completed with an additional 430,000 million pesetas. The investments would be implemented according to schedule, according to Ignácio Bayón.

49. The government also mentioned that in the coming months three new generating plants and one nuclear plant (Almaraz) would be placed in service, permitting a savings of one million Tep in 1981. *El País*, 2 November 1980, 46.

50. *El País*, 26 September 1981, 40, and 6 December 1981, 53.

51. *El País*, 18 July 1981, 26–27.

52. *El País*, 3 December 1981.

## Chapter 4

1. Organization for Economic Co-Operation and Development, *OECD Economic Survey: Spain* (Paris: OECD, 1975), 25.

2. Organization for Economic Co-Operation and Development, *OECD Economic Survey: Spain* (Paris: OECD, 1976), 29.

3. Spanish government officials believed at the time that the energy crisis was to be short-lived. This was confirmed to me during the course of interviews with several men who had held key positions in energy policy-making during the Franco regime. Of special note were interviews with individuals in the Ministry of Industry and Energy. These beliefs were also collaborated in interviews with a university professor who was a cabinet-level official in the UCD government, a representative of CEPSA, and several high-ranking officials of CAMPSA.

4. *The Economist*, 14 February 1976.

5. *Business Week*, 25 October 1976, 50.

6. Ibid., 55.

7. Organization for Economic Co-Operation and Development, *OECD Economic Survey: Spain* (Paris: OECD, 1977), 27.

8. Miguel Acoca, "Domestic Economic Woes Propel Membership Bid," *European Community* 203 (1977): 213.

9. Joseph Harrison, *An Economic History of Modern Spain* (Manchester: Manchester University Press, 1978), 168.

10. Eric N. Baklanoff, *The Economic Transformation of Spain and Portugal* (New York: Praeger, 1978), 93.

11. *Business Week*, 23 January 1978, 41, and *Economist* 30 July 1977.

12. *Economist*, 15 October 1977, and OCED (1978), 24.

13. *Business Week*, 23 January 1978.

14. Constantine Christopher Menges, *Spain: The Struggle for Democracy Today* (Beverly Hills: Sage, 1978), 83.

15. Ibid., 34.

16. *The Economist*, 7 January 1979.

17. *Business Week*, 10 April 1978, 47.

18. Harrison, 168.

19. Industrial investment fell 8 percent in 1978 and by considerably more than that in industries worse hit by the slump such as construction and steel.

20. See Richard Barnechea Bergareche, "Fiscalidad y precios de venta al público de los productos petroliferos," *Información Comercial Española* 542: 43–62.

21. *El País*, 10 December 1980. See also José Borrell e Ignácio Gafo, "El monopólio de petróleos y los precios de los productos petroliferos: sistema de fijación de precios ex-refinería," *Información Comercial Española* 542 (1978): 15–30, and Enrique Miravet Garcia, "Fiscalidad del petroleo y derivados," *Hacienda Pública Española* 53 (1978): 121–32.

22. Baklanoff, 90.

23. Statement made by the Commerce Minister shortly before the three-peseta price increase

decided upon by the Council of Ministers on 4 December 1980. *El País*, 23 November 1980, and 5 December 1980.

24. *El País*, 3 December 1981.

25. "Los impuestos en España que afectan a la energía" (86). Santiago Reig Gisbert, *Hacienda Pública Española* 53 (1978): 83–96.

26. See José Camacho, "Tarifas, eléctricas y equipos de medida" (Madrid: E. T. Superior de Ingenieros Agrónomos, 1978), and José Rodríquez de Pablo, "Costes y tarifas de la energía eléctrica," *Información Comercial Española* 542: 71–102.

27. Elio Núñez García, "Pricing Spanish Electricity," Ph.D. diss. University of Minnesota, 1972, 101–2. This study attempts to find "the appropriate level and the structure of a tariff that would take into account the different costs involved in supplying energy at different time periods." This work also includes a description of the generator-to-use delivery system in Spain.

28. Natural-gas prices, like those of petroleum and coal, were regulated by the Ministry of Industry and Energy. This regulation capacity applies to products sold by Empresa Nacional del Gas, S.A. (Enagas), Butano S.A., and Catalunya de Gas y Electricidad. All ministry decrees are published in the *Boletín Oficial del Estado*.

29. William T. Salisbury in *Spain in the Twentieth-Century World: Essays on Spanish Diplomacy, 1898–1978* ed. James W. Cortada (Westport, Conn.: Greenwood Press, 1980), 114.

30. Published interview with Juan António Garcia Díez, UCD Commerce Secretary, *El País*, 23 November 1980.

31. Several officials of the Ministry of Industry and Energy openly acknowledged this during the course of personal interviews. They never attempted to justify such projections but simply stated that they were being corrected. They also stated that earlier policymakers ignored these economic, technical, and political obstacles because the government officials uncritically formalized initial requests by the electrical companies. The policymakers wished not to offend the electricity industry by adjusting the estimates, particularly since these figures were only part of a very general policy blueprint.

32. PEN-75, 176.

33. PEN-75, 178.

34. PEN-75, 179.

35. See Pedro Costa Morata, *Energía: el fraude y el debate* (Barcelona: Gaya Ciencia, 1978), 109–16, and Federación de Energía UGT-ICEF, *La crisis nuclear: una alternativa socialista para España*, (Madrid: H. Blume Ediciones, 1981), 109–16.

36. "The feeling that there is over-investment in transmission, which appears when looking at isolated links of the system, has to be qualified by taking into account that an alternating-current system must keep synchronism among all generators on the system. This synchronism depends on the power angle among the bus bars—the more investment on lines the lower the power angle required to push a certain amount of energy on the line and the greater the stability. For a system like the Spanish one, which was plagued by synchronism problem in the late 1960's, it is difficult to say that there is over-investment. Perhaps better coordination will eventually achieve the same service security at lower cost" (Núñez García, 68).

37. *El País*, 18 October 1980, 48.

38. The Italian National Hydrocarburates Corporation (ENI) was created in 1953. By the late 1950s it controlled production and prospecting for gas, oil, and petroleum products as well as artificial rubber, fertilizers, and a variety of petrochemicals.

39. See Jerónimo Sánchez Blanco, "El Instituto Nacional de Hidrocarburos: Necesidad de un debate / y 2," *El País* (23 July 1981). Also see "El INH funcionara como una empresa, según Claudio Boada," *El País*, (26 June, 55, and "Chequeo al ente de hidrocarburos," *El Nuevo Lunes*, 22–28 June 1981, 14, 19. During a series of personal interviews, critics argued that INH was not initially created through parliamentary channels so as to minimize open discussions of overall energy policies. These critics included a researcher in the Centro de Estudios Socio-Ecológicos, a PSOE activist and civil servant in the Ministry of Industry and Energy, and a PSOE member of parliament and the party's spokesman on energy. In other interviews, INH's technical secretary argued that no need existed for parliamentary debate during the early stages of INH's creation. He stated that parliamentary approval was eventually necessary to make the legal transfer of INI's funds to INH. Critics responded to this by stating that several years of operation

before the parliamentary debate would unfairly remove the question of whether or not INH should actually exist.

40. *El Nuevo Lunes*, 22–28 June 1981, 14.

41. Such memories of the past regime's practices were expressed to me during several interviews, including ones with a PSOE ex-deputy of parliament on 21 September 1981 and HISPANOIL's scheduling and shipping manager on 28 July 1981. Both interviews were conducted in Madrid.

42. *El Nuevo Lunes*, 20–26 July 1981.

43. The first directive team included Miguel Boyer as Director of Planning, Manuel Pérez Olea as secretary general, António Hoyos as director of legal matters, José de Miguel as director of internal matters, and Rafael Spottorno as director of external matters.

44. *Business Week*, 30 January 1978.

45. *El País*, 7 July 1981.

46. *El País*, 26 June 1981, 55.

47. Personal interview with the technical secretary of INH, conducted in Madrid on 10 September 1981.

## Chapter 5

1. Amigos de la Tierra, *Modelo energético de tránsito: Respuesta ecologista al Plan Energético Nacional* (Madrid: Ediciones Miraguano, 1979).

2. As stated in interviews with authors and political activists associated with Amigos de la Tierra on 14 and 16 July 1981 in Madrid.

3. Worthy of special mention, given its comprehensiveness, is Pedro Costa Morata, *Energía: El fraude y el debate* (Barcelona: Gaya Ciencia, 1978). See also Pedro Costa Morata, *Nuclearizar España* (Barcelona: Los Libros de la Frontera, 1976); Vicens Fisas Armengol, *Centrales Nucleares* (Madrid: Campo Abierto Ediciones, 1978); and Mário Gabiria, *La Lucha Antinuclear* (Donostia, Spain: Campo Abierto Ediciones, 1978).

4. This point was openly admitted during the course of several interviews both with members of these groups and with Spanish officials participating directly in energy policy-making. These interviews included leaders of Amigos de la Tierra, a Spanish academic associated with the antinuclear movement, a high-ranking official in Energy Planning in the Ministry of Industry and Energy, and a PSOE activist and bureaucrat in the Ministry of Industry and Energy.

5. Miguel Marandarian, manager of Iberduero's nuclear- and thermal-energy division, denied the plant threatened the area's ecology: "The water at Lemóniz will be heated by one degree. This will mean that some species of fish will go away but others which like warmer water will take their place" (*Newsweek*, 24 April 1978).

6. Interview conducted on 7 October 1981 in Vitoria with a representative of Euskadiko Ezkerra to the Basque Autonomous Parliament.

7. *Newsweek*, 24 April 1978, 12, and supported in a personal interview on 15 July 1981 in Madrid with an author and academic involved in the anti-nuclear movement.

8. See, for example, *El País*, 25 July and 17 September 1981.

9. *Newsweek*, 24 April 1978, 12.

10. Herri Batasuna parliamentary deputies Jon Idigoras, Inaki Aldekoa, Txomin Ziloaga, and Santi Brouard all participated in the large demonstration in Bilbao against Lemóniz on 29 August 1981 (*El País*, 30 August 1981).

11. Euskadiko Ezkerra, *Programa de lucha y de gobierno* (Bilbao: Printzen, 1980), 53–61.

12. Statement made during a personal interview conducted on 7 October 1981 in Vitoria with a representative of Euskadiko Ezkerra to the Basque Autonomous Parliament.

13. *El País*, 19 March and 7 April 1982.

14. *Nuclear News*, February 1987, 61–80.

15. Mario Onaindia Natxiondo, *Otra herencia más: plan energético nacional* (Bilbao: Printzen, 1978). Sr. Onaindia, the leader of the extreme left Basque party Euskadiko Eskerra, told me that despite the appearance of his name, he was not the work's author. Due to legal technicalities associated with the nonlegalized status of the party during the book's writing, his name appeared

instead of Javier Olavere's. Sr. Olavere confirmed during a personal interview that he had in fact chaired the party's committee responsible for this work.

16. Ibid., 8.

17. Costa Morata (1978) 123–30, discusses the CCOO's position vis-à-vis nuclear energy, harshly criticizing their pro-nuclear position.

18. Expressed during a personal interview conducted in Madrid on 17 September 1981 at UGT headquarters with several members of UGT's Federated Technical Commission of Industrial Energy and a former PSOE member of the Chamber of Deputies.

19. Ibid., 17 September 1981.

20. UGT-ICEF, Federación de Energía, *La crisis nuclear: Una alternativa socialista para España* (Madrid: H. Blume, 1981).

21. Federaciones de Energía y Mineria de la UGT, *Alternativa energética: Una solución socialista para España* (Madrid: H. Blume, 1981).

22. UGT interview, 17 September 1981.

23. Forum Atomico Español, Jornadas de Primavera, Juan Luis Calleja conference, (Madrid: May, 1978), 18–19.

24. Party statements, April 1977, taken from *Programas económicos de los partidos políticos*.

25. This general point was made consistently during numerous personal interviews conducted with PSOE party officials and members.

26. Personal interview conducted with a member of the Central Committee of the Spanish Communist Party, conducted on 8 October 1981.

27. PSOE's Javier Solana quoted in *Primera Plana*, 1 February 1978.

28. PSOE's Tierno Galvan quoted in *Primera Plana*, 1 February 1978.

29. Ibid.

30. Ibid.

31. Quoted in *Informaciones*, 20 March 1978.

32. See Santiago Vilanova, *El sindrome nuclear: El accidente del Harrisburg y el riesgo nuclear en España* (Barcelona: Bruguera, 1980).

33. This discussion on the party's position on PEN during the parliamentary debates relies quite extensively on UGT's *Alternativa energética*, 55–58.

34. UGT's *Alternativa energética*.

35. Ibid.

36. This point was reinforced during a personal interview with PSOE's energy spokesman in the Congress of Deputies.

37. Instituto Nacional de Industria, "Debate parliamentario sobre el Plan Energético Nacional" (Madrid: Dirección de Estudios, Centro de Documentación, 1979), 57.

38. Javier Solana Madariaga, "Alternativa socialista al PEN," *Papeles De Economía Española* 14 (May 1983): 14–20.

39. Ibid.

40. The responses recorded in the following tables were solicited by these questions:

The Arab-Jewish War has produced a world gasoline shortage that can affect Spain: which of these measures do you consider our authorities should adopt on this matter?

1. Rationing, that is to say, a limitation of the amount each driver may buy.
2. Prohibit the driving of cars on Sundays.
3. Prohibit the driving of cars one weekday, other than Sunday.
4. Place speed limits on traffic, given that less gasoline is consumed at lower speeds.
5. Alternate traffic, even days for cars with even license plates, odd days for those with odd plates.
6. Don't know, no response.

Along the same lines, do you think that a measure will not be needed because you don't consider it necessary, or that some of these restrictions should be implemented?

1. None.
2. Various.
3. Don't know, no response.

The question posed in the June 1979 questionnaire was the following:

> Finally, speaking about the energy crisis and the need to face this crisis by limiting or not limiting gasoline consumption, are you personally in agreement that some of the steps I'm going to read to you are taken or do you not believe in taking steps to limit gasoline consumption?
>
> 1. Raise gasoline prices so people will consume less.
> 2. Ration gasoline by means of a quota per driver.
> 3. Establish turns in such a manner that half the cars may be driven on even days, the other half on odd days.
> 4. Don't adhere to taking measures in order to limit gasoline consumption.
> 5. Don't know, no response.

41. This Spanish government-sponsored survey was conducted by means of a personal interview in the home of the respondent with a structured questionnaire. The sample size of 1,223 was stratified according to sex, age, occupation, region, and city size. The interviews were conducted by R.N.C. Sondeos, S.A. (Red Nacional de Campo) between 10 and 30 July 1979.

42. Personal interviews conducted in Madrid with several key energy policymakers. These included the general subdirector of Energy Planning in the Ministry of Industry and Energy and the technical secretary of the National Institute of Hydrocarbons, who was an ex-commissioner of Energy in the Ministry of Industry and Energy. See also Ramón Leonato Marsal, "Posibilidades energéticas de España," *Boletín Informativo* (Madrid: Fundación Juan March) 94 (1980), and Francisco Pascual Martínez, "La energía nuclear y su futuro," *Boletín Informativo* (Madrid: Fundación Juan March) 92 (1980).

43. Personal interviews with numerous energy policy officials during 1981. They held positions in planning in the Ministry of Industry and Energy and included the head of the technical cabinet of the Commission of Energy and Mineral Resources in the Ministry of Industry and Energy, one of the central authors PEN-82 in the Ministry of Industry and Energy, the head of exploration in the state's delegation in CAMPSA, and an official of the Center for Energy Studies.

44. See Javier Solana's criticism of PEN in the 1979 parliamentary debates (Instituto Nacional de Industria, Ibid.).

45. Ramón Querol, "La crisis energética: diagnóstico y alternativas" (Madrid: Fundación Humanismo y Democracia, 1980).

46. *El País*, 5 December 1980, 55.

47. Stated in the course of numerous personal interviews with members of these parties, groups, and other individuals. In addition to the interviews noted above with members of the Spanish Socialist Workers Party, the Spanish Communist Party, Euskadiko Eskerra, and Amigos de la Tierra, this point surfaced in interviews with a general subdirector of the official bank; a professor who conducts research on energy policy, and who later became general technical secretary of the Ministry of the Presidency; a director in CAMPSA; and a high official of UNESA.

48. This impressionistic statement is based on extensive interviews with many Spanish political activists and government leaders.

## Chapter 6

1. Statements based on personal interviews conducted on 17 September 1981 at UGT headquarters with several members of UGT's Federated Technical Commission of Industrial Energy and a political leader of PSOE.

2. UGT, Federaciones de Energía y Minéria de la UGT, *Alternativa energética: Una solución socialista para España* (Madrid: H. Blume, 1981), 130.

3. In this chapter, I admittedly use only circumstantial evidence to support the argument that a financial oligarchy existed in Spain and that it continued to play a central role in Spanish energy policy-making.

4. References made during many personal interviews conducted in Spain, including several with high-level government officials in economics and politics conducted in June 1983. Other works on Spain also mention this oligarchy. For example, Richard Gunther et al., in *Spain After Franco: The Making of a Competitive Party System*, (University of California Press, 1986), make numerous references to the activities and the role that the oligarchy played in Spain's transition to democracy. For example, in quoting one of the people he interviewed, he refers directly to "the great economic oligarchy" in discussing the relationship between party membership and economic actors. While these authors prefer to refer to it as the "Spanish business class" (144), they acknowledge the existence of Spain's financial oligarchy throughout their analysis on, for example, 74, 87–88, 144, and 174. In his *The Triumph of Democracy in Spain* (Methuen, 1986), Paul Preston also directly refers to an economic oligarchy (76).

5. See Juan Múñoz, *El poder de la banca en España* (Algorta: Zero, 1969), 307–10, and Ramón Tamames, *La lucha contra los monopolios* (Madrid, 1970), 323–52.

6. Tamames (1970), 356–416.

7. UNESA's role as a coordinator of the Spanish electrical industry was confirmed during the course of numerous interviews, including those with several officials of UNESA in its Madrid headquarters in July and September 1981 and during the summers of 1983 and 1984.

8. Stated in a personal interview in Madrid on 27 July 1981 in the CAMPSA headquarters with two high-level officials.

9. The best exception to this is found in Juan J. Linz, "A Century of Politics and Interests in Spain," in *Organizing Interests in Western Europe*, Suzanne Berger, ed. (Cambridge: Cambridge University Press, 1981).

10. For a discussion of the families comprising Spain's financial elite, see Linz, 1981.

11. Figures calculated from data presented in Ramón Tamames, *Estructura económica de España*, 17th edition (Madrid: Alianza, 1986), 604.

12. Torrero (1982), 93.

13. See, for example, Banco de Bilboa, *Informe y Memoria* (Bilboa: Banco de Bilboa, 1982).

14. Personal interviews with several bank officials on 20 July 1981. Among these was one individual who was also a university professor, author, and researcher on energy policy. Another was a former member of parliament.

15. Interviews with officials from CAMPSA.

16. Linkage between the political-financial oligarchy and industrialization began its intensification period in 1959. For example, before that time, INI had been financed through budgetary appropriations. After 1959, savings banks were required to invest in bonds issued by INI. This avoided tax increases and even further intertwined Spanish banking interests with the state economic decision-making concerns.

17. Throughout my interviews in Spain, many officials in government ministries continually stressed their role as "technical" rather than "political" decision-makers. While it may be difficult not to be engaged in politics when policy is being made, these officials consistently insisted that their expertise, education, and experience removed them from politics. They generally appeared to view politics as party activities and partisan affairs. While U.S. scholars may not fully appreciate this distinction between technical and political activity, these Spanish officials appeared quite comfortable making the distinction. Language helps to "hide" behind this "technical" self-description in that the Spanish word "política" implies both the English words "politics" and "policy."

18. See Paul H. Lewis, "The Spanish Ministerial Elite, 1938–1969," *Comparative Politics* 5:95–96.

19. Lewis (1972), 100.

20. Ibid.

21. Richard Gunther, *Public Policy in a No-Party State* (Berkeley: University of California Press, 1980), 182.

22. Ibid., 217.

23. Described during the course of a personal interview with a professor of the University of Navarra who had conducted extensive research on Spain's energy resources and public policy in energy. The respondent openly acknowledged his affinity with Opus Dei.

24. For a discussion of this period of the transition, see Victor Alba, *Transition in Spain:*

*Franco to Democracy,* trans. Barbara Lotito (New Brunswick, N.J.: Transaction Books, 1978) John F. Coverdale, *The Political Transformation of Post-Franco Spain* (New York: Praeger, 1979); José Maravall, *Transition to Democracy in Spain* (New York: St. Martin's Press, 1982); Raymond Carr and Juan P. Fusi, *Dictatorship to Democracy* (London: Allen & Unwin, 1979); Robert Graham, *Spain: Change of a Nation* (London: Michael Joseph, 1984); Paul Preston, *The Triumph of Democracy in Spain* (New York: Methuen, 1986); and Donald Share, *The Making of Spanish Democracy* (New York: Praeger, 1986).

25. Linz (1981), 400.

26. The UCD, it should be remembered, was initially an electoral coalition of twelve separate parties, along with many independents formed before the 1977 election. This fusion into a single party occurred under the leadership and prodding of President Suárez.

27. Adapted from Linz (1980), 109–110.

28. *El País,* 26 September 1981, 39.

29. UGT-ICEF, Federación de Energía, *La crisis nuclear: una alternativa socialista para España* (Madrid: H. Blume, 1981), 199–200.

30. UGT interview cited in footnote one.

31. *El País,* 17 December 1980, 14.

32. *El País,* 9 December 1980, 57.

33. A desire for better control of the State's representation in the economy through public companies and better economic planning remains alive, as was demonstrated in discussions on the question during PSOE's twenty-ninth Congress in October 1981 (*El País,* 10 September 1981).

34. Giuseppe Di Palma, "Founding Coalitions in Southern Europe: Legitimacy and Hegemony," *Government and Opposition* 15:182.

35. PSOE's only serious threat to take a nonmoderate stance came in May 1979, when Felipe González resigned as party secretary during an internecine dispute over the party's identification with Marxism. Moderation prevailed, and Felipe reemerged as the party's undisputed leader during a special congress held four months later.

36. Linz (1981), 401.

37. It is interesting to note that PSOE has gone out of its way not to use the term "nationalization." They prefer to use the term "appropriation."

38. Rumasa's secretive style of business is described in José María Bernáldez's *El Señor Rumasa* (Barcelona: Playa & Janés, 1983).

39. Javier Solana Madariaga, "Alternativa socialista al PEN," *Papeles De Económica Española* 14 (1983): 14–20.

## Chapter 7

1. See, for example, Vicens Fisas, *Centrales nucleares: Imperialismo, tecnológico, proliferación nuclear* (Madrid: Campo Abierto Ediciones, 1978); Pedro Costa Morata, *Nuclearizar España* (Barcelona: Los Libros De La Frontera, 1976); and Vicens Fisas Armengol, *Despilfarro y control de la energía* (Barcelona: Edita, 1981), chap. 3.

2. Personal interview with a representative of the Partido Comunista De España (Marxista-Leninista) in the party headquarters in Madrid on 22 September 1981.

3. It should be noted that no attempt is made here to give a complete background of the IEA. Such discussions are available elsewhere. Early information on the IEA includes "The New International Energy Agency of OECD," *The OECD Observer* 73 (January-February 1975): 20–25, Ulf Lantzke, "The OECD and Its International Energy Agency," *Daedalus* (Fall 1975): 217–28, reprinted in *The Oil Crisis,* ed. Raymond Vernon (New York: W. W. Norton, 1976), 217–27; Ulf Lantzke, "International Co-Operation on Energy-Problems and Prospects," *The World Today* 32:83–94; Charles F. Doran, "International Energy Agency: Myth of the Collective Consumer Response" in *Myth, Oil, and Politics: Introduction to the Political Economy of Petroleum* (New York; The Free Press, 1977). See also Mason Willrich and Melvin A. Conant, "The International Energy Agency: An Interpretation and Assessment," *American Journal of International Law* 71 (1977): 199–223. Richard Scott, "Innovation in International Organization: The International

Energy Agency," *Hastings International and Comparative Law Review* 1 (1977): 1–56, outlines the IEA's institutions and legal arrangements. Robert O. Keohane, "The International Energy Agency: State Influence and Transgovernmental Politics," *International Organizations* 32 (1978): 929–51, discusses the IEA's formal decision-making mechanisms. Davis B. Bobrow and Robert T. Kudrle's "Energy R & D: in Tepid Pursuit of Collective Goods," *International Organization* 33 (1979): 149–75, on R & D contains a good history of IEA and the organizational and bureaucratic politics with it.

4. The OECD members that did not belong to the IEA were Finland, France, and Iceland.

5. The Economist Intelligence Unit, Ltd., *Spain: Economic Prospects to 1985* (London: EIU, 1981).

6. The question of the IEA's influence is by no means as controversial as, say, the nationalization of the private electrical industry or nuclear power. Nor is it the centerpiece of Spanish energy planning.

7. "Debate parlamentario sobre el Plan Energético Nacional," *Boletín de Documentación Económica, Especial No. 49*, (Dirección de Estudios, Centro de Documentación, Instituto Nacional de Industria, November 1978), 22.

8. Ibid., 35–37.

9. Ibid., 121.

10. Personal interview conducted on 30 July 1981 at the Ministry of Industry and Energy in Madrid.

11. *El País*, 10 December 1980, in which he highlighted Spain's plan to go beyond the IEA's recommendations of doubling coal production by 1990.

12. UGT-ICEF, Federación de Energía, *La crisis nuclear: Una alternativa socialista para España* (Madrid: H. Blume, 1981), 154.

13. Pedro Costa Morata, *Energía: El fraude y el debate* (Barcelona: Gaya Ciencia, 1978), 101.

14. Christophen Tugendhat and Adrian Hamilton. *Oil: The Biggest Business* (London: Eyre Methuen, 1975) 101. See also Henry R. Nau, "The Evolution of U.S. Foreign Policy in Energy: From Alliance Politics to Politics-as-Usual," in *International Energy Policy*, eds. Robert M. Lawrence and Martin O. Heisler (Lexington, Mass.: Lexington Books, 1980). Few questions can be raised about the U.S. central role in the IEA.

15. Statement made during an interview with the Deputy Director of Corporate Development and Technology of INI who was also at the time a member of INH. The interview was conducted on 21 July 1981 in Madrid.

16. Prior to PSOE victory in October 1982, it and the PCE bitterly opposed the UCD's taking Spain into NATO. Political debate on this issue during essentially the 1980–82 period was one of Spain's most visible and heated controversies. Through a simple parliamentary majority, Spain became a member of NATO in late 1981 under the UCD leadership of Prime Minister Calvo Sotelo. During the 1982 election campaign, the PCE continued to oppose membership, advocating immediate withdrawal from this international organization. The PSOE argued both against membership and the procedure UCD used in bring Spain into NATO. Hence the PSOE promised, if elected, to hold a national referendum on the country's future in NATO. Once elected, the Socialists reversed positions under the leadership of Felipe González. This left the PCE as the only major party opposing Spain's NATO membership. The PSOE government sidestepped the referendum promise for several years while Felipe González mapped out a strategy to take his newfound position to the voters. The prime minister did find a successful strategy. Despite most opinion polls, the Spanish electorate voted to remain in NATO in a national referendum held in early 1986. The issue, for all practical purposes, has now been laid to rest. On the entire question of Spain and NATO, see, for example, Fernando de Salas López, *¿Nos interesa la Otan?* (Madrid: Imprenta Julian Benita, 1981), and Thomas Carothes, "Spain, Nato, and Democracy," *The World Today* 37 (July/August 1981): 298–303.

17. Personal interviews with several current and former representatives in the Congress of Deputies. Interviews were conducted in September 1981.

18. See UGT-ICEF (1981), Ibid., and Amigos de la Tierra, *Modelo energético de tránsito: respuesta ecologista al Plan Energético Nacional* (Madrid: Ediciones Miraguano, 1979).

19. See Hanns Maull, *Europe and World Energy* (London: Butterworths, 1980), 158–72, for a good and detailed discussion of how this procedure operates.

20. Ibid., 164.

21. Interview with the Deputy Director of Corporate Development and Technology of INI.
22. Ibid.
23. Ibid.
24. Wilfred Kohl, "The United States, Western Europe, and the Energy Problem," *Journal of International Affairs* 30 (1976): 90.
25. *El País*, 10 December 1980.
26. Ibid., Wilfred Kohl, 92.
27. See Bobrow and Kudrle, 1979.
28. Ministerio de Industria y Energía, *Plan Energético Nacional: informe de situación* (October 1980), 52.
29. *El País*, 23 September 1981.
30. IEA, *Annual Report on Energy Research, Development and Demonstration: Activities of the IEA 1980–81* (Paris: OECD, 1981), 10.
31. IEA, *Annual Report on Energy Research, Development and Demonstration: Activities of the IEA, 1977–78* (Paris: OECD, 1978), 8.
32. Interview with the Deputy Director of Corporate Development and Technology of INI, July 1981.
33. Personal interviews conducted with several Spanish officials in the International Energy Agency in Paris, France in August, 1981.
34. IEA, *Annual Report on Energy Research, Development and Demonstration: Activities of the IEA, 1980–81* (Paris: OECD, 1982), 8.
35. Stated in one form or another in several personal interviews with numerous Spanish officials of energy policy.
36. IEA, *Energy Policies and Programmes of IEA Countries, 1978 Review* (Paris: OECD, 1979).
37. Ibid.
38. Vicente Gil Sordo, "Modelo de planificación 'MARKAL' de la energía," *Economia Industrial* 183 (1979): 39–47 (Madrid: Servicio de Publicaciones, Ministerio de Industria y Energía).
39. Stated by this official in the Ministry of Industry and Energy during a personal interview conducted in Madrid in July 1981.
40. Ibid.
41. Juan Alegre Marcet, "Previsión sobre la demanda de energía en España hasta el año 2000," *Boletín Informativo* 99: 3–22 (Madrid: Fundación Juan March, 1980).
42. Interviews with Spanish officials in the IEA in Paris.
43. Personal interview with the Deputy Director of Corporate Development and Technology of INI.
44. IEA (1978), 147.
45. IEA (1979), 120.
46. IEA (1980), 186.
47. Ibid. (1980), 248.
48. Ibid., 250.
49. Personal interviews with numerous Spanish energy officials, throughout the early 1980s.
50. Personal interviews with the Deputy Director of Corporate Development and Technology in INI in Madrid and several Spanish officials in the International Energy Agency in Paris.
51. Noreng Øystein, *Oil Politics in the 1980's: Patterns of International Cooperation* (New York: McGraw-Hill, 1978), 117.
52. Ibid, 122, 126–28.
53. *El País*, 21 November 1980.

## Chapter 8

1. The PSOE government, unlike Spain's previous governments, has been more open in many respects to the criticisms against its policies. For example, transcripts of the full parliamentary debates at both the committee and plenary stage are printed with the plan itself by the Ministry of Industry and Energy in the *Plan Energético Nacional 1983–1992*.
2. See Jerónimo Zaragoza (1984), "La puesta en marcha del Plan Energético Nacional," *Econ-*

216 Notes

*omistas: Boletín del Colegio* 11 (December): 85–86. This was also acknowledged to me in an interview in Madrid with the subdirector general of energy planning of the Ministry of Industry and Energy on 28 June 1985.

   3. Euskadi, the Basque Country, has a parallel institution, the Center of Energy and Mineral Savings and Development (CADEM).

   4. Personal interview with an official of the IDAE conducted on 5 July 1985 in Madrid.

   5. Discussed in a personal interview with the Executive Vice-President and Director of the Technical Cabinet of CAMPSA in Madrid, Spain, 27 June 1985.

   6. Also in terms of reorganization in the petroleum industry, PEN-83 led to Hispanoil's absorption of Eniepsa. This is an important step in the PSOE's attempt to maximize through increased coordination foreign and domestic exploration for oil.

   7. *Actualidad Económica,* 12 May 1983, 20.

   8. *El País,* 5 May 1983.

   9. *El País,* 11 June 1984.

   10. *BOE,* 29 December 1984, No. 312, 37461–37464.

   11. *El País,* 29 January 1985; *El País,* 25 June 1987, 51.

   12. *El País,* 29 January 1985.

   13. *El País,* 11 June 1984; 29 January 1985; and 25 June 1987.

   14. *El País,* 25 June 1987, 51.

   15. Javier Solana Madariaga, "Alternativa Socialista al PEN," *Papeles de Economía Española* 14 (1983): 14–20.

   16. See UGT-ICEF, Federación de Energía, *La crisis nuclear: Una alternativa socialista para España* (Madrid: H. Blume, 1981); and UGT, Federaciones de Energía y Mineria de la UGT, *Alternativa energética: una solución socialista para España* (Madrid: H. Blume, 1981).

   17. *El País,* 5 April 1985.

   18. *Nuclear News,* March 1987, 78–79.

   19. *Económica Actualidad,* 7 March 1985.

   20. *Económica Actualidad,* 7 March 1985.

   21. *Nuclear News,* March 1987, 78.

   22. *El País,* 1985, 337.

   23. On energy and Spain's entry into the EEC see, *El petróleo en la Comunidad Económica Europea: Suplemento de la Memoria 1985* (Madrid: Ministerio de Economica y Hacienda, Delegacion del Gobierno en CAMPSA, 1986).

## Chapter 9

   1. See my "Economics, Democracy, and Spanish Elections," *Political Behavior* 6 (December 1984): 353–67. Reprinted in *Economic Conditions and Electoral Outcomes,* ed. Heinz Eulau and Michael S. Lewis-Beck (New York: Agathon Press, 1985).

   2. See my "Spanish Macroeconomic Policy: Considerations of a Generalized Reaction Function, 1960–1979," unpublished manuscript. See also OECD, *Economic Surveys: Spain* (Paris: OECD, yearly).

   3. See Sima Lieberman, *The Contemporary Spanish Economy: A Historical Perspective* (London: George Allen & Unwin, 1982); see also Eric N. Baklanoff, *The Economic Transformation of Spain and Portugal* (New York: Praeger, 1978); Alison Wright, *The Spanish Economy 1959–1979* (New York: Holmes and Meier, 1977); R. Poveda, "Política monetaria y financeria," in *Política Económica de España,* ed. Luis Gámir (Madrid: Alianza Universidad, 1980), 71–132; Thomas D. Lancaster, "The Spanish Economy: The Transition and Prospects for Stability," in *Spain's Prospects: Reports on a Spanish Institute-Tinker Foundation Executive Seminar,* ed. Kenneth Maxwell (New York: The Spanish Institute, 1985); and Ramón Tamames, *Estructura económica de España,* 17 edición (Madrid: Alianza, 1986).

   4. See, for example, the early "classics" in this literature: William D. Nordhaus, "The Political Cycle," *Review of Economic Studies* 42 (1975): 169–90; Edward R. Tufte, *Political Control of the Economy* (Princeton, N.J.: Princeton University Press, 1978); Bruno S. Frey, "Politico-Economic Models and Cycles," *Journal of Public Economics* 9 (1978): 1–18; C. Duncan MacRae,

"A Political Model of the Business Cycle," *Journal of Political Economy* 85 (1977): 239–63. See also James E. Alt and K. Alec Chrystal, *Political Economics* (Berkeley: University of California Press, 1983), chap. 5. For a more comparative perspective, see *Economic Conditions and Electoral Outcomes: The United States and Western Europe,* ed. Heinz Eulau and Michael S. Lewis-Beck (New York: Agathon Press, 1985); and Michael S. Lewis-Beck, "Comparative Economic Voting: Britain, France, Germany, Italy," *American Journal of Political Science* 30 (1986): 315–46. For work on Spain, see Thomas D. Lancaster and Michael S. Lewis-Beck, "The Spanish Voter: Tradition, Economics, Ideology," *Journal of Politics* 48 (1986): 648–74; and Peter McDonough, Samuel Barnes, and Antonio López Pina, "Economic Policy and Public Opinion in Spain," *American Journal of Political Science* 30 (1986): 446–79.

5. In the U.S., research includes John Manley, *The Politics of Finance* (Boston: Little, Brown, 1970); John Ferejohn, *Pork Barrel Politics* (Stanford: Stanford University Press, 1974); William A. Niskanen, *Bureaucracy and Representative Government* (Chicago: Aldine-Atherton, 1971); and articles in *Budgets and Bureaucrats: The Sources of Government Growth,* ed. Thomas E. Borcherding (Durham, N.C.: Duke University Press, 1977). Samples of more comparative work can be seen in Bruce Cain, John Ferejohn, and Morris Fiorina, *The Personal Vote: Constituency Service and Electoral Independence* (Cambridge, Mass.: Harvard University Press, 1987); and my "Electoral Structures and Pork Barrel Politics," *International Political Science Review* 7 (1986): 67–81.

6. Richard Gunther, *Public Policy in a No-Party State* (Berkeley: University of California Press, 1980).

7. In the area of taxation policy, see my "A Price for Entry: the European Community, Spain, and the Value-added Tax," presented at the 1983 Annual Meeting of the American Political Science Association; Juan Zurdo, *El impuesto sobre el valor añadido en la CEE* (Madrid: Instituto de Estudios Economicos, 1981); and José Santacana Jubillar, *El I.V.A.: España y el Mercado Común* (Barcelona: Bosch, 1982).

8. See my "Toward an Assessment of the Spanish Social Security System," presented at the Fourth European Studies Conference, Omaha, Nebraska, October 1979; *Problemas actuales de la Seguridad Social en España,* ed. Javier de Istúriz, Victorino Anguera, Emilio Fontela, Alfonso Mantero (Madrid: Instituto de Estudios Económicos, 1981); and Ministerio de Trabajo y Seguridad Social, *Jornados Tecnicas Sobre Seguridad Social* (Madrid: Servico de Publicaciones, 1984).

9. Based on a series of about fifteen personal interviews on the Spanish social security system. The respondents were selected from a wide range of institutions, participants, and researchers involved in the system. They included individuals in the Instituto de Estudios Económicos, the Instituto de Estudios de Sanidad, the secretary of the Committee on Labor Relations for the Confederación Española de Organizaciones Empresariales, the subdirector of planning of the Ministry of Health and Social Security, the general secretary of the Confederación de Sanitarios Privados, and the cabinet chief of the Ministry of Health and Social Security. All interviews were conducted in Madrid in 1981, 1982, and 1985.

10. Personal interview with the faculty director, La Escuela de A.T.S., conducted on 28 September 1981.

11. OECD, *Revenue Statistics of OECD Member Countries* (Paris: OECD, 1982).

# Bibliography

Acoca, Miguel. "Domestic Economic Woes Propel Membership Bid." *European Community* 203, 1977.

Alba, Victor. *Transition in Spain: Franco to Democracy*, trans. Barbara Lotito. New Brunswick, N.J.: Transaction Books, 1978.

Alegre Marcet, Juan. "Previsión sobre la demanda de energía en España hasta el año 2000." *Boletín Informativo* Madrid: Fundación Juan March 99 (1980): 3–22.

Alt, James E., and K. Alec Chrystal. *Political Economics*. Berkeley: University of California Press, 1983.

Amigos de la Tierra. *Modelo energético de tránsito: respuesta ecologista al Plan Energético Nacional*. Madrid: Ediciones Miraguano, 1979.

Amsden, Jon. *Collective Bargaining and Class Conflict in Spain*. London: Weidenfeld and Nicolson, 1972.

Amodia, José. *Franco's Political Legacy: From Fascism to Facade Democracy*. London: Penguin Books, 1977.

Anderson, Charles W. *The Political Economy of Modern Spain: Policy-Making in an Authoritarian System*. Madison: The University of Wisconsin Press, 1970.

Apter, David E. *The Politics of Modernization*. Chicago: University of Chicago Press, 1965.

Arango, E. Ramón. *The Spanish Political System: Franco's Political Legacy*. Boulder, Colo.: Westview Press, 1978.

Artigues, Daniel. *El Opus Dei en España, 1928–1962*. París: Ruedo Ibérico, 1971.

Banco Urquijo, Servicio de Estudios en Barcelona. *El Petróleo en Cataluña: análisis económico*. Vol. 2. Madrid: Editorial Moneda y Crédito, 1969.

Baklanoff, Eric N. "Spain and the Atlantic Community: A Study of Incipient Integration and Economic Development." *Economic Development and Cultural Change* 16 (1968): 588–602.

Baklanoff, Eric N. *The Economic Transformation of Spain and Portugal*. New York: Praeger, 1978.

Banco de Bilbao. *Informe Económico: 1980*. Bilbao: Servicio de Estudios, 1981.

Banco de Bilbao. *Informe y Memoria*. Bilbao: Banco de Bilbao, 1982.

Barceló Rico-Avelló, Gabriel. *La Energía y su impacto social*. Madrid: Editorial Index, 1976.

Barceló Rico-Avelló, Gabriel. *La energía en la edificación: política energética y ahorro de energía*. Madrid: Editorial Index, 1978.

Barnechea Bergareche, Richard. "Fiscalidad y precios de venta al público de los productos petroliferos." *Información Comercial Española* 542 (1978): 43–62.

Barnes, Samuel H., Peter McDonough, and Antonio López Pina. "The Development of Partisanship in New Democracies: The Case of Spain." *American Journal of Political Science* 29 (1985): 695–720.

Belmonte, José. *La Constitución: texto y contexto.* Madrid: Prensa Española, 1979.

Beltran, Miguel. *La elite burocrática española.* Madrid: Fundación Juan March/Ariel, 1977.

Bendix, Reinhard. *Nation-Building and Citizenship.* New York: John Wiley, 1964.

Bengoechea, J. A., J. A. Sagardoy, and David Leon Blanco. *El poder sindical en España.* Barcelona, 1982.

Bernáldez, José María. *El Señor Rumasa.* Barcelona: Playa & Janés, 1983.

Bill, James A., and Robert L. Hardgrave, Jr. *Comparative Politics: The Quest for Theory,* 1973, 1981.

Black, C. E. *The Dynamics of Modernization.* New York: Harper and Row, 1966.

Bobrow, Davis B., and Robert T. Kudrle. "Energy R & D: In Tepid Pursuit of Collective Goods." *International Organization* 33 (1979): 149–75.

Bookchin, Murray. *The Spanish Anarchists: The Heroic Years, 1868–1936.* New York: Harper Colophon Books, 1977.

Borcherding, Thomas E., ed. *Budgets and Bureaucrats: The Sources of Government Growth.* Durham: Duke University Press, 1977.

Borrell Fontelles, José. "Notas sobre la estructura de la industria del refino en España." *Información Comercial Española* 542 (October 1978): 31–40.

Borrell Fontelles, José. "El Petróleo en España: Posibilidades prospecciones, suministros exteriores." *Boletín Informativo* (Madrid: Fundación Juan March) 87 (1979).

Borrell, José, and Ignácio Gafo. "El monopolio de petróleos y los precios de los productos petrolíferos: sistema de fijación de precios ex-refínería." *Información Comercial Española* 542 (1978): 15–30.

Boyd, Carolyn P., and James M. Boyden. "The Armed Forces and the Transition to Democracy in Spain." In *Politics and Change in Spain,* eds. Thomas D. Lancaster and Gary Prevost. New York: Praeger, 1985.

Brenan, Gerald. *The Spanish Labyrinth: An Account of the Social and Political Background of the Spanish Civil War.* 1943. Reprint. New York: Cambridge University Press, 1970.

Busquets Bragulat, Julio. *El militar de carrera en España.* 2d ed. Barcelona, 1971.

Busquets Bragulat, Julio. *Pronunciamientos y golpes de Estado en España.* Barcelona, 1982.

Caciagli, Mario. "Spain: Parties and the Party System in the Transition." *West European Politics* 7 (1984): 84–98. Reprinted in *The New Mediterranean Democracies: Regime Transition in Spain, Greece and Portugal,* ed. Geoffrey Pridham. London: Frank Cass, 1984.

Cain, Bruce, John Ferejohn, and Morris Fiorina. *The Personal Vote: Constituency Service and Electoral Independence.* Cambridge, Mass.: Harvard University Press, 1987.

Camacho, José. *Tarifas eléctricas y equipos de medida.* Madrid: E. T. Superior de Ingenieros Agronomos, 1978.

CAMPSA. *Memoria.* Madrid: Ministerio de Economía y Hacienda, 1976.

CAMPSA. *Memoria.* Madrid: Ministerio de Economía y Hacienda, 1985.

Carothes, Thomas. "Spain, Nato, and Democracy." *The World Today* 37 (1981): 298–303.

Carr, Raymond, and Juan P. Fusi. *Spain: Dictatorship to Democracy.* London: George Allen & Unwin, 1979.

Centro de Estudios de la Energía. *Opinión pública y ahorro de energía.* Madrid: Ministerio de Industria y Energía, 1980.

Chilcote, Ronald H. *Theories of Comparative Politics.* Boulder, Colo.: Westview Press, 1981.

Comisaría del Plan de Desarrollo Económico y Social. *III (Tercer) plan de desarrollo, 1972–1975.* Madrid: Imprenta Nacional del Boletín Oficial del Estado, 1971.

Cortada, James W., ed. *Spain in the Twentieth-Century World: Essays on Spanish Diplomacy 1898–1978.* Westport, Conn.: Greenwood Press, 1980.

Costa Morata, Pedro. *Nuclearizar España.* Barcelona: Los Libros De La Frontera, 1976.

Costa Morata, Pedro. *Energía: el fraude y el debate.* Barcelona: Gaya Ciencia, 1978.

Coverdale, John F. *The Political Transformation of Post-Franco Spain.* New York: Praeger, 1979.

de Blas, Andres. *Introducción al sistema político Español.* Barcelona: Teide, 1983.

de Esteban, Jorge, and Luis López Guerra. *Los partidos politicos en la España actual.* Barcelona, 1982.

de Isturiz, Javier, Victorino Anguera, Emilio Fontela, and Alfonso Mantero, eds. *Problemas actuales de la Seguridad Social en España.* Madrid: Instituto de Estudios Económicos, 1981.

del Campo, Salustiano, José Felix Texanos, and Walter Santín. "The Spanish Political Elite: Permanency and Change." In *Does Who Governs Matter? Elite Circulation in Contemporary Societies,* ed. Moshe M. Czudnowski. DeKalb: Northern Illinois University Press, 1982.

de Miguel, Amando. *Sociología del franquismo.* Barcelona: 1975.

de Pablo, José Rodríquez. "Costes y tarifas de la energía eléctrica." *Información Comercial Española* 542 (1978): 71–102.

de Salas López, Fernando. *¿Nos interesa la Otan?* Madrid: Imprenta Julian Benita, 1981.

Diéz, Alfonso Valeriano Heras. *Oferta electoral.* Madrid: Piesa, 1977.

Di Palma, Giuseppe. "Founding Coalitions in Southern Europe: Legitimacy and Hegemony." *Government and Opposition* 15: (1980): 162–89.

Dixon, William J., and Bruce E. Moon. "The Military Burden and Basic Human Needs." *Journal of Conflict Resolution.* 30 (1986): 660–84.

Doran, Charles F. *Myth, Oil, and Politics: Introduction to the Political Economy of Petroleum.* New York: The Free Press, 1977.

EIU. *Spain: Economic Prospects to 1985, Special Report No. 114.* London: The Economist Intelligence Unit, 1981.

El País. *Anuario El País*. Madrid: Ediciones El Pais, 1985.

Esparraguera Martínez, José Luis and Javier Molina Fajardo. *El futuro de la energía en España y su problématica*. Madrid: Estudios del Instituto de Desarrollo Económica, 1970.

Esteban, Joan. "The Economic Policy of Francoism: An Interpretation." In *Spain In Crisis*, ed. Paul Preston. London: The Harvester Press, 1976.

Eulau, Heinz, and Michael S. Lewis-Beck. *Economic Conditions and Electoral Outcomes: The United States and Western Europe*. New York: Agathon Press, 1985.

Euskadiko Ezkerra. *Programa de lucha y de gobierno*. Bilbao: Printzen, 1980.

Ferejohn, John. *Pork Barrel Politics*. Stanford: Stanford University Press, 1974.

Fisas Armengol, Vicens. *Centrales nucleares: imperialismo, tecnológico y proliferación nuclear*. Madrid: Campo Abierto Ediciones, 1978.

Fisas, Vicenç. *El poder militar en España*. Barcelona, 1979.

Fisas Armengol, Vicens. *Despilfarro y control de la energía*. Barcelona: Edita Ediciones, 1981.

Frey, Bruno S. "Politico-Economic Models and Cycles." *Journal of Public Economics* 8 (1978).

Gabiria, Mário. *La lucha antinuclear*. Donostia, Spain: Hórdago, S.A., 1979.

Gallagher, Charles F. *Spain, Development, and the Energy Crisis*. AUFS West European series, vol 8, no. 8. New York: American Universities Field Staff Report, 1973.

Gallo, Max. *História de la España franquista*. París, 1971.

Gámir, Luis. *Política económica de España*. Madrid: Alianza Universidad, 1980.

Garcia-Conde Cenal, J. R. "El Carbón, sus posibilidades de utilización en España." *Boletín Informativo* (Madrid: Fundación Juan March) 89 (1980).

Gil Sordo, Vicente. "Modelo de planificación 'MARKAL' de la energía." *Economía Industrial* 183 (1979): 39–47. Madrid: Servicio de Publicaciones, Ministerio de Industria y Energía.

González Ortiz, Primo. "Problemas de la energía." *Cuadernos de Política Económica* 4 (1981): Centro de Estudios y Comunicación Económica.

Graham, Robert. *Spain: Change of a Nation*. London: Michael Joseph, 1984.

Grayson, L. E. *National Oil Companies*. New York: John Wiley & Sons, 1981.

Gunther, Richard. *Public Policy in a No-Party State*. Berkeley: University of California Press, 1981.

Gunther, Richard, Giacomo Sani, and Goldie Shabad. *The Making of a Competitive Party System*. Berkeley: University of California Press, 1986.

Hagopian, Mark N. *Regimes, Movements, and Ideologies*. New York: Longman, 1978.

Harrison, Joseph. *An Economic History of Modern Spain*. Manchester: Manchester University Press, 1978.

Hermet, Guy. *The Communists in Spain*. Lexington, Mass.: Lexington Books, 1974.

Holt, Robert T., and John E. Turner. *The Political Basis of Economic Development: An Exploration in Comparative Political Analysis*. Princeton: Van Nostrand, 1966.

Huntington, Samuel A. *Political Order in Changing Societies*. New Haven: Yale University Press, 1968.

IESA. *The Spanish Energy Sector.* Barcelona: Instituto de Estudios Superiores de la Empresa, 1981.

IEA. *Annual Report on Energy Research, Development and Demonstration: Activities of the IEA, 1977-78.* Paris: OECD, 1978.

IEA. *Energy Policies and Programmes of IEA Countries, 1977 Review.* Paris: OECD, 1978b.

IEA. *Energy Policies and Programmes of IEA Countries, 1978 Review.* Paris: OECD, 1979.

IEA. *Annual Report on Energy Research, Development and Demonstration.* Paris: OECD, 1979.

IEA. *Energy Policies and Programmes of IEA Countries: 1979 Review.* Paris: OECD, 1980.

IEA. *Annual Report on Energy Research, Development and Demonstration: Activities of the IEA, 1980-81.* Paris: OECD, 1981.

IEA. *Energy Policies and Programmes of IEA Countries: 1980 Review.* Paris: OECD, 1981b.

IEA. *Energy Balances of OECD Countries 1975/1979.* Paris: OECD, 1981c.

Instituto Nacional de Industria. "Debate parlamentario sobre el Plan Energético Nacional." Madrid: Dirección de Estudios, Centrol de Documentación, 1979.

International Bank for Reconstruction and Development. *The Economic Development of Spain.* Baltimore: Johns Hopkins Press, 1963.

Jackson, Gabriel. *The Spanish Republic and the Civil War: 1931-1939.* Princeton, N.J.: Princeton University Press, 1965.

Jackson, Gabriel, ed. *The Spanish Civil War: Domestic Crisis or International Conspiracy?* Chicago: Quadrangle Books, 1972.

Keohane, Robert O. "The International Energy Agency: State Influence and Transgovernmental Politics." *International Organizations* 32 (1978): 929-51.

Kern, Robert W. *Red Years/Black Years: A Political History of Spanish Anarchism 1911-1937.* Philadelphia: Institute for the Study of Human Issues, 1978.

Kohl, Wilfrid L. "The United States, Western Europe, and the Energy Problem." *Journal of International Affairs* 30 (1976): 81-96.

Lancaster, Thomas D. "Economics, Democracy, and Spanish Elections." *Political Behavior* 6: 353-67. Reprinted in *Economic Conditions and Electoral Outcomes,* ed. Heinz Eulau and Michael S. Lewis-Beck. New York: Agathon Press, 1984.

Lancaster, Thomas D. "The Spanish Economy: The Transition and Prospects for Stability." In *Spain's Prospects: Reports on a Spanish Institute-Tinker Foundation Executive Seminar,* ed. Kenneth Maxwell. New York: The Spanish Institute, 1985.

Lancaster, Thomas D. "Spanish Public Policy and Financial Power." In *Politics and Change in Spain,* ed. Thomas D. Lancaster and Gary Prevost. New York: Praeger, 1985.

Lancaster, Thomas D. "Electoral Structures and Pork Barrel Politics." *International Political Science Review* 7 (1986): 67-81.

Lancaster, Thomas D., and Micheal W. Giles. "Spain," in *Legal Traditions and Systems: An International Handbook,* ed. Alan N. Katz. Westport, Conn.: Greenwood Press, 1986.

Lancaster, Thomas D., and Michael S. Lewis-Beck. "The Spanish Voter: Tradition, Economics, Ideology." *Journal of Politics* 48 (1986): 648–74.

Lancaster, Thomas D., and Gary Prevost. *Politics and Change in Spain.* New York: Praeger, 1985.

Lantzke, Ulf. "The OECD and its International Energy Agency." *Daedalus* 104 (1975): 217–28. Reprinted in *The Oil Crisis,* ed. Raymond Vernon. New York: W. W. Norton, 1976.

Lantzke, Ulf. "International co-operation on energy—problems and prospects." *The World Today* 32 (1976): 84–94.

Lasso de la Vega, Raimundo. "La economía del carbón." *Economía Industrial* 149 (1976): 48–58.

Leichter, Howard M. "Political Regime and Public Policy: A Study of Two Philippine Cities." Ph.D. diss., The University of Wisconsin, 1973.

Leichter, Howard M. *A Comparative Approach to Policy Analysis: Health Care Policy in Four Nations.* Cambridge: Cambridge University Press, 1979.

Leonato Marsal, Ramón. "Posibilidades energéticas de España." *Boletín Informativo* (Madrid: Fundación Juan March) 94 (1980).

Lewis, Paul H. "The Spanish Ministerial Elite, 1938–1969." *Comparative Politics* 5 (1973): 83–106.

Lewis-Beck, Michael S. "Comparative Economic Voting: Britain, France, Germany, Italy." *American Journal of Political Science* 30 (1986): 315–46.

Lieberman, Sima. *The Contemporary Spanish Economy: A Historical Perspective.* London: George Allen & Unwin, 1982.

Linz, Juan J. "An Authoritarian Regime: Spain." In *Cleavages, Ideologies, and Party Systems,* ed. E. Allardt and Y. Littunen. Helsinki: Academic Bookstore, 1964. Also appeared in *Mass Politics: Studies in Political Sociology,* ed. E. Allardt and S. Rokkan. New York: The Free Press, 1970.

Linz, Juan J. "From Falange to Movimiento-organización: The Spanish Single Party and the Franco Regime, 1936–1968." In *Authoritarian Politics in Modern Societies: The Dynamics of Established One Party System.,* ed. Samuel P. Huntington and Clement H. Moore. New York: Basic Books, 1970.

Linz, Juan J. "Opposition In and Under an Authoritarian Regime." In *Regimes and Oppositions,* ed. Robert A. Dahl. New Haven: Yale University Press, 1973.

Linz, Juan J. "Legislatures in Organic Statist-Authoritarian Regimes—The Case of Spain." In *Legislatures in Development: Dynamics of Change in New and Old States,* ed. Joel Smith and Lloyd D. Musolf. Durham, N.C.: Duke University Press, 1979.

Linz, Juan J. "The New Spanish Party System." In *Electoral Participation: A Comparative Analysis,* ed. Richard Rose. Beverly Hills: Sage, 1980.

Linz, Juan J. "A Century of Politics and Interests in Spain." In *Organizing Interests in Western Europe: Pluralism, Corporatism and the Transformation of Politics,* ed. Suzanne Berger. Cambridge: Cambridge University Press, 1981.

Linz, Juan J., and Miguel de Amando. *Los Empresarios ante el poder público.* Madrid: Instituto de Estúdios Políticos, 1966.

Linz, Juan J., and José R. Montero, eds. *Crisis y cambio: electores y partidos en la*

*España de los años ochenta.* Madrid: Centro de Estúdios Constitucionales, 1986.

Linz, Juan J., Manuel Gómez-Reino, Francisco A. Orizo, and Dario Vila. *Informe sociológico sobre el cambio político en España, 1975–1981.* Madrid: Fundación Foessa, 1981.

MacRae, C. Duncan. "A Political Model of the Business Cycle." *Journal of Political Economy* 85 (1977): 239–63.

Magana Vázquez, R. "El carbón español en el futuro energético." *Información Comercial Española* 501 (1975): 57–67.

Malefakis, Edward. *Agrarian Reform and Peasant Revolution in Spain: Origins of the Civil War.* New Haven: Yale University Press, 1970.

Manley, John. *The Politics of Finance.* Boston: Little, Brown, 1970.

Maravall, José. *Dictatorship and Political Dissent: Workers and Students in Franco's Spain.* New York: St. Martin's Press, 1979.

Maravall, José. *Transition to Democracy in Spain.* New York: St. Martin's Press, 1982.

Marin Quemada, José María. *Política Petrolífera Española.* Madrid: Confederación Española de Cajas de Ahorros, 1978.

Marin Quemada, José María. "Política de Energía." In *Política Económica de España,* vol. 2, ed. Luis Gámir. Madrid: Alianza Editorial, 1980.

Martín Sanz, Dionisio. *En las Cortes españolas: crítica del segundo plan de desarrollo.* Madrid: Afrodisio Aguado, 1969.

Martín Sanz, Dionisio. *La planificación española en la olimpiada de las ideologias. Crítica del III Plan de Desarrollo.* Madrid: Afrodisio Aguado, 1972.

Maull, Hanns. *Europe and World Energy.* London: Butterworths, 1980.

McDonough, Peter, Samuel H. Barnes, and Antonio López Pina. "The Legitimacy of Democracy in Spain." *American Political Science Review* 80 (1986): 735–60.

McDonough, Peter, Samuel H. Barnes, and Antonio López Pina. "Economic Policy and Public Opinion in Spain." *American Journal of Political Science* 30 (1986): 446–79.

McDonough, Peter, and Antonio López Pina. "Continuity and Change in Spanish Politics." In *Electoral Change in Advanced Industrial Democracies,* ed. Russell J. Dalton, Scott C. Flanagan, and Paul Allen Beck. Princeton: Princeton University Press, 1984.

Menges, Constantine Christopher. *Spain: The Struggle for Democracy Today.* Beverly Hills: Sage, 1978.

Medhurst, Kenneth N. *Government in Spain: The Executive at Work.* Oxford: Pergamon Press, 1973.

Migdal, Joel S. *Peasants, Politics, and Revolution: Pressures Toward Political and Social Change in the Third World.* Princeton: Princeton University Press, 1974.

Ministerio de Económica y Hacienda. *El petróleo en la Comunidad Económica Europea: Suplemento de la Memoria 1985.* Madrid: Delegación del Gobierno en CAMPSA, 1986.

Ministerio de Industria. *Sintesis del Plan Energético Nacional 1975–1985.* Madrid: January 1975.

Ministerio de Industria. *Estadística de Energía Eléctrica, 1977.* Madrid: Ministerio de Industria, 1977.

Ministerio de Industria y Energía. *Plan Energético Nacional: 1978/1987*. Madrid: Servicio de Publicaciones, 1978.
————. *Plan Energético Nacional: informe de situación*. Madrid: Comisaría de la Energía y Recursos Minerales, October 1980.
————. *Plan Energético Nacional: Balance de actuaciones*. Madrid: Comisaría de la Energía Y Recursos Minerales, July 1981.
————. *Plan Energético Nacional 1983–1992*, vols. 1 and 2. Madrid: Ministerio de Industria y Energía, Secretaría General de la Energía y Recursos Minerales, 1984.
Ministerio de Trabajo y Seguridad Social. *Jornadas Téchnicas Sobre Seguridad Social*. Madrid: Servicio de Publicaciones, 1984.
Miravet Garcia, Enrique. "Fiscalidad del petróleo y derivados." *Hacienda Publica Española* 53 (1978): 121–32.
Moncada, A. *El Opus Dei: una interpretación*. Madrid: Indice, 1974.
Moon, Bruce E., and William J. Dixon. "Politics, the State, and Basic Human Needs: A Cross-national Study." *American Journal of Political Science* 29 (1985): 661–94.
Moore, Barrington, Jr. *Social Origins of Dictatorship and Democracy: Lord and Peasant in the Making of the Modern World*. Boston: Beacon Press, 1966.
Morales, José Luis, and Juan Celada. *La alternativa militar: el golpismo despues de Franco*. Madrid: 1981.
Moya Valganon, Carlos. "Las elites económicas y el desarrollo español," Campo Urbano, *La España* 1:188.
Mujal-León, Eusebio. *Communism and Political Change in Spain*. Bloomington: Indiana University Press, 1983.
Muñoz, Juan. *El poder de la banca en España*. Algorta: Zero, 1969.
Nau, Henry R. "The Evolution of U.S. Foreign Policy in Energy: From Alliance Politics to Politics-as-Usual." In *International Energy Policy*, ed. Robert M. Lawrence and Martin O. Heisler. Lexington, Mass.: Lexington Books, 1980.
Niskanen, William. *Bureaucracy and Representative Government*. Chicago: Aldine-Atherton, 1971.
Nordhaus, William D. "The Political Business Cycle." *Review of Economic Studies* 42 (1975): 169–190.
North, Douglas C. *Structure and Change in Economic History*. New York: W. W. Norton, 1981.
Nuclear Energy Agency. *Nuclear Power and Public Opinion*. Paris: OECD, 1984.
Núñez García, Elio. "Pricing Spanish Electricity." Ph.D. diss., University of Minnesota, 1972.
OECD. *Main Economic Indicators*. Paris: OECD.
OECD. *OECD Economic Survey: Spain*. Paris: OECD.
OECD. "The New International Energy Agency of OECD." *The OECD Observer* 73 (1975): 20–25.
OECD. *Energy Balances of OECD Countries 1960/1974*. Paris: OECD, 1976.
OECD. *Revenue Statistics of OECD Member Countries*. Paris: OECD, 1982.
OECD. *Energy Balances of OECD Countries, 1970–1985*. Paris: OECD, 1987.

Onaindia Natxiondo, Mario. *Otra herencia más: Plan Energético Nacional.* Bilbao: Printzen, 1978.

Organski, A. F. K. *The Stages of Political Development.* New York: Alfred A. Knopf, 1965.

Øystein, Noreng. *Oil Politics in the 1980's: Patterns of International Cooperation.* New York: McGraw-Hill, 1978.

Pascual Martínez, Francisco. "La energía nuclear y su futuro." *Boletín Informativo* (Madrid: Fundación Juan March) 92 (1980).

Payne, Stanley. *Franco's Spain.* New York: Thomas Y. Crowell, 1967.

Payne, Stanley. *Politics and Society in Twentieth-Century Spain.* New York: New Viewpoints, 1976.

Payne, Stanley G. *The Spanish Revolution: A Study of the Social and Political Tensions that Culminated in the Civil War in Spain.* New York: W. W. Norton, 1970.

Penniman, Howard R., and Eusebio M. Mujal-León. *Spain at the Polls, 1977, 1979, and 1982.* Durham: Duke University Press, 1985.

Pérez Díaz, Victor. "Políticas económicas y pautas sociales en la España de la transición: la doble cara del neocorporatismo." In *España: un presente para el futuro,* ed. E. Garcia de Enterria. Madrid: Instituto de Estudios Económicas, 1984.

Pike, Frederick B. "The New Corporatism in Franco's Spain and Some Latin American Perspectives." In *The New Corporatism: Social-Political Structures in the Iberian World,* ed. Pike and Thomas Stritch. Notre Dame: University of Notre Dame Press, 1974.

Preston, Paul, ed. *Spain in Crisis: The Evaluation and Decline of the Franco Regime.* London: The Harvester Press, 1976.

Preston, Paul. *The Triumph of Democracy in Spain.* London: Methuen, 1986.

Prevost, Gary. "Contemporary Spanish Anarchism." *Social Anarchism* (Winter 1982): 22–32.

Prevost, Gary. "Change and Continuity in the Spanish Labor Movement." *West European Politics* (Winter 1984). 7:80–94.

Pryor, Frederic L. *Public Expenditures in Communist and Capitalist Nations.* London: Allen & Unwin, 1968.

Pye, Lucian W. *Aspects of Political Development.* Boston: Little, Brown, 1966.

Ramírez Jiménez, Manuel. *Los grupos de presión en la Segunda República Española.* Madrid: Tecnos, 1969.

Reig, Gisbert, Santiago. "Los impuestos en España que afectan a la energía." *Hacienda Pública Española* 53 (1978): 83–96.

Robinson, Richard A. H. *The Origins of Franco's Spain: the Right, the Republic and Revolution, 1931–1936.* Newton Abbot: David and Charles, 1970.

Roman, Manuel. *The Limits of Economic Growth in Spain.* New York: Praeger, 1971.

Saez Alba, A. *La Asociación Catolica Nacional de Propagandistas y el caso del Correo de Andalucia.* París: Ruedo Ibérico, 1974.

Salmore, Barbara Gitlin. "Political Structure, Economic Development and Social Security Policies: A Cross-National Study." Ph.D. diss., Rutgers University.

Sánchez Agesta, Luis. *El sistema político de la Constitución Española de 1978.* 3d ed. Madrid: Editora Nacional, 1984.

Sánchez Goyanes, E. *El sistema constitucional español*. Madrid: Paranfino, 1981.

Sánchez Goyanes, E. *Constitución Española Comentada*. 12th ed. Madrid: Paranfino, 1981.

Santacana Jubillar, José. *El I.V.A.: España y el Mercado Común*. Barcelona: Bosch, 1982.

Schmitter, Philippe. *Corporatism and Public Policy in Authoritarian Portugal*. Beverly Hills: Sage, 1975.

Schwartz, Pedro. "Politics First: The Economy after Franco." *Government and Opposition* 11 (1976): 84–103.

Schwartz, Pedro, and M. J. González. *Una historia del Instituto Nacional de Industria*. Madrid: Editorial Tecnos, 1978.

Scott, Richard. "Innovation in International Organization: The International Energy Agency." *Hastings International and Comparative Law Review* 1 (1977): 1–56.

Serrano, Angel, and Juan Muñoz. "La configuración del sector eléctrico y el negocio de la construcción de las centrales nucleares." *Ruedo Ibérico* (1979): 63–66.

Sevilla Segura, J. V. *Economía política de la crisis española*. Barcelona: Editorial Critica, 1985.

Share, Donald. *The Making of Spanish Democracy*. New York: Praeger, 1986.

*Situación*. "La planificación energética en España." August 1979: 34–48.

Solana Madariaga, Javier. "Alternativa socialista al PEN." *Papeles de Economía Española* 14 (1983): 14–20.

Tamames, Ramón. *La lucha contra los monopolios*. Madrid, 1970.

Tamames, Ramón. *La oligarquía financiera en España*. Barcelona: Editorial Planeta, 1977.

Tamames, Ramón. *Introducción a la economía española*. 12th edición. Madrid: Alianza Editorial, 1978.

Tamames, Ramón. *Estructura económica de España*. Madrid: Alianza Universidad, 1980.

Tamames, Ramón. *Estructura económica de España*. 17th edición. Madrid: Alianza Editorial, 1986.

Téllez de Peralta, António. "El gas natural en España." *Boletín Informativo* (Fundación Juan March) 96 (September 1980): 3–16.

Tezanos, José Felix. *Estructura de clases y conflictos de poder en la España post-Franquista*. Madrid, 1978.

Theberge, James D. "Spanish Industrial Development Policy in the Twentieth Century." In *Spain in the 1970's: Economics, Social Structure, and Foreign Policy*, ed. William T. Salisbury and Theberge. New York: Praeger, 1976.

Thomas, Hugh. *The Spanish Civil War*. New York: Harper, 1961.

Trythall, J. W. D. *Franco: A Biography*. London: Rupert Hart-Davis, 1970.

Tufte, Edward R. *Political Control of the Economy*. Princeton, N.J.: Princeton University Press, 1978.

Tugendhat, Christophen, and Adrian Hamilton. *Oil: The Biggest Business*. London: Methuen, 1975.

UGT-ICEF, Federación de Energía. *La crisis nuclear: una alternativa socialista para España*. Madrid: H. Blume Ediciones, 1981.

UGT, Federaciones de Energía y Mineria de la UGT. *Alternativa energética: una solu-*

*ción socialista para España*. Madrid: H. Blume Ediciones, 1981.

UNESA. *Memoria Estadística Eléctrica 1980*. Madrid: UNESA, 1981.

Vilanova, Santiago. *El síndrome nuclear: El accidente de Harrisburg y el riesgo nuclear en España*. Barcelona: Editorial Bruguera, S.A., 1980.

Watters, William E. *An International Affair: Non-Intervention in the Spanish Civil War, 1936–1939*. New York: Exposition Press, 1971.

Weyman-Jones, T. *Energy in Europe: Issues and Policies*. London: Methuen, 1986.

Whitaker, Arthur P. *Spain and Defense of the West, Ally and Liability*. New York: Praeger, 1961.

Wiarda, Howard J. "The Aftermath of the Trujillo Dictatorship: The Emergence of a Pluralist Political System in the Dominican Republic." Ph.D. diss., The University of Florida.

Wiarda, Howard J. *Corporatism and Development: the Portuguese Experience*. Amherst: University of Massachusetts Press, 1977.

Wiarda, Howard J., ed. *New Directions in Comparative Politics*. Boulder, Colo.: Westview Press, 1985.

Wilensky, Harold L. *The Welfare State and Equality*. Berkeley: University of California Press, 1975.

Willrich, Mason, and Melvin A. Conant. "The International Energy Agency: An Interpretation and Assessment." *American Journal of International Law* 71 (1977): 199–223.

Wirth, John D. *Latin American Oil Companies and the Politics of Energy* (Lincoln: University of Nebraska Press, 1985).

Witney, Fred. *Labor Policy and Practices in Spain*. New York: Praeger, 1965.

Wright, Alison. *The Spanish Economy 1959–1979*. New York: Holmes & Meier Publishers, 1977.

Ynfante, J. *La prodigiosa aventura del Opus Dei: génesis y desarrollo de la Santa Mafia*. París: Ruedo Ibérico, 1970.

Ynfante, Jesus. *El ejército de Franco y de Juan Carlos*. París, 1976.

Zaragoza, Jerónimo. "La puesta en marcha del Plan Energético Nacional." *Economistas: Boletín del Colegio* 11 (December 1984): 85–86.

Zurdo, Juan. *El impuesto sobre el valor añadido en la CEE*. Madrid: Instituto de Estudios Económicos, 1981.

# Index